Reads Well With Others

Contains *Unshelved* comic strips originally published on the *Unshelved* website from April 1, 2013 to September 25, 2014. *Conference Tips* originally published in *ALA CogNotes* newspapers in June 2013, January 2014, and June 2014.

ISBN-13: 978-1-937914-06-6

First printing: January 2015

Printed in China.

Reads Well With Others

an ▬UNSHELVED▬ collection by
Gene Ambaum & Bill Barnes

**OVERDUE
MEDIA**
Seattle

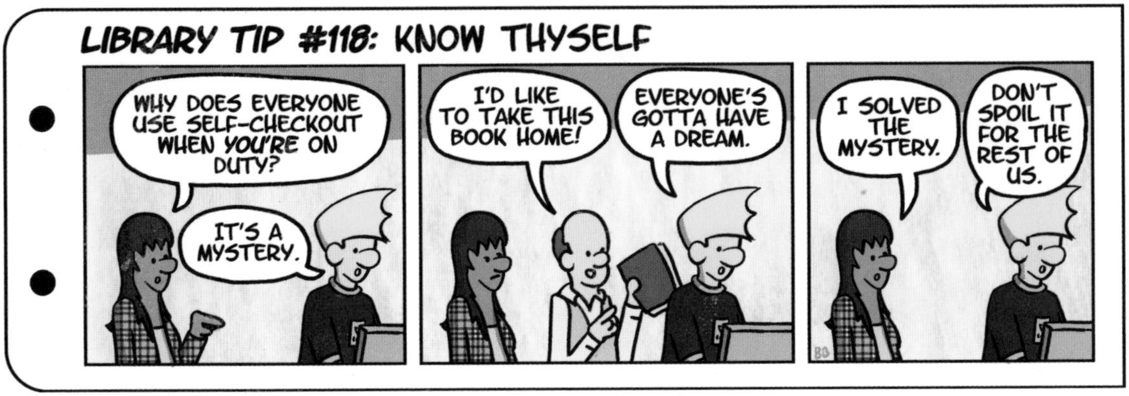
LIBRARY TIP #118: KNOW THYSELF
WHY DOES EVERYONE USE SELF-CHECKOUT WHEN YOU'RE ON DUTY?
IT'S A MYSTERY.
I'D LIKE TO TAKE THIS BOOK HOME!
EVERYONE'S GOTTA HAVE A DREAM.
I SOLVED THE MYSTERY.
DON'T SPOIL IT FOR THE REST OF US.
BB

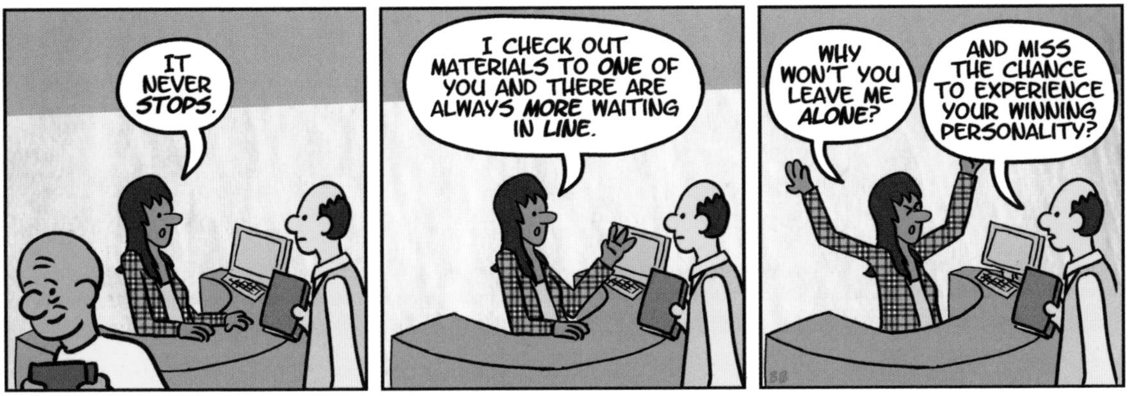
IT NEVER STOPS.
I CHECK OUT MATERIALS TO ONE OF YOU AND THERE ARE ALWAYS MORE WAITING IN LINE.
WHY WON'T YOU LEAVE ME ALONE?
AND MISS THE CHANCE TO EXPERIENCE YOUR WINNING PERSONALITY?
BB

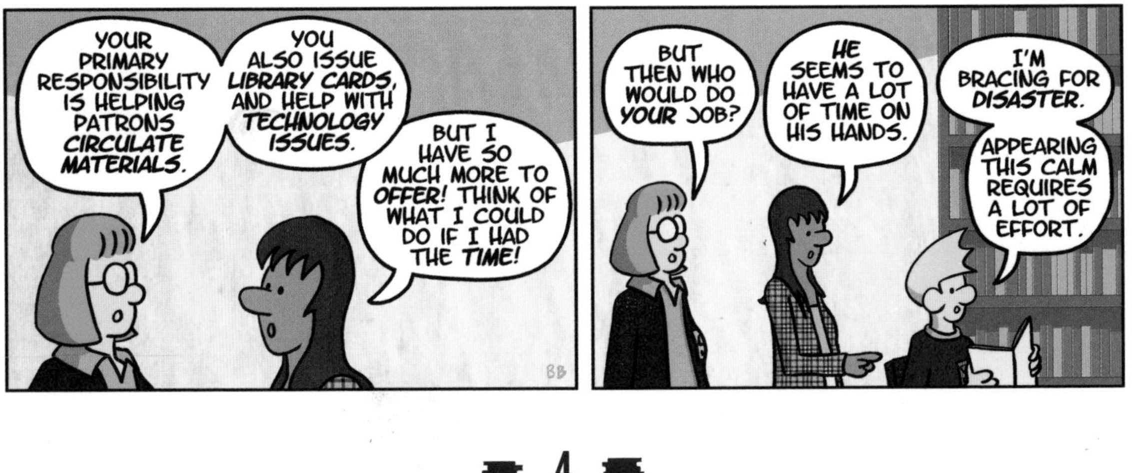
YOUR PRIMARY RESPONSIBILITY IS HELPING PATRONS CIRCULATE MATERIALS.
YOU ALSO ISSUE LIBRARY CARDS, AND HELP WITH TECHNOLOGY ISSUES.
BUT I HAVE SO MUCH MORE TO OFFER! THINK OF WHAT I COULD DO IF I HAD THE TIME!
BB
BUT THEN WHO WOULD DO YOUR JOB?
HE SEEMS TO HAVE A LOT OF TIME ON HIS HANDS.
I'M BRACING FOR DISASTER.
APPEARING THIS CALM REQUIRES A LOT OF EFFORT.

Reads Well With Others

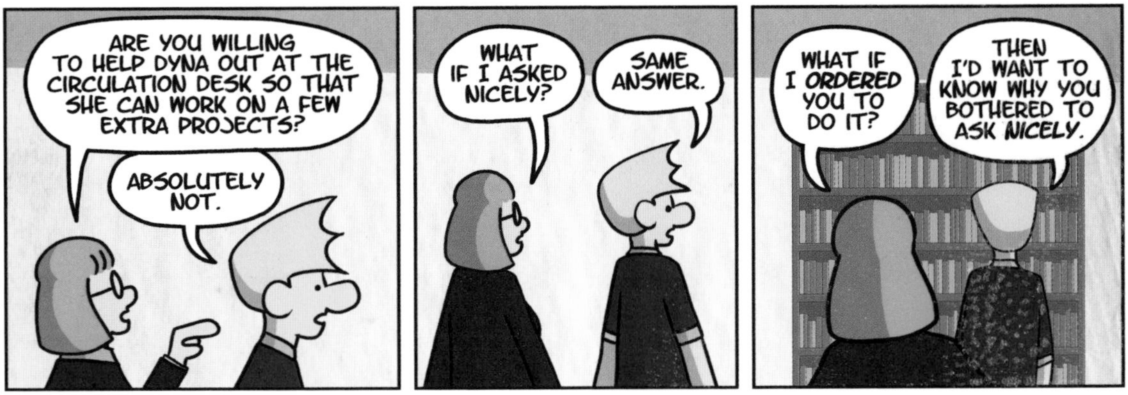
ARE YOU WILLING TO HELP DYNA OUT AT THE CIRCULATION DESK SO THAT SHE CAN WORK ON A FEW EXTRA PROJECTS?
ABSOLUTELY NOT.
WHAT IF I ASKED NICELY?
SAME ANSWER.
WHAT IF I ORDERED YOU TO DO IT?
THEN I'D WANT TO KNOW WHY YOU BOTHERED TO ASK NICELY.

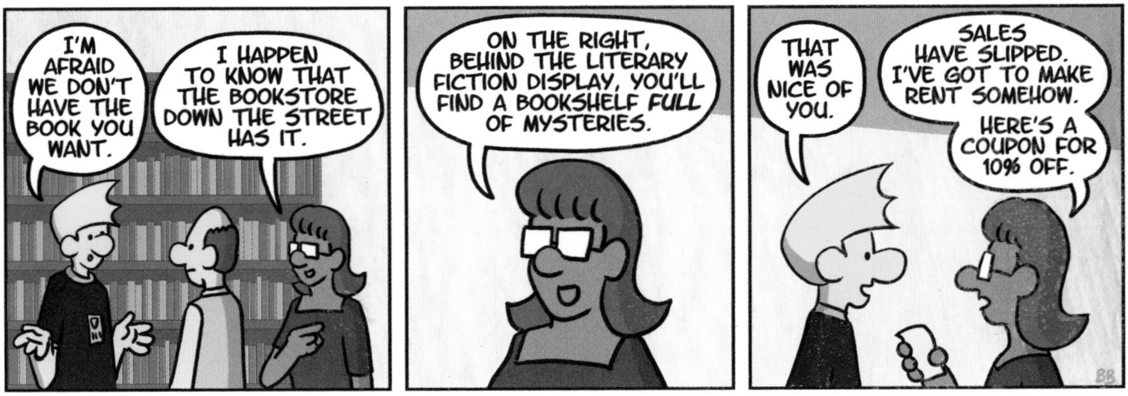
I'M AFRAID WE DON'T HAVE THE BOOK YOU WANT.
I HAPPEN TO KNOW THAT THE BOOKSTORE DOWN THE STREET HAS IT.
ON THE RIGHT, BEHIND THE LITERARY FICTION DISPLAY, YOU'LL FIND A BOOKSHELF FULL OF MYSTERIES.
THAT WAS NICE OF YOU.
SALES HAVE SLIPPED. I'VE GOT TO MAKE RENT SOMEHOW.
HERE'S A COUPON FOR 10% OFF.
BB

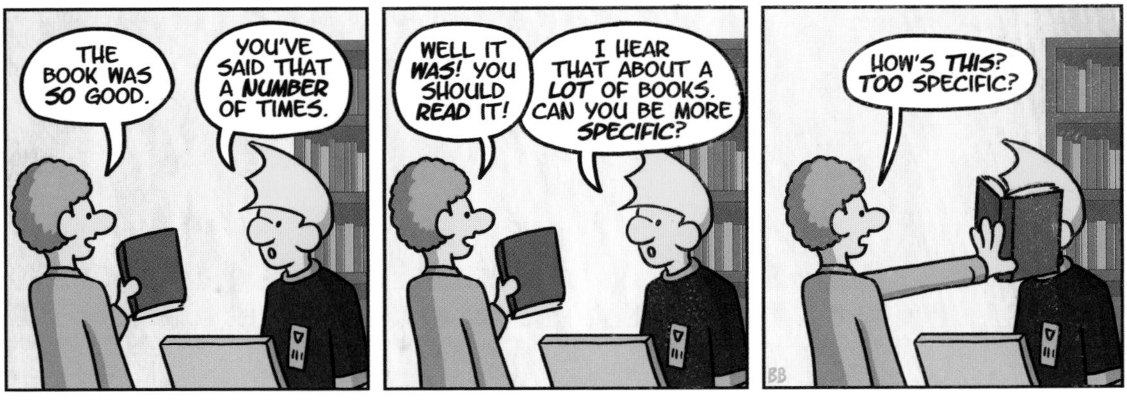
THE BOOK WAS SO GOOD.
YOU'VE SAID THAT A NUMBER OF TIMES.
WELL IT WAS! YOU SHOULD READ IT!
I HEAR THAT ABOUT A LOT OF BOOKS. CAN YOU BE MORE SPECIFIC?
HOW'S THIS? TOO SPECIFIC?
BB

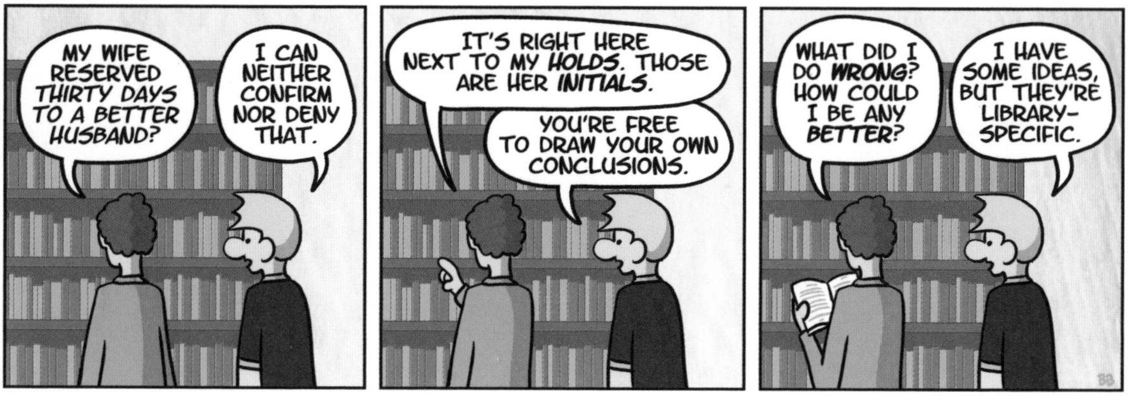
MY WIFE RESERVED THIRTY DAYS TO A BETTER HUSBAND?
I CAN NEITHER CONFIRM NOR DENY THAT.
IT'S RIGHT HERE NEXT TO MY HOLDS. THOSE ARE HER INITIALS.
YOU'RE FREE TO DRAW YOUR OWN CONCLUSIONS.
WHAT DID I DO WRONG? HOW COULD I BE ANY BETTER?
I HAVE SOME IDEAS, BUT THEY'RE LIBRARY-SPECIFIC.
BB

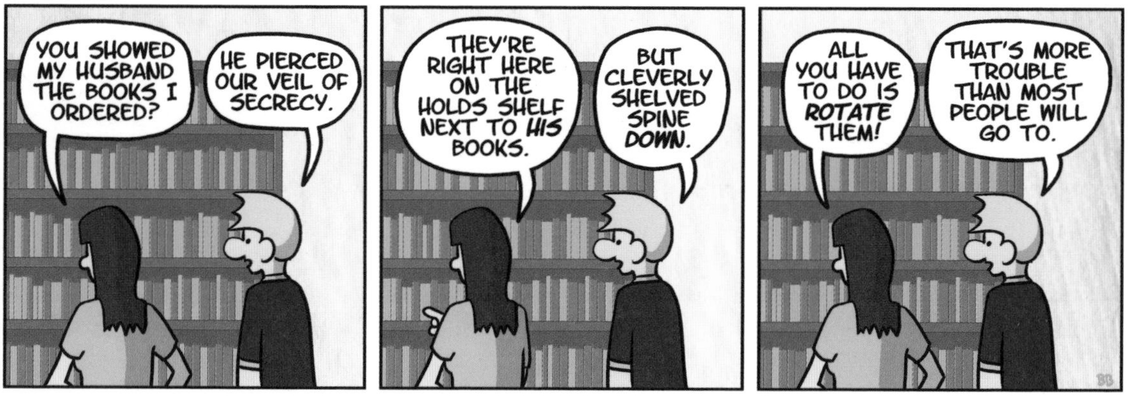
YOU SHOWED MY HUSBAND THE BOOKS I ORDERED?
HE PIERCED OUR VEIL OF SECRECY.
THEY'RE RIGHT HERE ON THE HOLDS SHELF NEXT TO HIS BOOKS.
BUT CLEVERLY SHELVED SPINE DOWN.
ALL YOU HAVE TO DO IS ROTATE THEM!
THAT'S MORE TROUBLE THAN MOST PEOPLE WILL GO TO.
BB

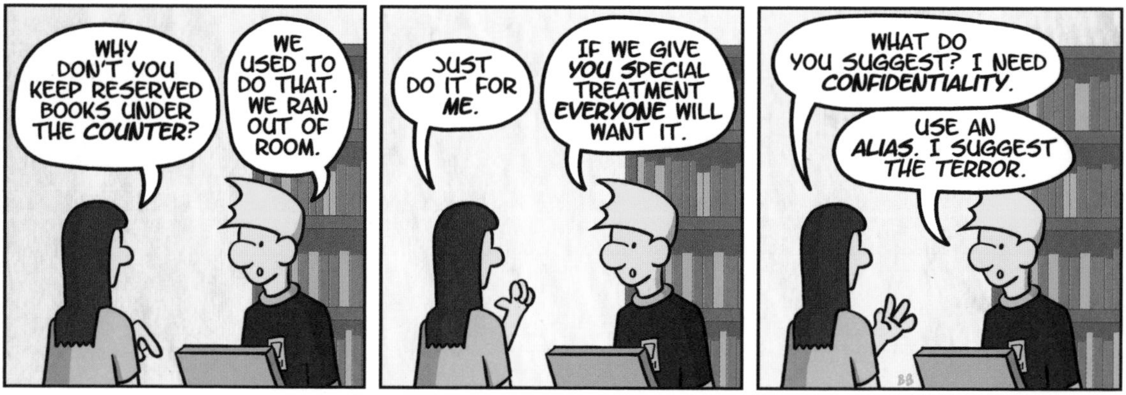
WHY DON'T YOU KEEP RESERVED BOOKS UNDER THE COUNTER?
WE USED TO DO THAT. WE RAN OUT OF ROOM.
JUST DO IT FOR ME.
IF WE GIVE YOU SPECIAL TREATMENT EVERYONE WILL WANT IT.
WHAT DO YOU SUGGEST? I NEED CONFIDENTIALITY.
USE AN ALIAS. I SUGGEST THE TERROR.
BB

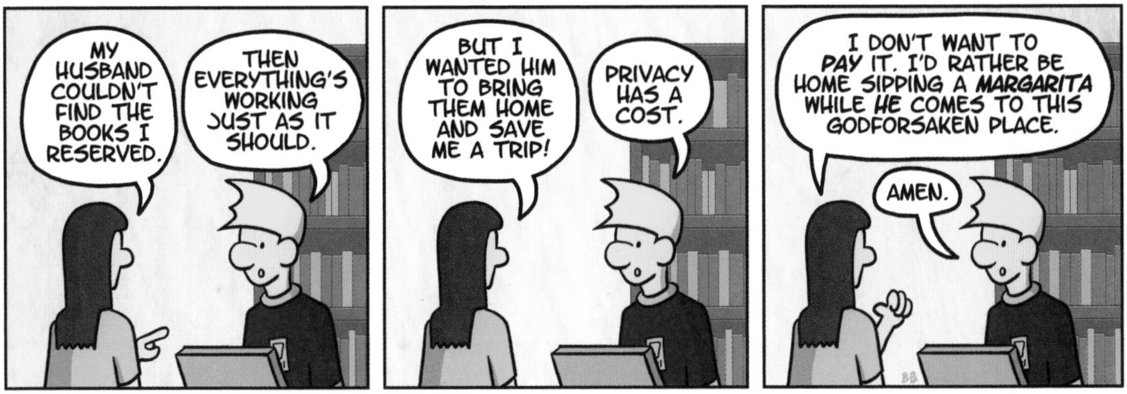
MY HUSBAND COULDN'T FIND THE BOOKS I RESERVED.
THEN EVERYTHING'S WORKING JUST AS IT SHOULD.
BUT I WANTED HIM TO BRING THEM HOME AND SAVE ME A TRIP!
PRIVACY HAS A COST.
I DON'T WANT TO PAY IT. I'D RATHER BE HOME SIPPING A MARGARITA WHILE HE COMES TO THIS GODFORSAKEN PLACE.
AMEN.

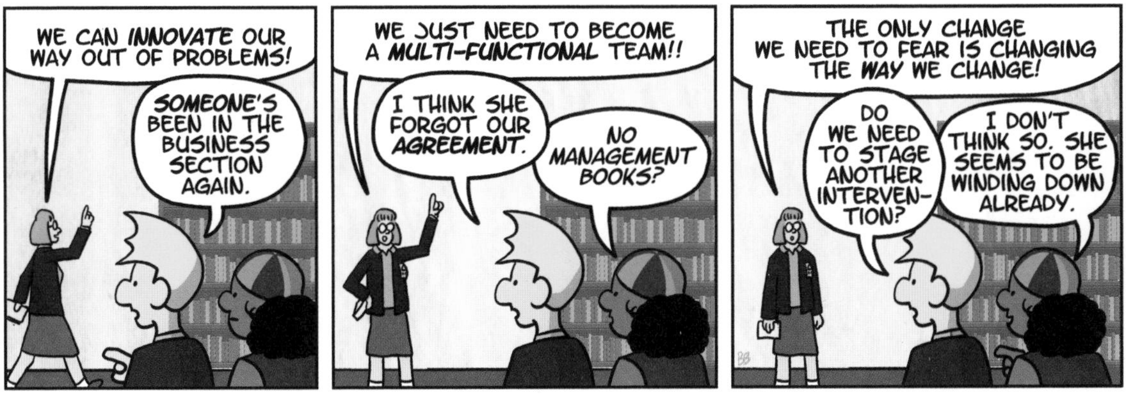
WE CAN INNOVATE OUR WAY OUT OF PROBLEMS!
SOMEONE'S BEEN IN THE BUSINESS SECTION AGAIN.
WE JUST NEED TO BECOME A MULTI-FUNCTIONAL TEAM!!
I THINK SHE FORGOT OUR AGREEMENT.
NO MANAGEMENT BOOKS?
THE ONLY CHANGE WE NEED TO FEAR IS CHANGING THE WAY WE CHANGE!
DO WE NEED TO STAGE ANOTHER INTERVENTION?
I DON'T THINK SO. SHE SEEMS TO BE WINDING DOWN ALREADY.

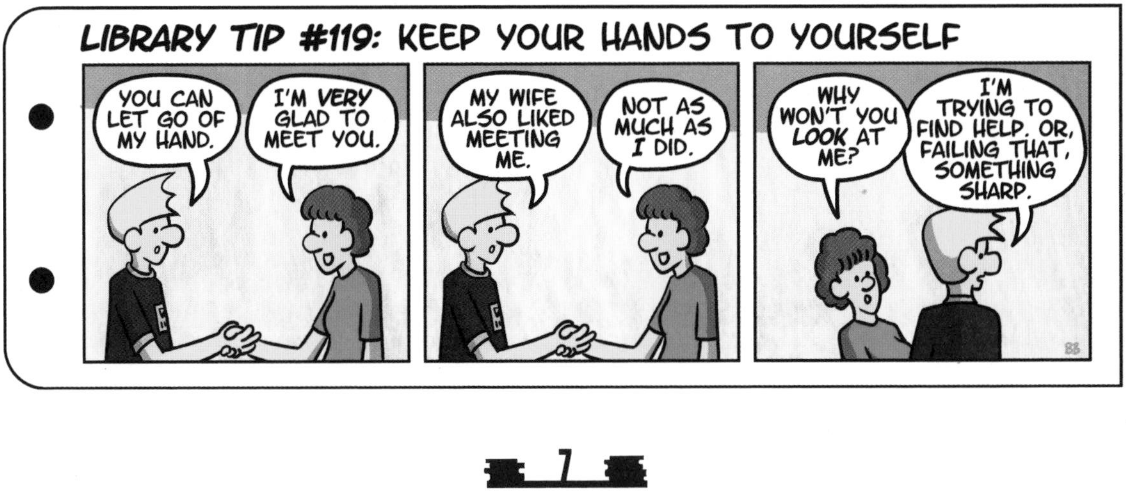
LIBRARY TIP #119: KEEP YOUR HANDS TO YOURSELF
YOU CAN LET GO OF MY HAND.
I'M VERY GLAD TO MEET YOU.
MY WIFE ALSO LIKED MEETING ME.
NOT AS MUCH AS I DID.
WHY WON'T YOU LOOK AT ME?
I'M TRYING TO FIND HELP. OR, FAILING THAT, SOMETHING SHARP.

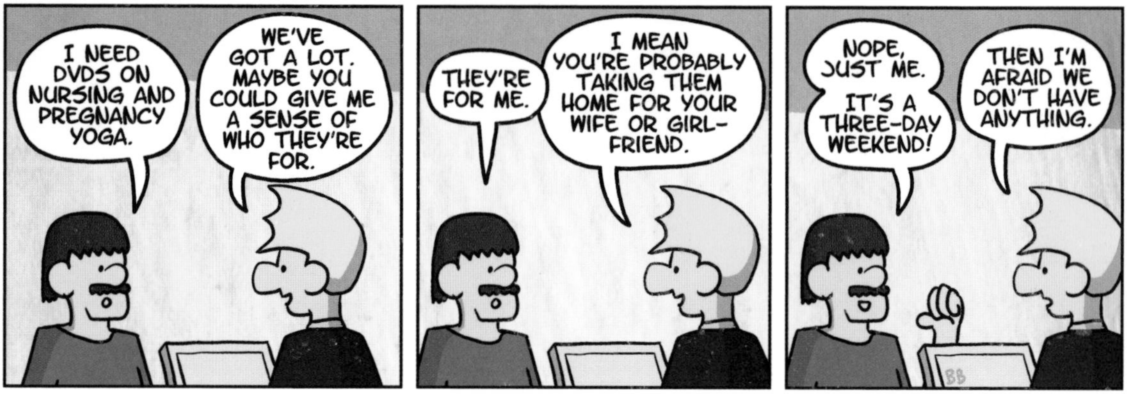
I NEED DVDS ON NURSING AND PREGNANCY YOGA.
WE'VE GOT A LOT. MAYBE YOU COULD GIVE ME A SENSE OF WHO THEY'RE FOR.
THEY'RE FOR ME.
I MEAN YOU'RE PROBABLY TAKING THEM HOME FOR YOUR WIFE OR GIRL-FRIEND.
NOPE, JUST ME.
IT'S A THREE-DAY WEEKEND!
THEN I'M AFRAID WE DON'T HAVE ANYTHING.
BB

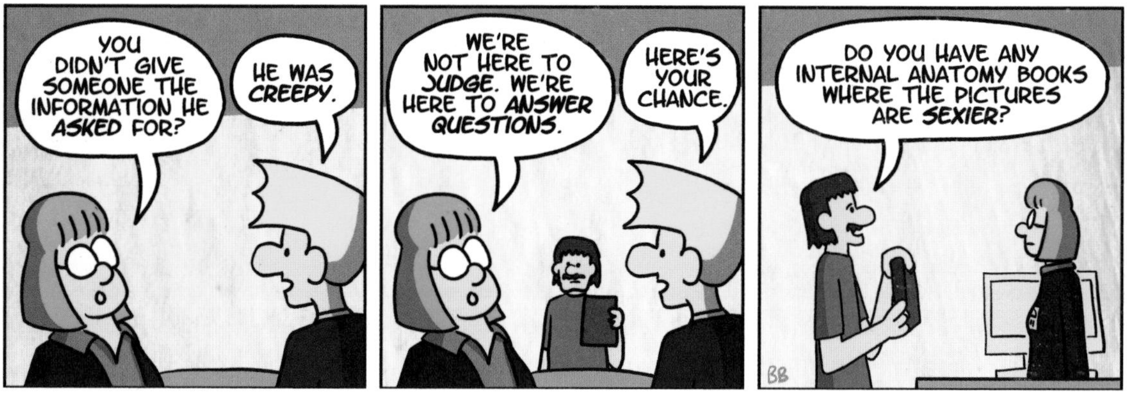
YOU DIDN'T GIVE SOMEONE THE INFORMATION HE ASKED FOR?
HE WAS CREEPY.
WE'RE NOT HERE TO JUDGE. WE'RE HERE TO ANSWER QUESTIONS.
HERE'S YOUR CHANCE.
DO YOU HAVE ANY INTERNAL ANATOMY BOOKS WHERE THE PICTURES ARE SEXIER?
BB

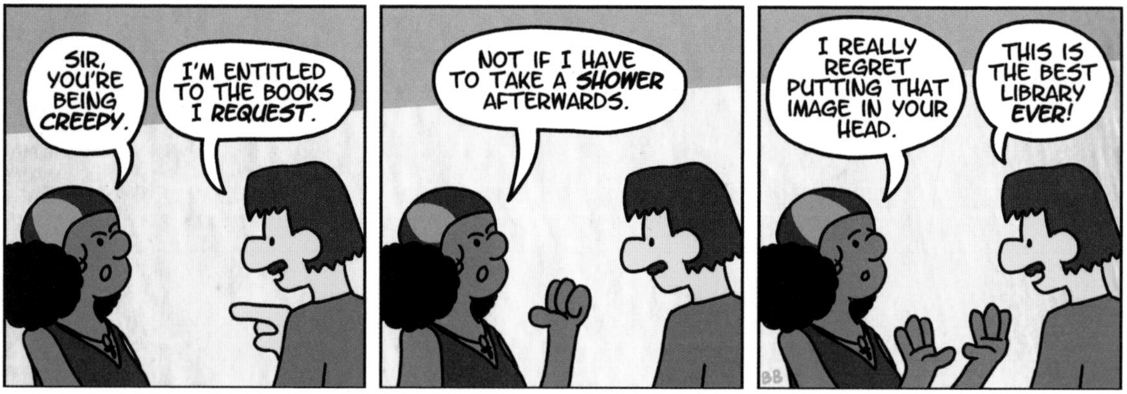
SIR, YOU'RE BEING CREEPY.
I'M ENTITLED TO THE BOOKS I REQUEST.
NOT IF I HAVE TO TAKE A SHOWER AFTERWARDS.
I REALLY REGRET PUTTING THAT IMAGE IN YOUR HEAD.
THIS IS THE BEST LIBRARY EVER!
BB

Reads Well With Others

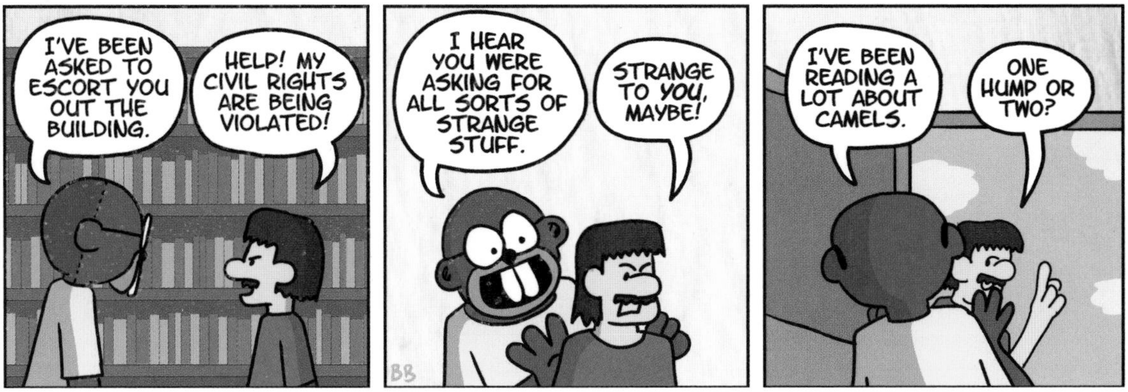
I'VE BEEN ASKED TO ESCORT YOU OUT THE BUILDING.
HELP! MY CIVIL RIGHTS ARE BEING VIOLATED!
I HEAR YOU WERE ASKING FOR ALL SORTS OF STRANGE STUFF.
STRANGE TO *YOU*, MAYBE!
BB
I'VE BEEN READING A LOT ABOUT CAMELS.
ONE HUMP OR TWO?

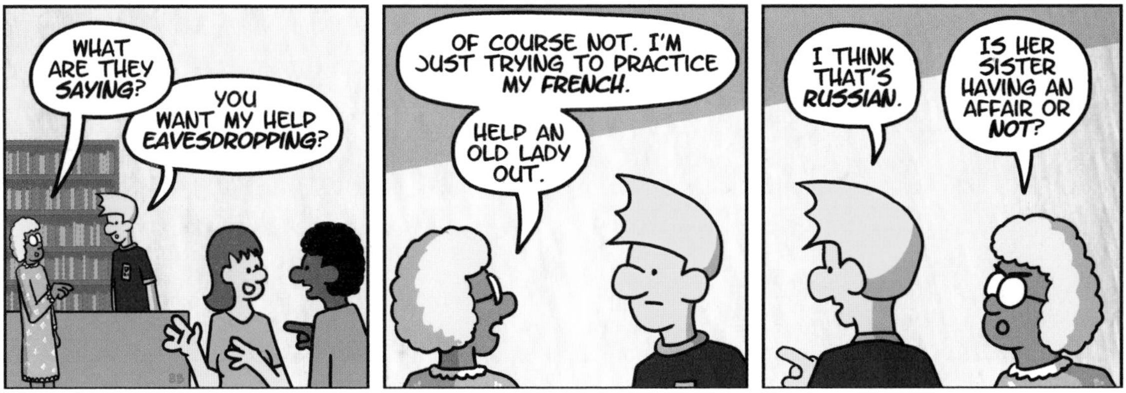
WHAT ARE THEY *SAYING*?
YOU WANT MY HELP *EAVESDROPPING*?
BB
OF COURSE NOT. I'M JUST TRYING TO PRACTICE MY *FRENCH*.
HELP AN OLD LADY OUT.
I THINK THAT'S *RUSSIAN*.
IS HER SISTER HAVING AN AFFAIR OR *NOT*?

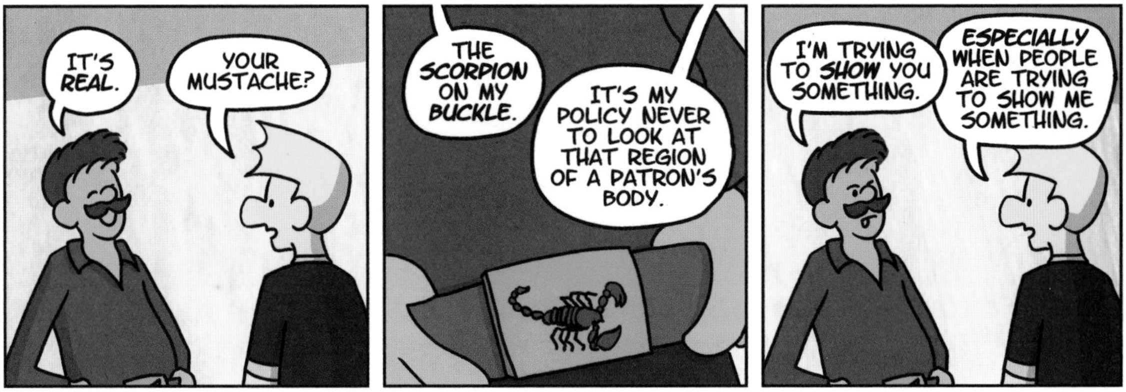
IT'S *REAL*.
YOUR MUSTACHE?
THE *SCORPION* ON MY *BUCKLE*.
IT'S MY POLICY NEVER TO LOOK AT THAT REGION OF A PATRON'S BODY.
I'M TRYING TO *SHOW* YOU SOMETHING.
ESPECIALLY WHEN PEOPLE ARE TRYING TO SHOW ME SOMETHING.

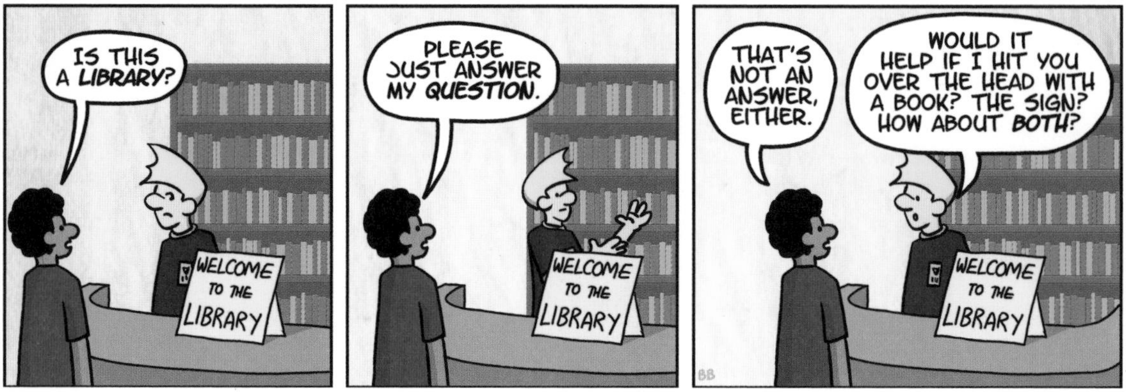
IS THIS A LIBRARY?
WELCOME TO THE LIBRARY
PLEASE JUST ANSWER MY QUESTION.
WELCOME TO THE LIBRARY
THAT'S NOT AN ANSWER, EITHER.
WOULD IT HELP IF I HIT YOU OVER THE HEAD WITH A BOOK? THE SIGN? HOW ABOUT BOTH?
WELCOME TO THE LIBRARY
BB

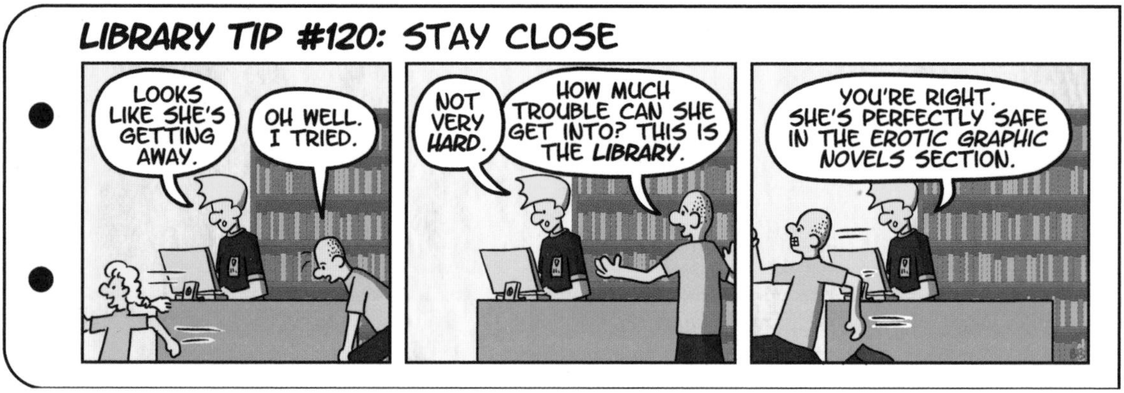
LIBRARY TIP #120: STAY CLOSE
LOOKS LIKE SHE'S GETTING AWAY.
OH WELL. I TRIED.
NOT VERY HARD.
HOW MUCH TROUBLE CAN SHE GET INTO? THIS IS THE LIBRARY.
YOU'RE RIGHT. SHE'S PERFECTLY SAFE IN THE EROTIC GRAPHIC NOVELS SECTION.
BB

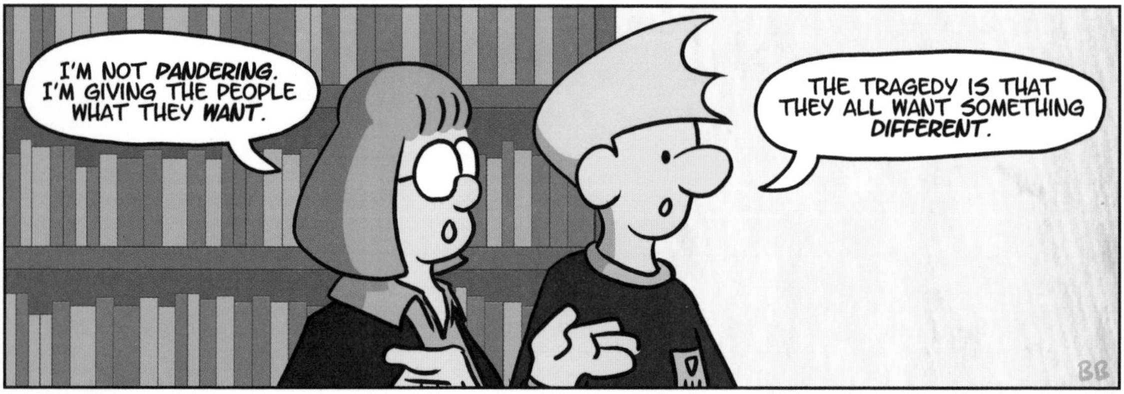
I'M NOT PANDERING. I'M GIVING THE PEOPLE WHAT THEY WANT.
THE TRAGEDY IS THAT THEY ALL WANT SOMETHING DIFFERENT.
BB

Reads Well With Others

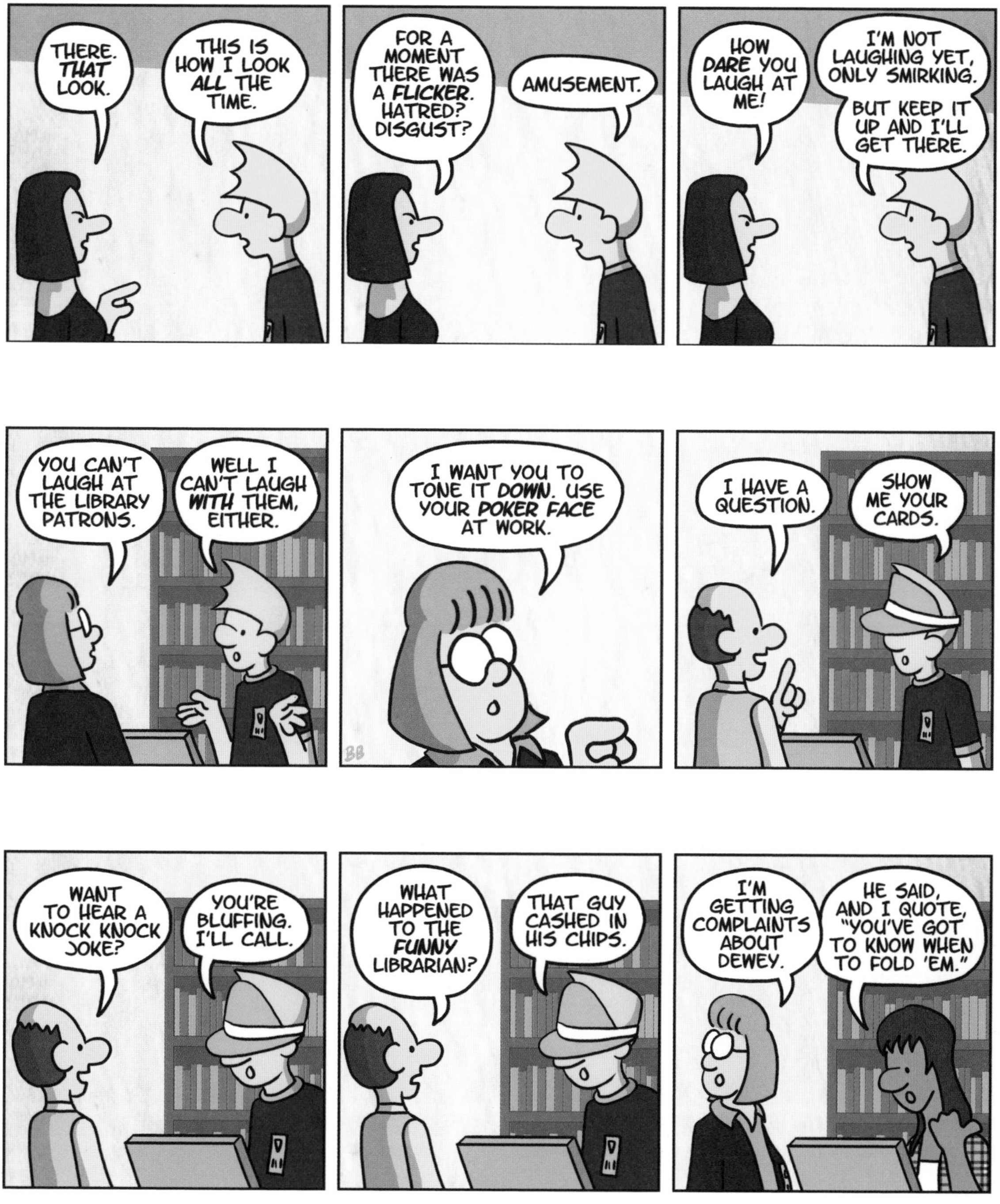
THERE. THAT LOOK.
THIS IS HOW I LOOK ALL THE TIME.
FOR A MOMENT THERE WAS A FLICKER. HATRED? DISGUST?
AMUSEMENT.
HOW DARE YOU LAUGH AT ME!
I'M NOT LAUGHING YET, ONLY SMIRKING.
BUT KEEP IT UP AND I'LL GET THERE.
YOU CAN'T LAUGH AT THE LIBRARY PATRONS.
WELL I CAN'T LAUGH WITH THEM, EITHER.
I WANT YOU TO TONE IT DOWN. USE YOUR POKER FACE AT WORK.
BB
I HAVE A QUESTION.
SHOW ME YOUR CARDS.
WANT TO HEAR A KNOCK KNOCK JOKE?
YOU'RE BLUFFING. I'LL CALL.
WHAT HAPPENED TO THE FUNNY LIBRARIAN?
THAT GUY CASHED IN HIS CHIPS.
I'M GETTING COMPLAINTS ABOUT DEWEY.
HE SAID, AND I QUOTE, "YOU'VE GOT TO KNOW WHEN TO FOLD 'EM."

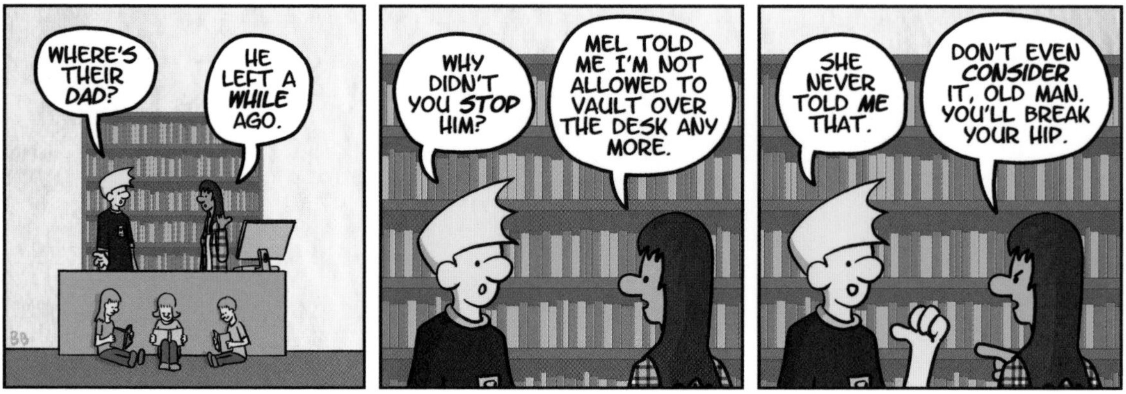
WHERE'S THEIR DAD?
HE LEFT A WHILE AGO.
WHY DIDN'T YOU STOP HIM?
MEL TOLD ME I'M NOT ALLOWED TO VAULT OVER THE DESK ANY MORE.
SHE NEVER TOLD ME THAT.
DON'T EVEN CONSIDER IT, OLD MAN. YOU'LL BREAK YOUR HIP.

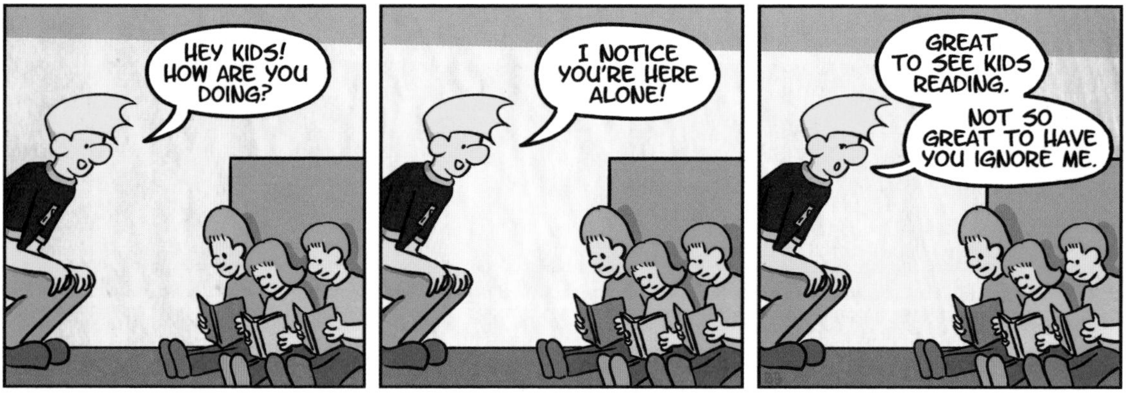
HEY KIDS! HOW ARE YOU DOING?
I NOTICE YOU'RE HERE ALONE!
GREAT TO SEE KIDS READING.
NOT SO GREAT TO HAVE YOU IGNORE ME.

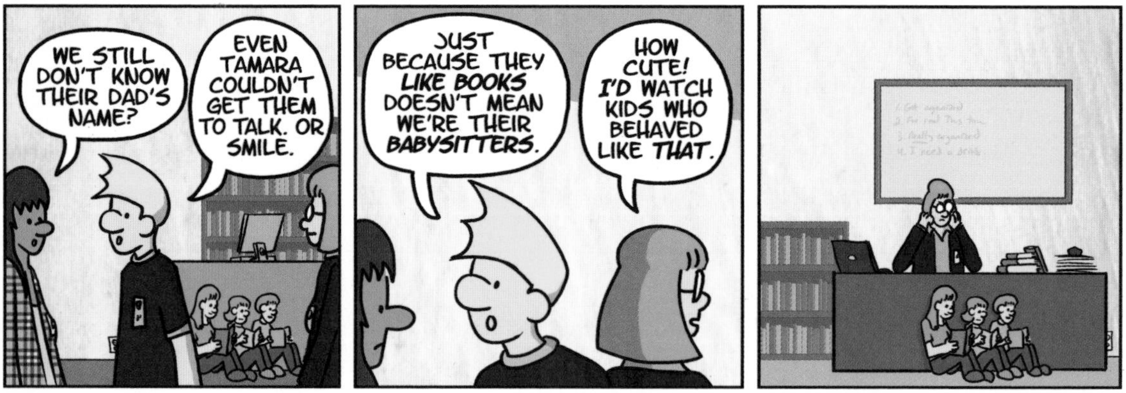
WE STILL DON'T KNOW THEIR DAD'S NAME?
EVEN TAMARA COULDN'T GET THEM TO TALK. OR SMILE.
JUST BECAUSE THEY LIKE BOOKS DOESN'T MEAN WE'RE THEIR BABYSITTERS.
HOW CUTE! I'D WATCH KIDS WHO BEHAVED LIKE THAT.

Reads Well With Others

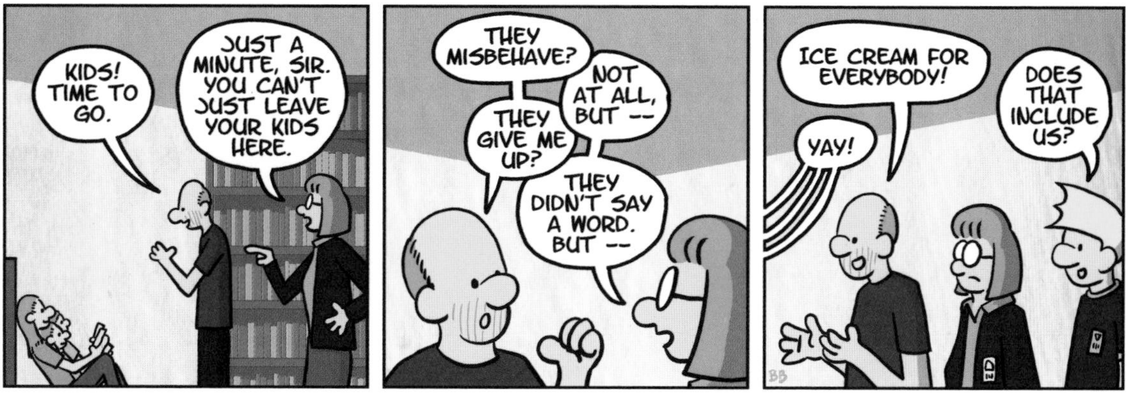
KIDS! TIME TO GO.
JUST A MINUTE, SIR. YOU CAN'T JUST LEAVE YOUR KIDS HERE.
THEY MISBEHAVE?
NOT AT ALL, BUT --
THEY GIVE ME UP?
THEY DIDN'T SAY A WORD. BUT --
ICE CREAM FOR EVERYBODY!
YAY!
DOES THAT INCLUDE US?
BB

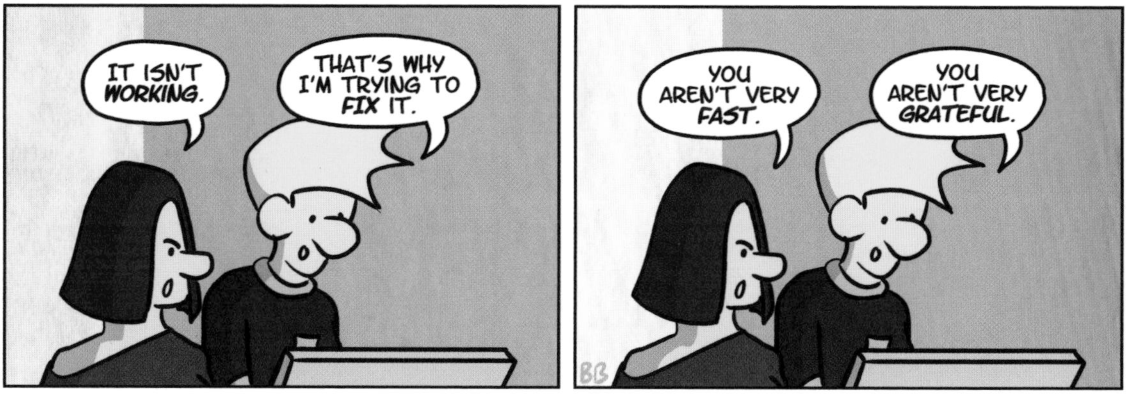
IT ISN'T WORKING.
THAT'S WHY I'M TRYING TO FIX IT.
YOU AREN'T VERY FAST.
YOU AREN'T VERY GRATEFUL.
BB

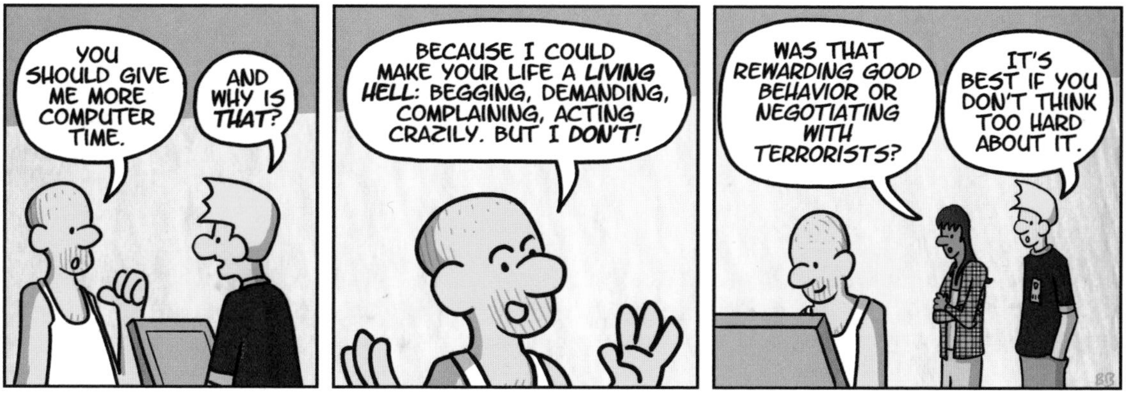
YOU SHOULD GIVE ME MORE COMPUTER TIME.
AND WHY IS THAT?
BECAUSE I COULD MAKE YOUR LIFE A LIVING HELL: BEGGING, DEMANDING, COMPLAINING, ACTING CRAZILY. BUT I DON'T!
WAS THAT REWARDING GOOD BEHAVIOR OR NEGOTIATING WITH TERRORISTS?
IT'S BEST IF YOU DON'T THINK TOO HARD ABOUT IT.
BB

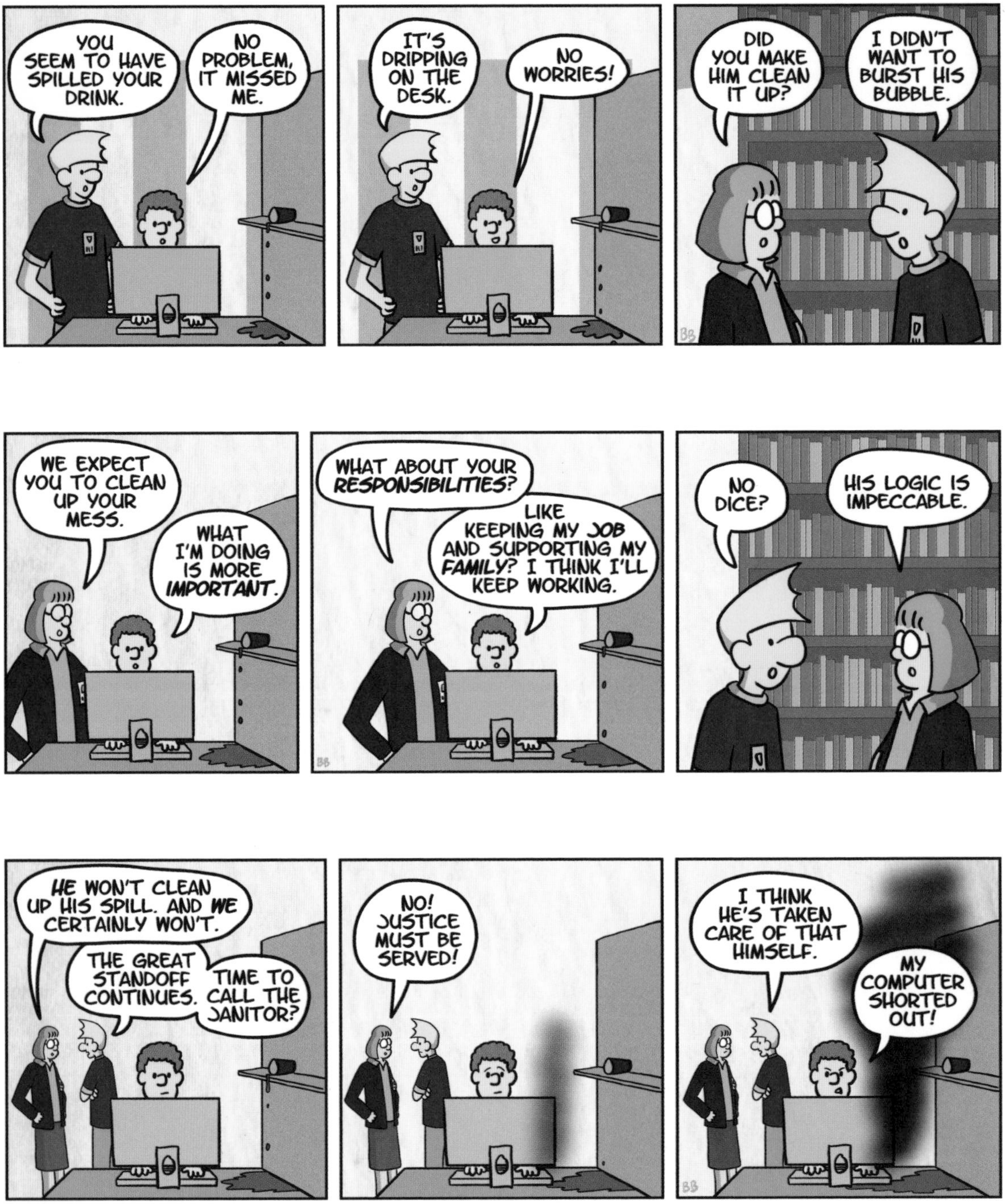
YOU SEEM TO HAVE SPILLED YOUR DRINK.
NO PROBLEM, IT MISSED ME.
IT'S DRIPPING ON THE DESK.
NO WORRIES!
DID YOU MAKE HIM CLEAN IT UP?
I DIDN'T WANT TO BURST HIS BUBBLE.
BB
WE EXPECT YOU TO CLEAN UP YOUR MESS.
WHAT I'M DOING IS MORE IMPORTANT.
WHAT ABOUT YOUR RESPONSIBILITIES?
LIKE KEEPING MY JOB AND SUPPORTING MY FAMILY? I THINK I'LL KEEP WORKING.
BB
NO DICE?
HIS LOGIC IS IMPECCABLE.
HE WON'T CLEAN UP HIS SPILL. AND WE CERTAINLY WON'T.
THE GREAT STANDOFF CONTINUES.
TIME TO CALL THE JANITOR?
NO! JUSTICE MUST BE SERVED!
I THINK HE'S TAKEN CARE OF THAT HIMSELF.
MY COMPUTER SHORTED OUT!
BB

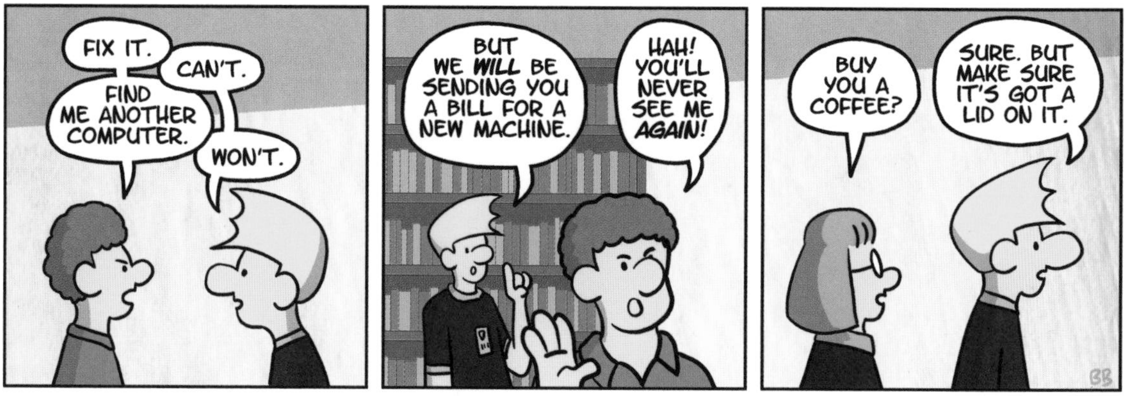
FIX IT.
CAN'T.
FIND ME ANOTHER COMPUTER.
WON'T.
BUT WE *WILL* BE SENDING YOU A BILL FOR A NEW MACHINE.
HAH! YOU'LL NEVER SEE ME *AGAIN!*
BUY YOU A COFFEE?
SURE. BUT MAKE SURE IT'S GOT A LID ON IT.
BB

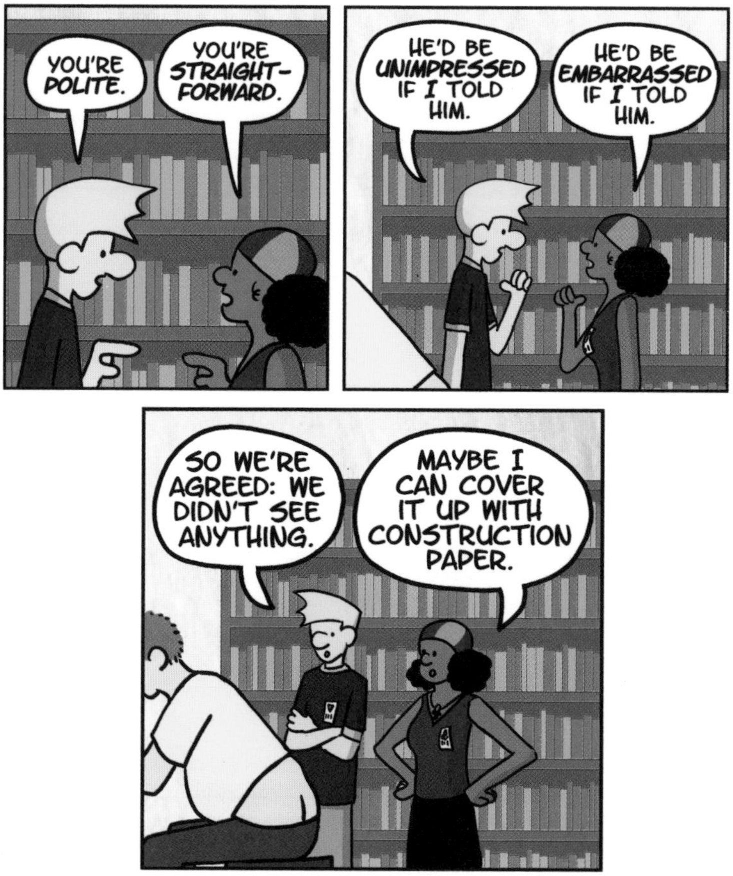
YOU'RE *POLITE.*
YOU'RE *STRAIGHT-FORWARD.*
HE'D BE *UNIMPRESSED* IF *I* TOLD HIM.
HE'D BE *EMBARRASSED* IF *I* TOLD HIM.
SO WE'RE AGREED: WE DIDN'T SEE ANYTHING.
MAYBE I CAN COVER IT UP WITH CONSTRUCTION PAPER.

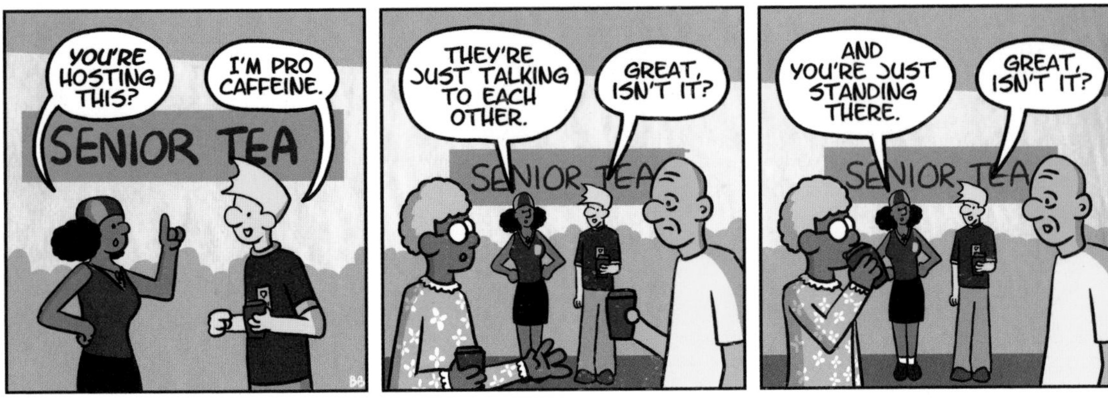
YOU'RE HOSTING THIS?
I'M PRO CAFFEINE.
SENIOR TEA
THEY'RE JUST TALKING TO EACH OTHER.
GREAT, ISN'T IT?
AND YOU'RE JUST STANDING THERE.
GREAT, ISN'T IT?

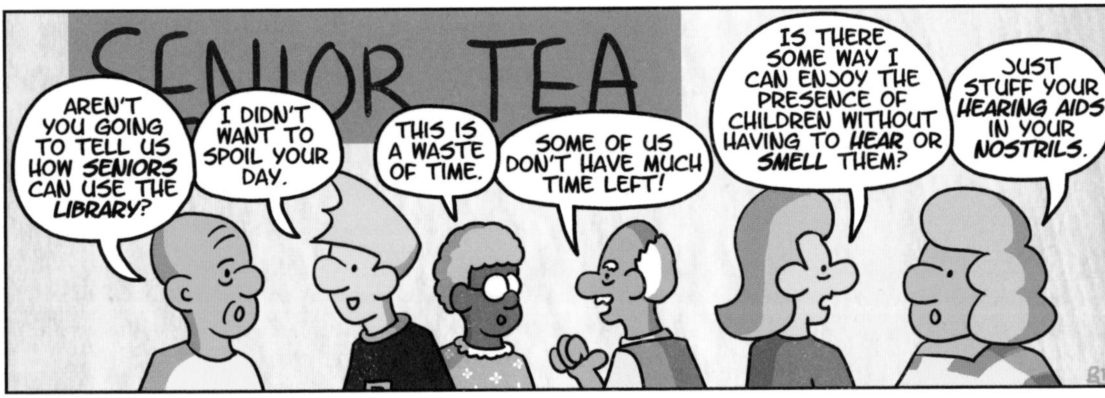
SENIOR TEA
AREN'T YOU GOING TO TELL US HOW SENIORS CAN USE THE LIBRARY?
I DIDN'T WANT TO SPOIL YOUR DAY.
THIS IS A WASTE OF TIME.
SOME OF US DON'T HAVE MUCH TIME LEFT!
IS THERE SOME WAY I CAN ENJOY THE PRESENCE OF CHILDREN WITHOUT HAVING TO HEAR OR SMELL THEM?
JUST STUFF YOUR HEARING AIDS IN YOUR NOSTRILS.

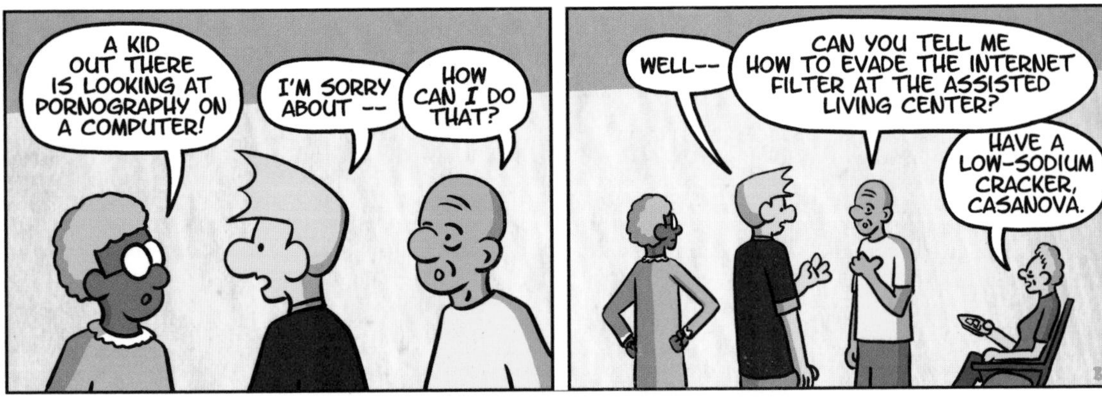
A KID OUT THERE IS LOOKING AT PORNOGRAPHY ON A COMPUTER!
I'M SORRY ABOUT --
HOW CAN I DO THAT?
WELL--
CAN YOU TELL ME HOW TO EVADE THE INTERNET FILTER AT THE ASSISTED LIVING CENTER?
HAVE A LOW-SODIUM CRACKER, CASANOVA.

Reads Well With Others

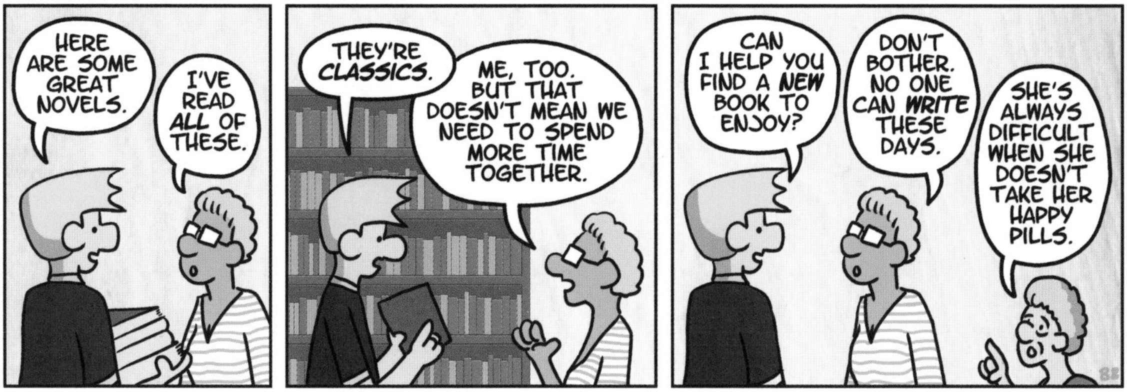
HERE ARE SOME GREAT NOVELS.
I'VE READ ALL OF THESE.
THEY'RE CLASSICS.
ME, TOO. BUT THAT DOESN'T MEAN WE NEED TO SPEND MORE TIME TOGETHER.
CAN I HELP YOU FIND A NEW BOOK TO ENJOY?
DON'T BOTHER. NO ONE CAN WRITE THESE DAYS.
SHE'S ALWAYS DIFFICULT WHEN SHE DOESN'T TAKE HER HAPPY PILLS.

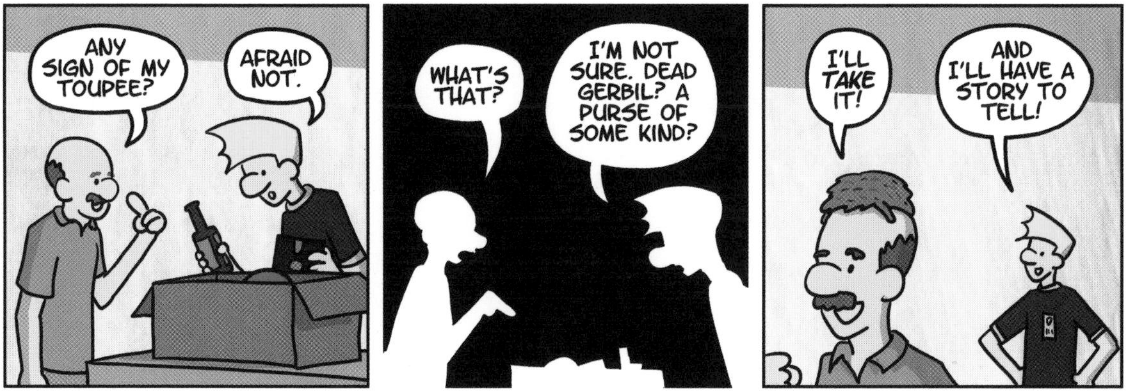
ANY SIGN OF MY TOUPEE?
AFRAID NOT.
WHAT'S THAT?
I'M NOT SURE. DEAD GERBIL? A PURSE OF SOME KIND?
I'LL TAKE IT!
AND I'LL HAVE A STORY TO TELL!

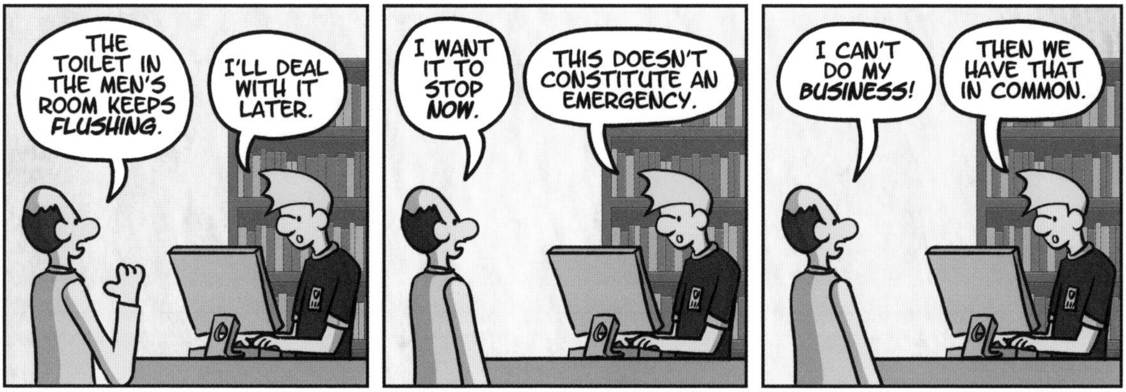
THE TOILET IN THE MEN'S ROOM KEEPS FLUSHING.
I'LL DEAL WITH IT LATER.
I WANT IT TO STOP NOW.
THIS DOESN'T CONSTITUTE AN EMERGENCY.
I CAN'T DO MY BUSINESS!
THEN WE HAVE THAT IN COMMON.

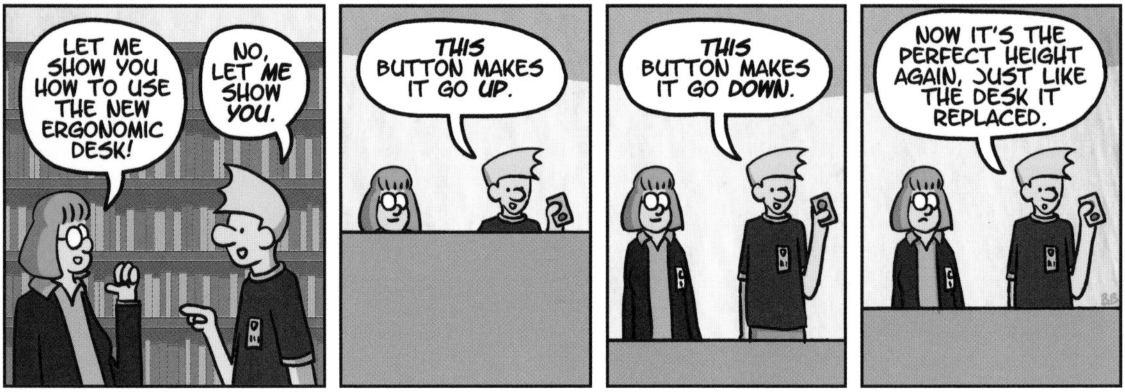
LET ME SHOW YOU HOW TO USE THE NEW ERGONOMIC DESK!
NO, LET ME SHOW YOU.
THIS BUTTON MAKES IT GO UP.
THIS BUTTON MAKES IT GO DOWN.
NOW IT'S THE PERFECT HEIGHT AGAIN, JUST LIKE THE DESK IT REPLACED.
BB

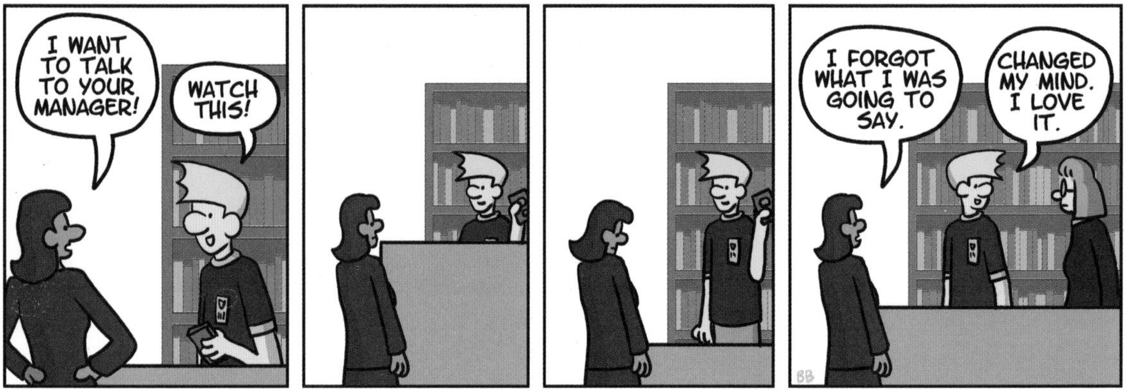
I WANT TO TALK TO YOUR MANAGER!
WATCH THIS!
I FORGOT WHAT I WAS GOING TO SAY.
CHANGED MY MIND. I LOVE IT.
BB

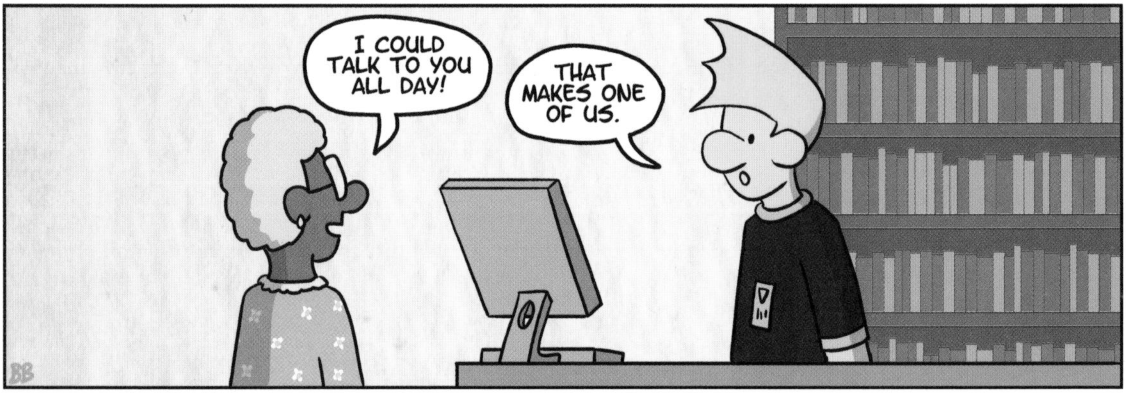
I COULD TALK TO YOU ALL DAY!
THAT MAKES ONE OF US.
BB

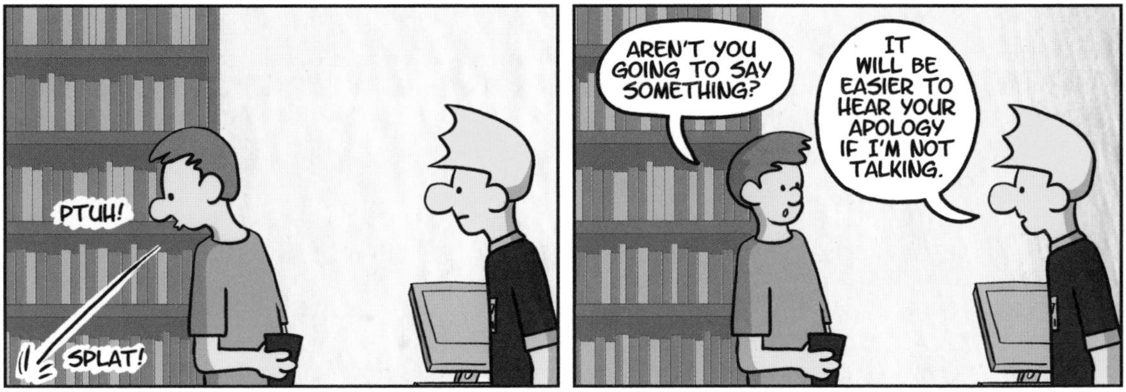
PTUH!
SPLAT!
AREN'T YOU GOING TO SAY SOMETHING?
IT WILL BE EASIER TO HEAR YOUR APOLOGY IF I'M NOT TALKING.

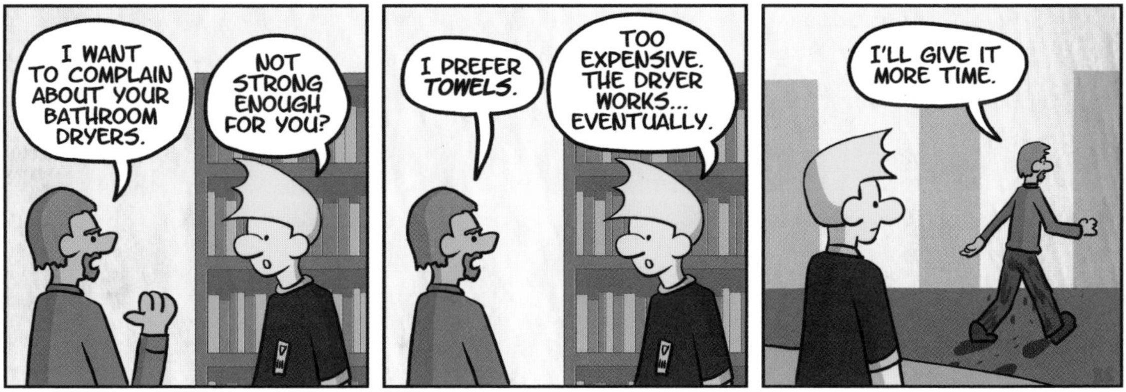
I WANT TO COMPLAIN ABOUT YOUR BATHROOM DRYERS.
NOT STRONG ENOUGH FOR YOU?
I PREFER TOWELS.
TOO EXPENSIVE. THE DRYER WORKS... EVENTUALLY.
I'LL GIVE IT MORE TIME.

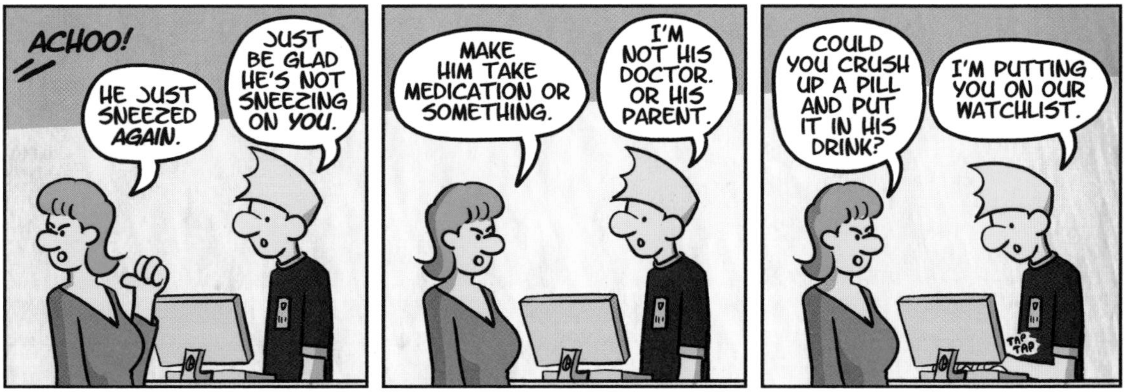
ACHOO!
HE JUST SNEEZED AGAIN.
JUST BE GLAD HE'S NOT SNEEZING ON YOU.
MAKE HIM TAKE MEDICATION OR SOMETHING.
I'M NOT HIS DOCTOR. OR HIS PARENT.
COULD YOU CRUSH UP A PILL AND PUT IT IN HIS DRINK?
I'M PUTTING YOU ON OUR WATCHLIST.
TAP TAP

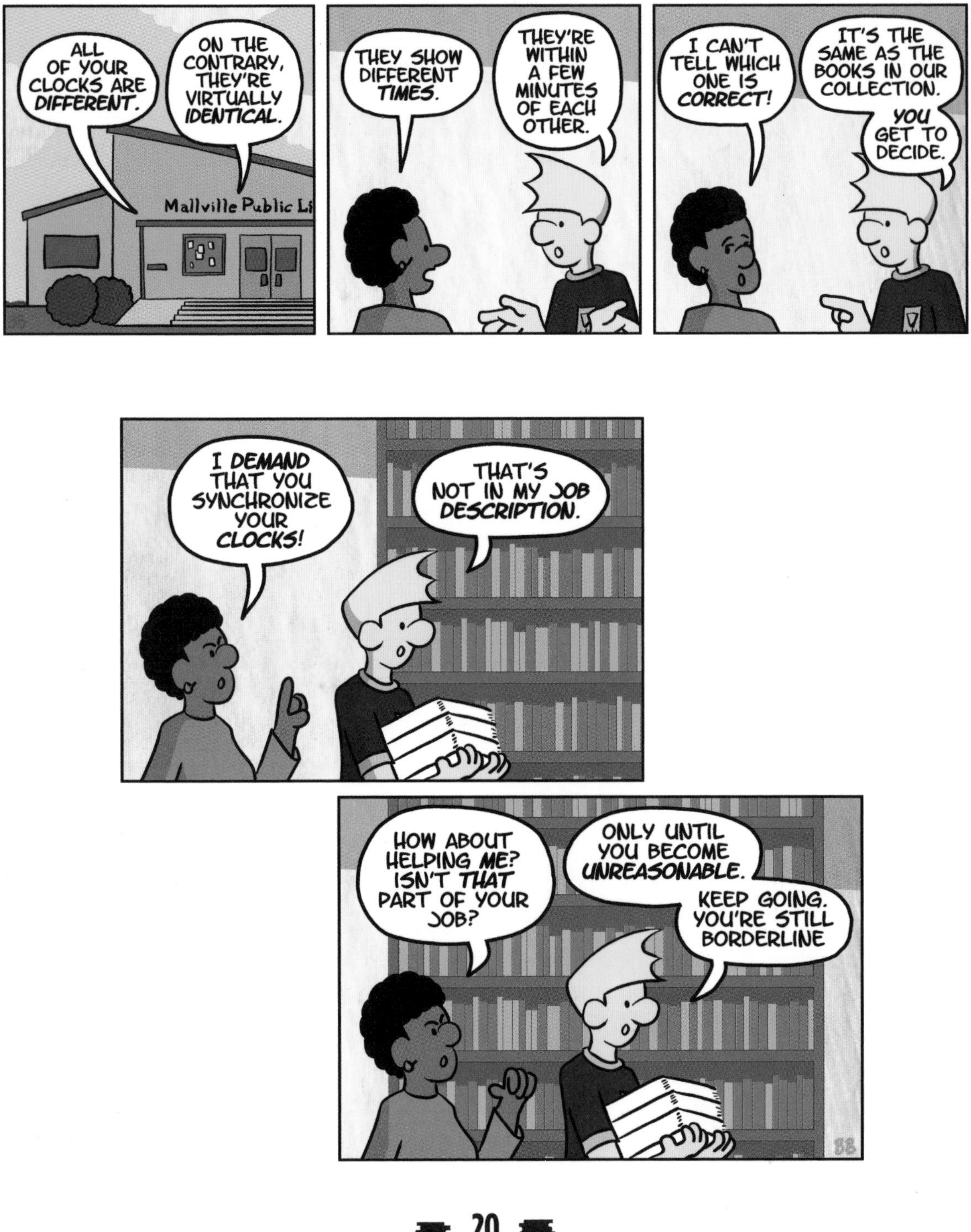
ALL OF YOUR CLOCKS ARE *DIFFERENT*.
ON THE CONTRARY, THEY'RE VIRTUALLY *IDENTICAL*.
Mallville Public Li
THEY SHOW DIFFERENT *TIMES*.
THEY'RE WITHIN A FEW MINUTES OF EACH OTHER.
I CAN'T TELL WHICH ONE IS *CORRECT*!
IT'S THE SAME AS THE BOOKS IN OUR COLLECTION.
YOU GET TO DECIDE.
I *DEMAND* THAT YOU SYNCHRONIZE YOUR *CLOCKS*!
THAT'S NOT IN MY *JOB DESCRIPTION*.
HOW ABOUT HELPING *ME*? ISN'T *THAT* PART OF YOUR JOB?
ONLY UNTIL YOU BECOME *UNREASONABLE*.
KEEP GOING. YOU'RE STILL BORDERLINE
BB

Reads Well With Others

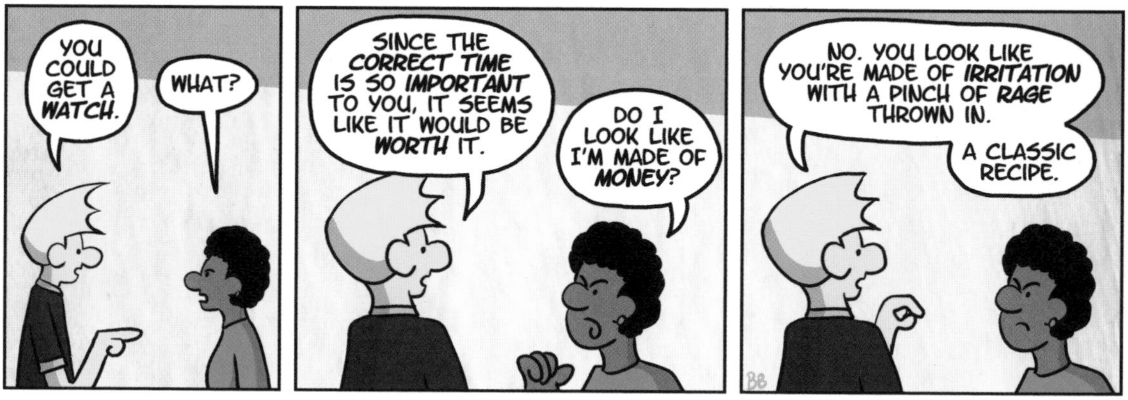
YOU COULD GET A WATCH.
WHAT?
SINCE THE CORRECT TIME IS SO IMPORTANT TO YOU, IT SEEMS LIKE IT WOULD BE WORTH IT.
DO I LOOK LIKE I'M MADE OF MONEY?
NO. YOU LOOK LIKE YOU'RE MADE OF IRRITATION WITH A PINCH OF RAGE THROWN IN.
A CLASSIC RECIPE.
BB

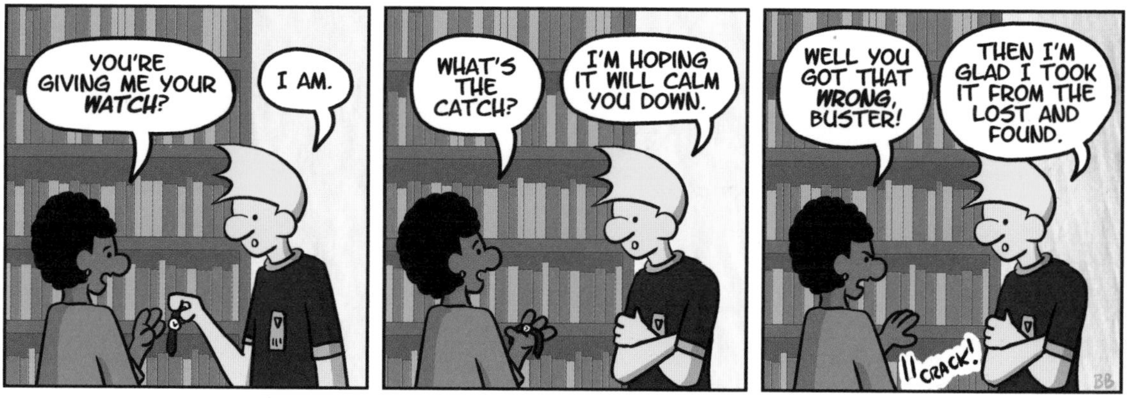
YOU'RE GIVING ME YOUR WATCH?
I AM.
WHAT'S THE CATCH?
I'M HOPING IT WILL CALM YOU DOWN.
WELL YOU GOT THAT WRONG, BUSTER!
THEN I'M GLAD I TOOK IT FROM THE LOST AND FOUND.
CRACK!
BB

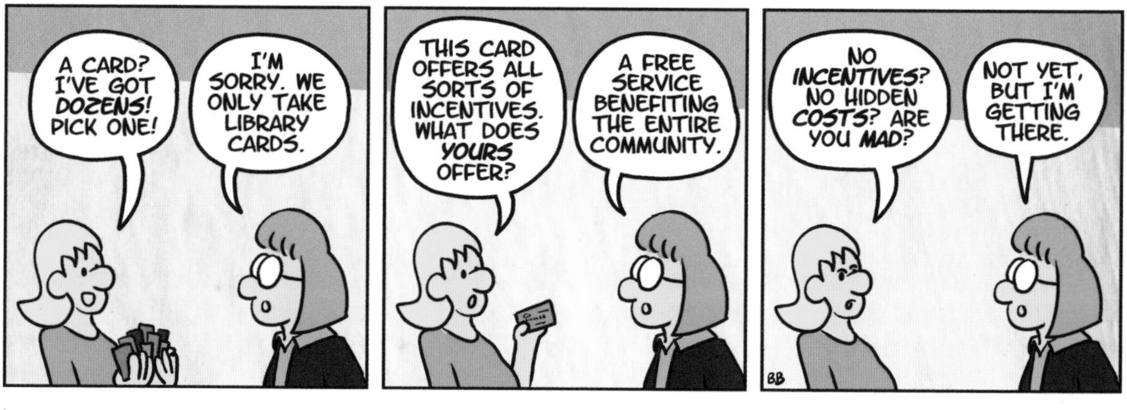
A CARD? I'VE GOT DOZENS! PICK ONE!
I'M SORRY. WE ONLY TAKE LIBRARY CARDS.
THIS CARD OFFERS ALL SORTS OF INCENTIVES. WHAT DOES YOURS OFFER?
A FREE SERVICE BENEFITING THE ENTIRE COMMUNITY.
NO INCENTIVES? NO HIDDEN COSTS? ARE YOU MAD?
NOT YET, BUT I'M GETTING THERE.
BB

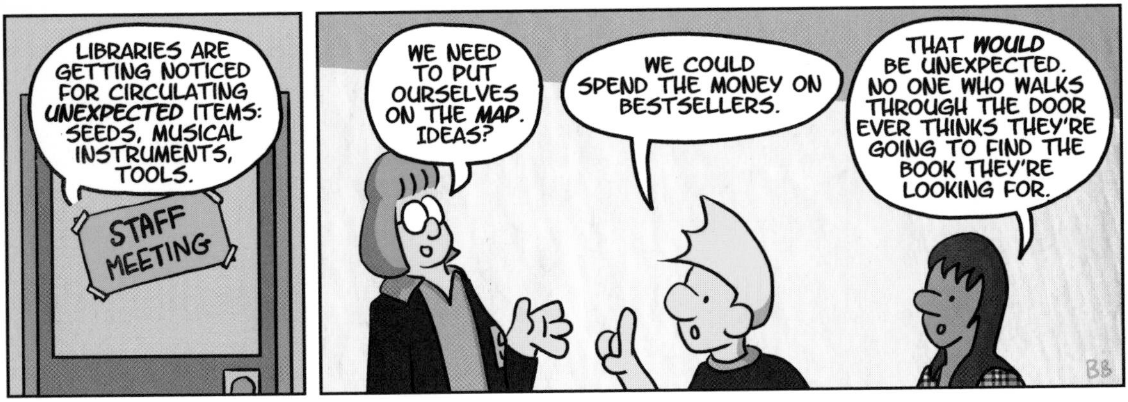
LIBRARIES ARE GETTING NOTICED FOR CIRCULATING UNEXPECTED ITEMS: SEEDS, MUSICAL INSTRUMENTS, TOOLS.
STAFF MEETING
WE NEED TO PUT OURSELVES ON THE MAP. IDEAS?
WE COULD SPEND THE MONEY ON BESTSELLERS.
THAT WOULD BE UNEXPECTED. NO ONE WHO WALKS THROUGH THE DOOR EVER THINKS THEY'RE GOING TO FIND THE BOOK THEY'RE LOOKING FOR.
BB

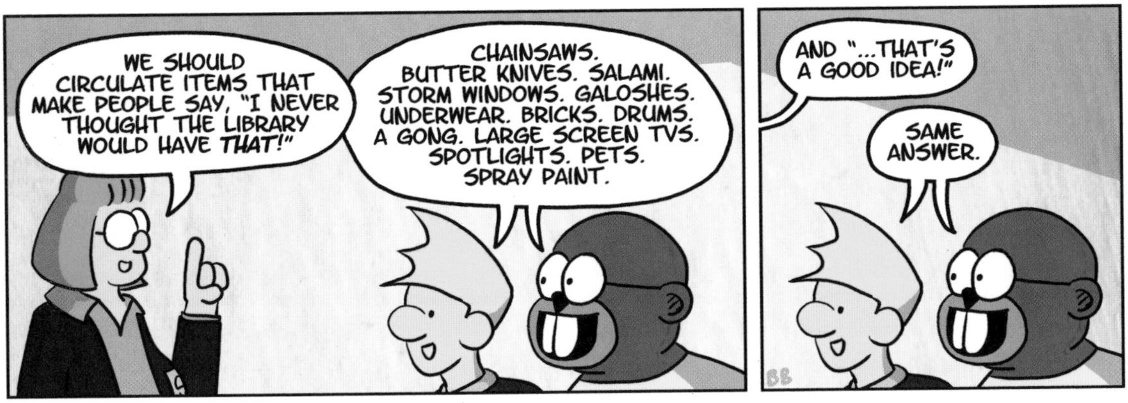
WE SHOULD CIRCULATE ITEMS THAT MAKE PEOPLE SAY, "I NEVER THOUGHT THE LIBRARY WOULD HAVE THAT!"
CHAINSAWS. BUTTER KNIVES. SALAMI. STORM WINDOWS. GALOSHES. UNDERWEAR. BRICKS. DRUMS. A GONG. LARGE SCREEN TVS. SPOTLIGHTS. PETS. SPRAY PAINT.
AND "...THAT'S A GOOD IDEA!"
SAME ANSWER.
BB

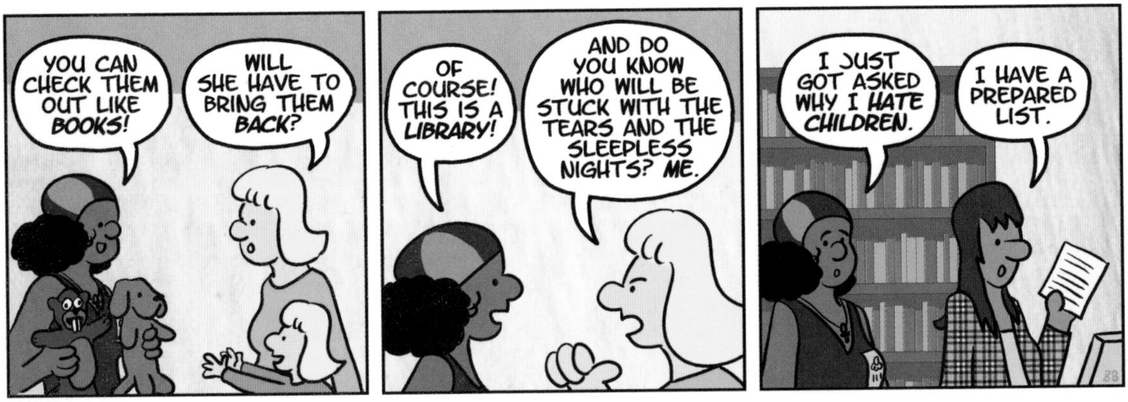
YOU CAN CHECK THEM OUT LIKE BOOKS!
WILL SHE HAVE TO BRING THEM BACK?
OF COURSE! THIS IS A LIBRARY!
AND DO YOU KNOW WHO WILL BE STUCK WITH THE TEARS AND THE SLEEPLESS NIGHTS? ME.
I JUST GOT ASKED WHY I HATE CHILDREN.
I HAVE A PREPARED LIST.
BB

Reads Well With Others

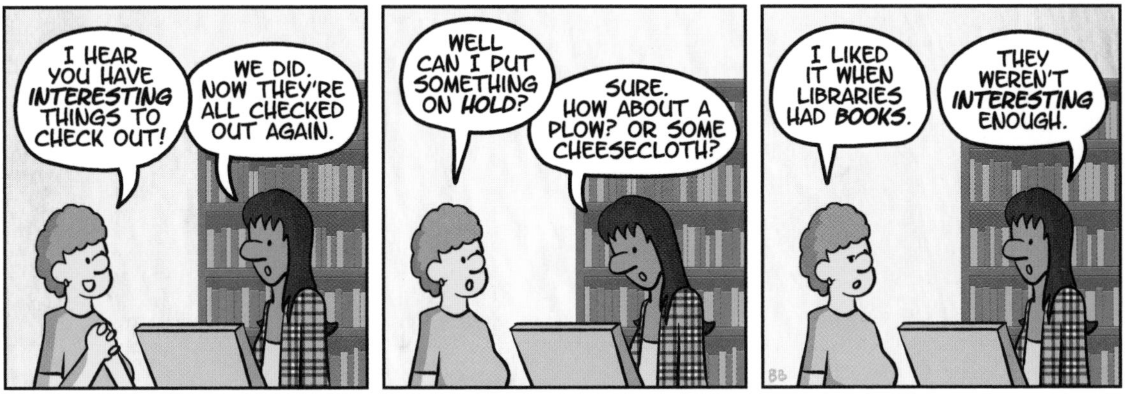
I HEAR YOU HAVE INTERESTING THINGS TO CHECK OUT!
WE DID. NOW THEY'RE ALL CHECKED OUT AGAIN.
WELL CAN I PUT SOMETHING ON HOLD?
SURE. HOW ABOUT A PLOW? OR SOME CHEESECLOTH?
I LIKED IT WHEN LIBRARIES HAD BOOKS.
THEY WEREN'T INTERESTING ENOUGH.
BB

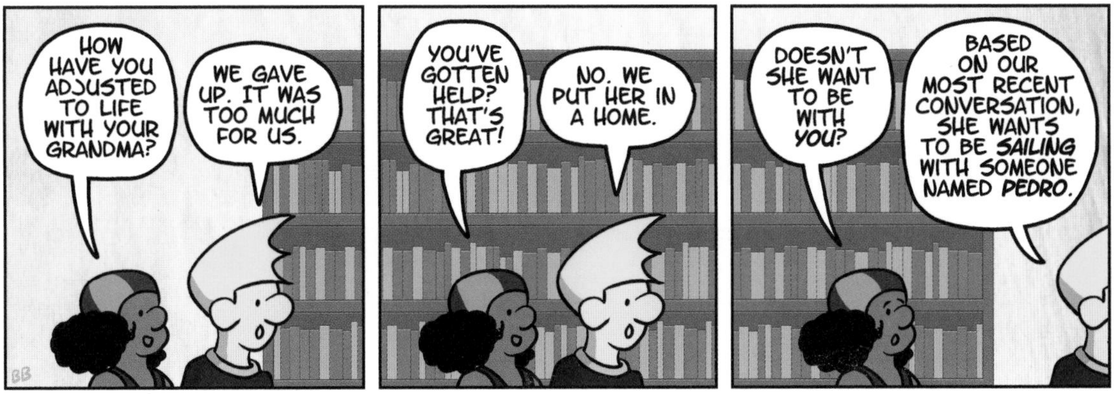
HOW HAVE YOU ADJUSTED TO LIFE WITH YOUR GRANDMA?
WE GAVE UP. IT WAS TOO MUCH FOR US.
BB
YOU'VE GOTTEN HELP? THAT'S GREAT!
NO. WE PUT HER IN A HOME.
DOESN'T SHE WANT TO BE WITH YOU?
BASED ON OUR MOST RECENT CONVERSATION, SHE WANTS TO BE SAILING WITH SOMEONE NAMED PEDRO.

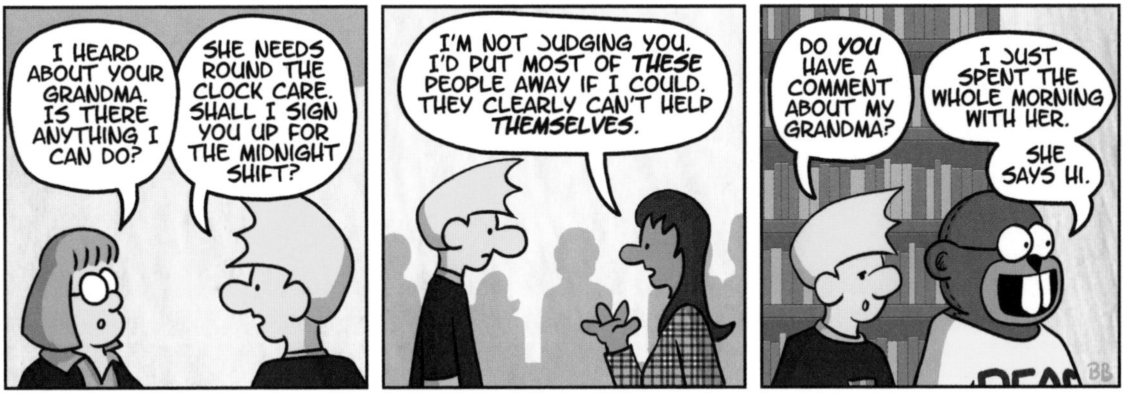
I HEARD ABOUT YOUR GRANDMA. IS THERE ANYTHING I CAN DO?
SHE NEEDS ROUND THE CLOCK CARE. SHALL I SIGN YOU UP FOR THE MIDNIGHT SHIFT?
I'M NOT JUDGING YOU. I'D PUT MOST OF THESE PEOPLE AWAY IF I COULD. THEY CLEARLY CAN'T HELP THEMSELVES.
DO YOU HAVE A COMMENT ABOUT MY GRANDMA?
I JUST SPENT THE WHOLE MORNING WITH HER.
SHE SAYS HI.
BB

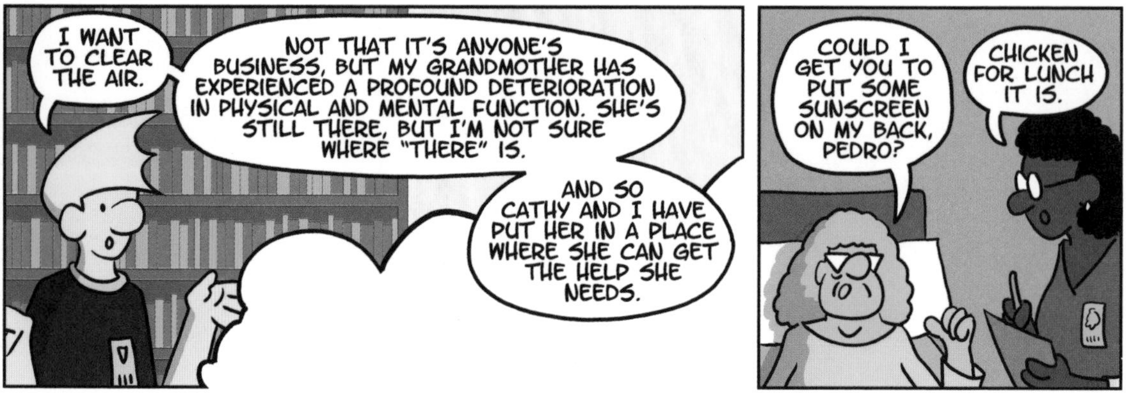
I WANT TO CLEAR THE AIR.
NOT THAT IT'S ANYONE'S BUSINESS, BUT MY GRANDMOTHER HAS EXPERIENCED A PROFOUND DETERIORATION IN PHYSICAL AND MENTAL FUNCTION. SHE'S STILL THERE, BUT I'M NOT SURE WHERE "THERE" IS.
AND SO CATHY AND I HAVE PUT HER IN A PLACE WHERE SHE CAN GET THE HELP SHE NEEDS.
COULD I GET YOU TO PUT SOME SUNSCREEN ON MY BACK, PEDRO?
CHICKEN FOR LUNCH IT IS.

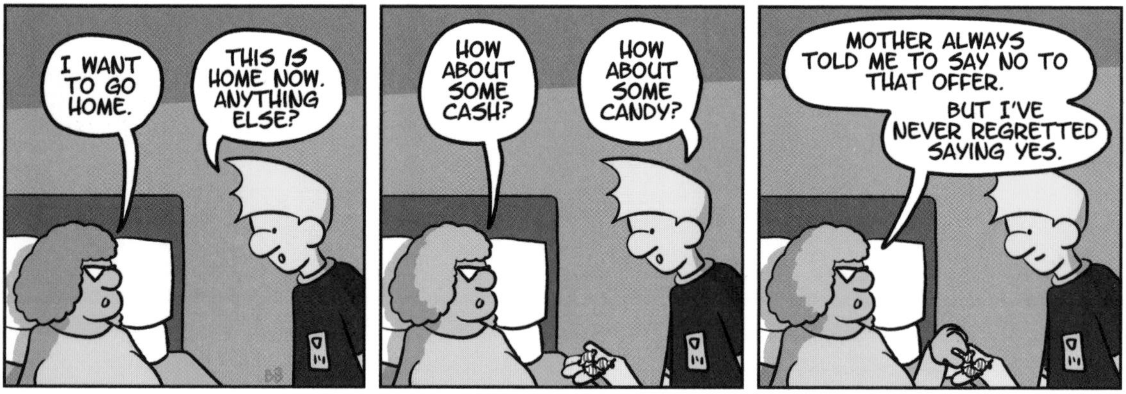
I WANT TO GO HOME.
THIS *IS* HOME NOW. ANYTHING ELSE?
HOW ABOUT SOME CASH?
HOW ABOUT SOME CANDY?
MOTHER ALWAYS TOLD ME TO SAY NO TO THAT OFFER.
BUT I'VE NEVER REGRETTED SAYING YES.

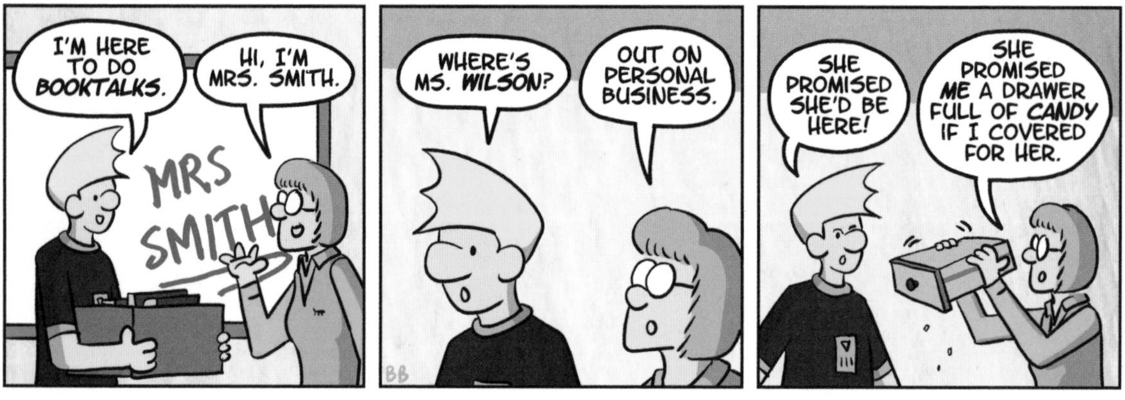
I'M HERE TO DO ***BOOKTALKS***.
HI, I'M MRS. SMITH.
MRS SMITH
WHERE'S MS. ***WILSON***?
OUT ON PERSONAL BUSINESS.
SHE PROMISED SHE'D BE HERE!
SHE PROMISED ***ME*** A DRAWER FULL OF ***CANDY*** IF I COVERED FOR HER.

Reads Well With Others

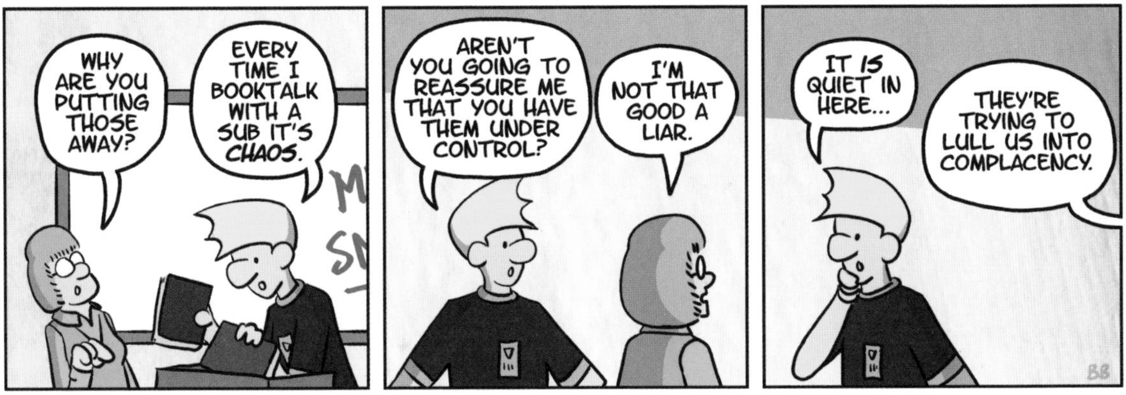
WHY ARE YOU PUTTING THOSE AWAY?
EVERY TIME I BOOKTALK WITH A SUB IT'S *CHAOS*.
AREN'T YOU GOING TO REASSURE ME THAT YOU HAVE THEM UNDER CONTROL?
I'M NOT THAT GOOD A LIAR.
IT *IS* QUIET IN HERE...
THEY'RE TRYING TO LULL US INTO COMPLACENCY.
BB

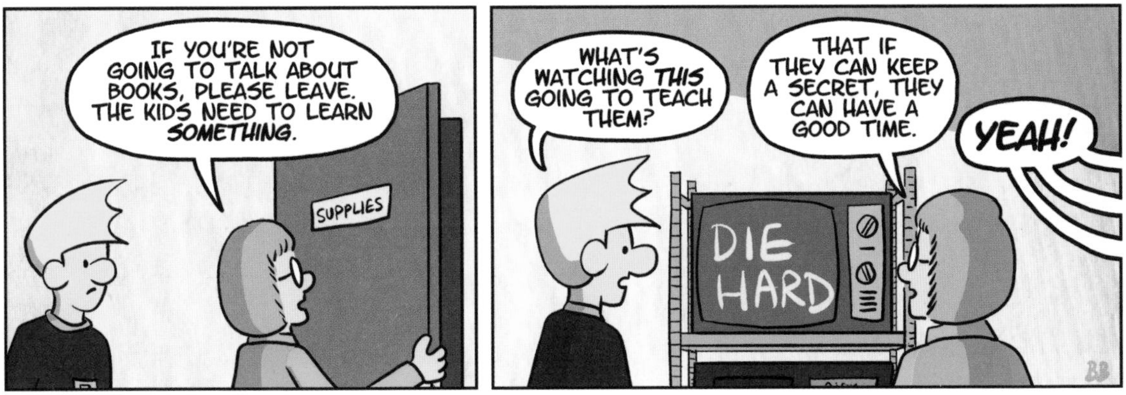
IF YOU'RE NOT GOING TO TALK ABOUT BOOKS, PLEASE LEAVE. THE KIDS NEED TO LEARN **SOMETHING**.
SUPPLIES
WHAT'S WATCHING **THIS** GOING TO TEACH THEM?
THAT IF THEY CAN KEEP A SECRET, THEY CAN HAVE A GOOD TIME.
YEAH!
DIE HARD
BB

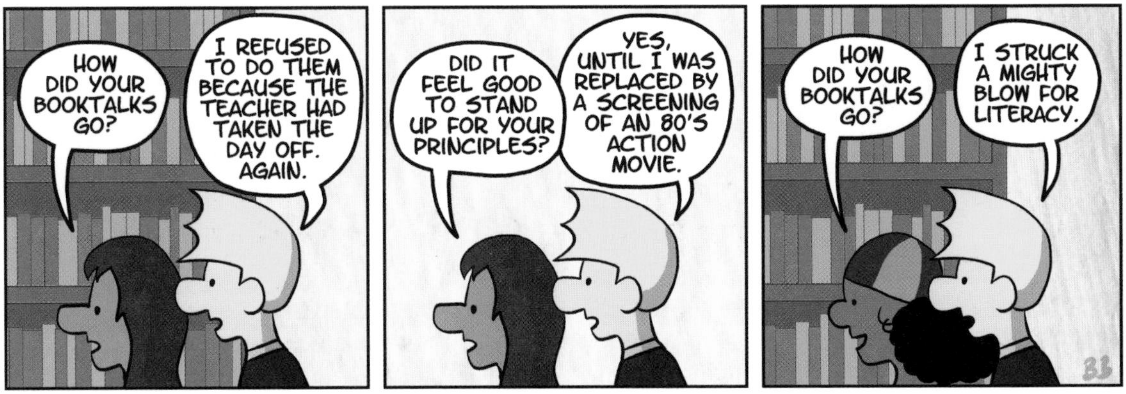
HOW DID YOUR BOOKTALKS GO?
I REFUSED TO DO THEM BECAUSE THE TEACHER HAD TAKEN THE DAY OFF. AGAIN.
DID IT FEEL GOOD TO STAND UP FOR YOUR PRINCIPLES?
YES, UNTIL I WAS REPLACED BY A SCREENING OF AN 80'S ACTION MOVIE.
HOW DID YOUR BOOKTALKS GO?
I STRUCK A MIGHTY BLOW FOR LITERACY.
BB

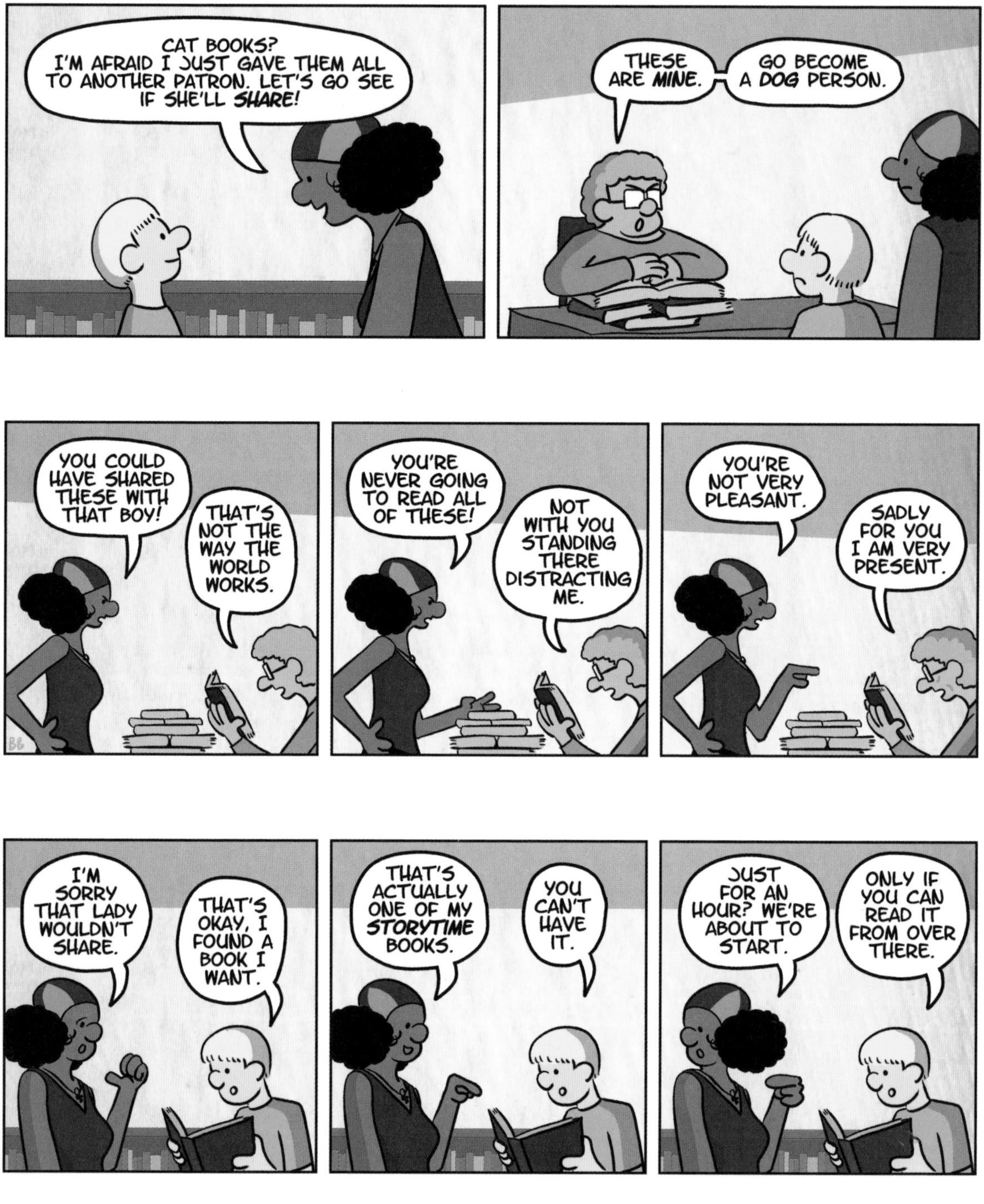
CAT BOOKS? I'M AFRAID I JUST GAVE THEM ALL TO ANOTHER PATRON. LET'S GO SEE IF SHE'LL **SHARE**!
THESE ARE **MINE**.
GO BECOME A **DOG** PERSON.
YOU COULD HAVE SHARED THESE WITH THAT BOY!
THAT'S NOT THE WAY THE WORLD WORKS.
YOU'RE NEVER GOING TO READ ALL OF THESE!
NOT WITH YOU STANDING THERE DISTRACTING ME.
YOU'RE NOT VERY PLEASANT.
SADLY FOR YOU I AM VERY PRESENT.
I'M SORRY THAT LADY WOULDN'T SHARE.
THAT'S OKAY, I FOUND A BOOK I WANT.
THAT'S ACTUALLY ONE OF MY **STORYTIME** BOOKS.
YOU CAN'T HAVE IT.
JUST FOR AN HOUR? WE'RE ABOUT TO START.
ONLY IF YOU CAN READ IT FROM OVER THERE.

Reads Well With Others

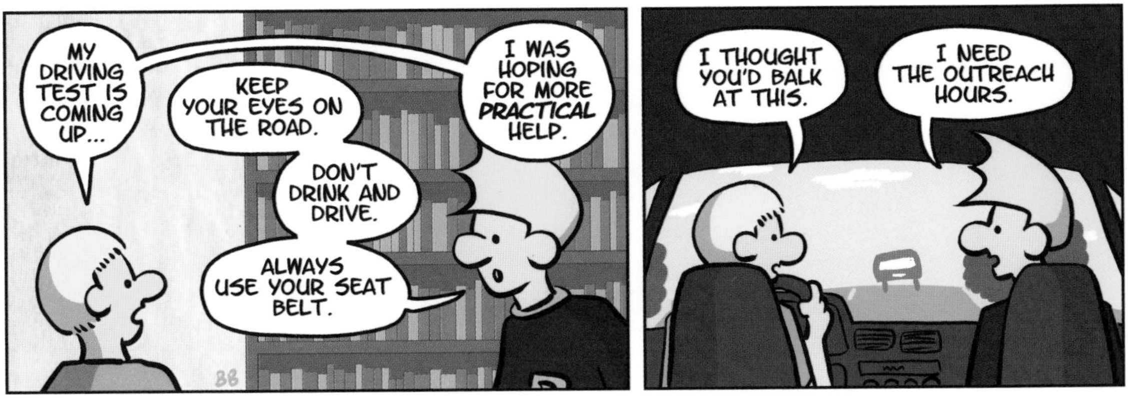
MY DRIVING TEST IS COMING UP...
KEEP YOUR EYES ON THE ROAD.
DON'T DRINK AND DRIVE.
ALWAYS USE YOUR SEAT BELT.
I WAS HOPING FOR MORE PRACTICAL HELP.
I THOUGHT YOU'D BALK AT THIS.
I NEED THE OUTREACH HOURS.
BB

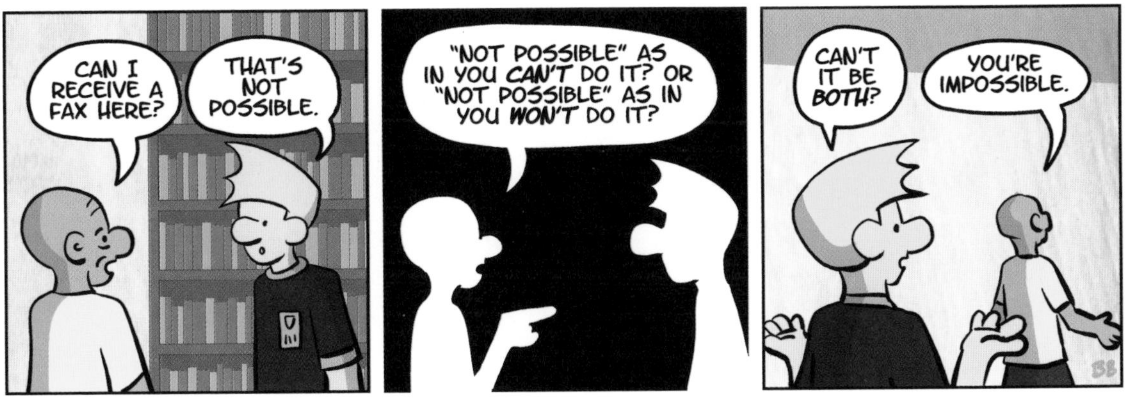
CAN I RECEIVE A FAX HERE?
THAT'S NOT POSSIBLE.
"NOT POSSIBLE" AS IN YOU CAN'T DO IT? OR "NOT POSSIBLE" AS IN YOU WON'T DO IT?
CAN'T IT BE BOTH?
YOU'RE IMPOSSIBLE.
BB

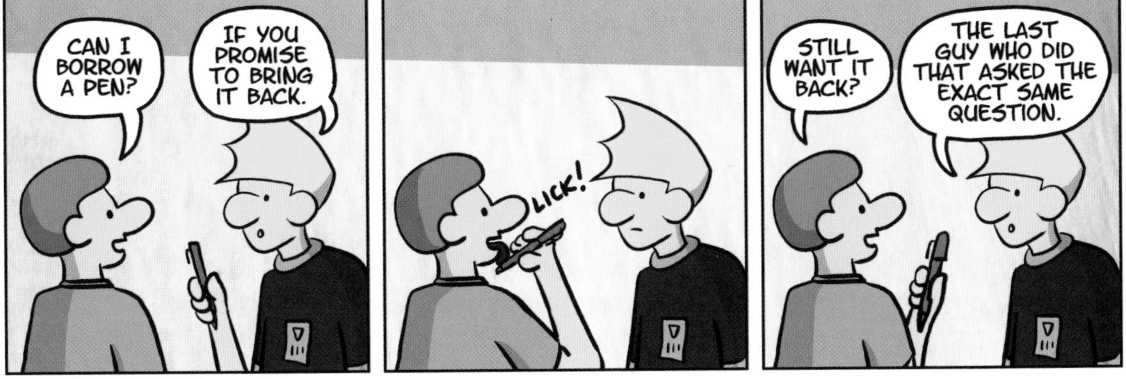
CAN I BORROW A PEN?
IF YOU PROMISE TO BRING IT BACK.
LICK!
STILL WANT IT BACK?
THE LAST GUY WHO DID THAT ASKED THE EXACT SAME QUESTION.

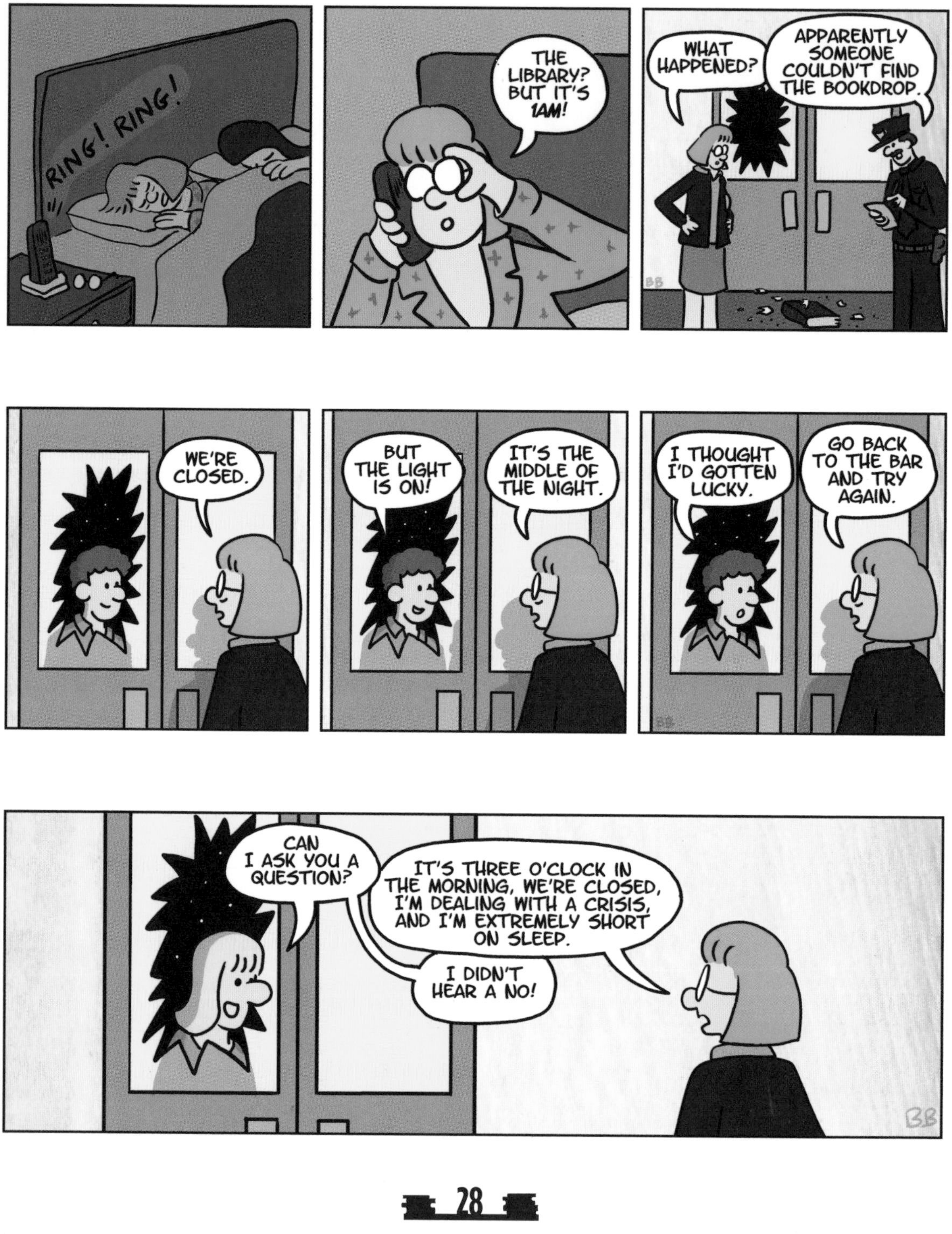
RING! RING!
THE LIBRARY? BUT IT'S 1AM!
WHAT HAPPENED?
APPARENTLY SOMEONE COULDN'T FIND THE BOOKDROP.
BB
WE'RE CLOSED.
BUT THE LIGHT IS ON!
IT'S THE MIDDLE OF THE NIGHT.
I THOUGHT I'D GOTTEN LUCKY.
GO BACK TO THE BAR AND TRY AGAIN.
BB
CAN I ASK YOU A QUESTION?
IT'S THREE O'CLOCK IN THE MORNING, WE'RE CLOSED, I'M DEALING WITH A CRISIS, AND I'M EXTREMELY SHORT ON SLEEP.
I DIDN'T HEAR A NO!
BB

Reads Well With Others

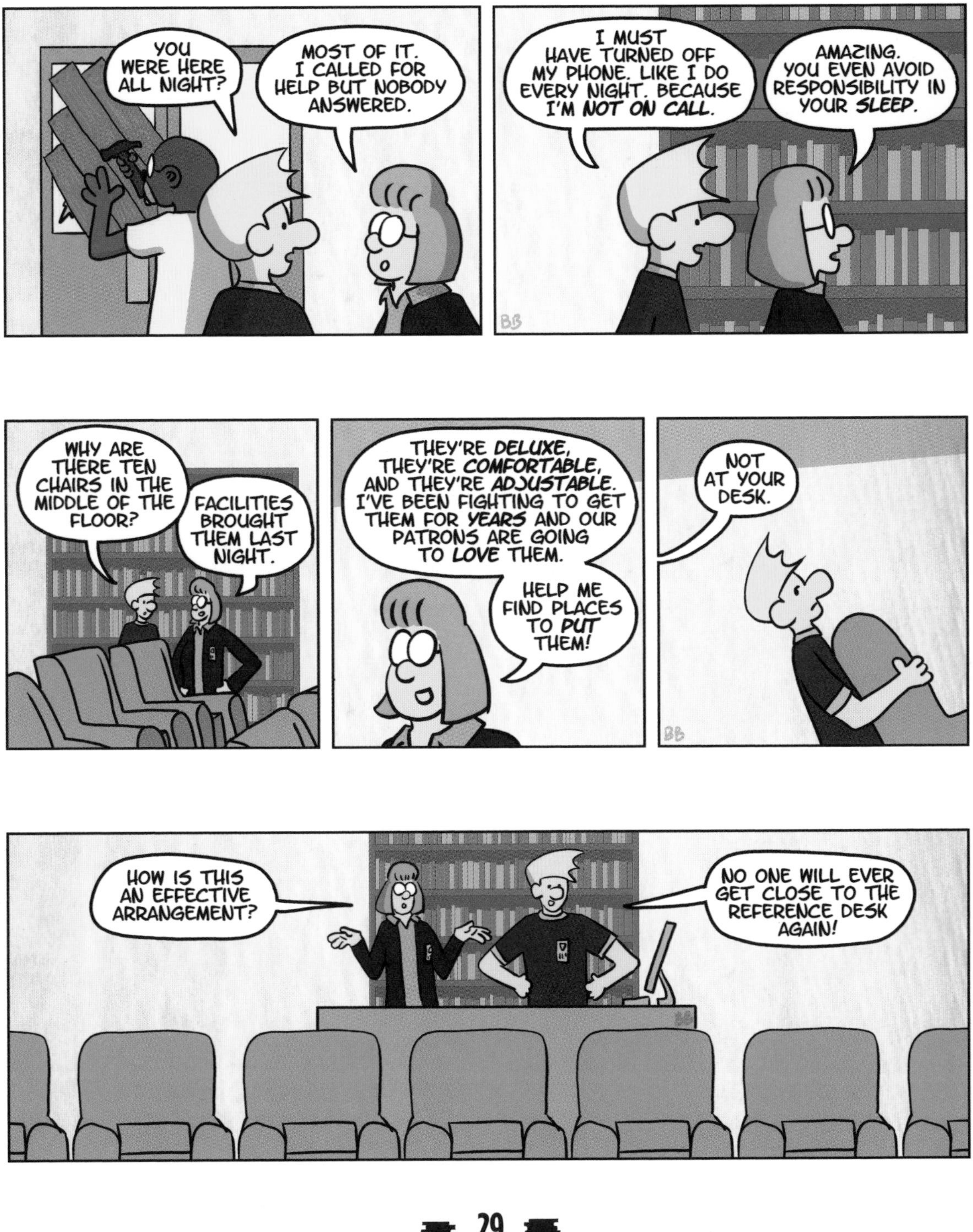

YOU WERE HERE ALL NIGHT?
MOST OF IT. I CALLED FOR HELP BUT NOBODY ANSWERED.
I MUST HAVE TURNED OFF MY PHONE. LIKE I DO EVERY NIGHT. BECAUSE I'M **NOT ON CALL**.
AMAZING. YOU EVEN AVOID RESPONSIBILITY IN YOUR **SLEEP**.
BB
WHY ARE THERE TEN CHAIRS IN THE MIDDLE OF THE FLOOR?
FACILITIES BROUGHT THEM LAST NIGHT.
THEY'RE **DELUXE**, THEY'RE **COMFORTABLE**, AND THEY'RE **ADJUSTABLE**. I'VE BEEN FIGHTING TO GET THEM FOR **YEARS** AND OUR PATRONS ARE GOING TO **LOVE** THEM.
HELP ME FIND PLACES TO **PUT** THEM!
NOT AT YOUR DESK.
BB
HOW IS THIS AN EFFECTIVE ARRANGEMENT?
NO ONE WILL EVER GET CLOSE TO THE REFERENCE DESK AGAIN!
BB

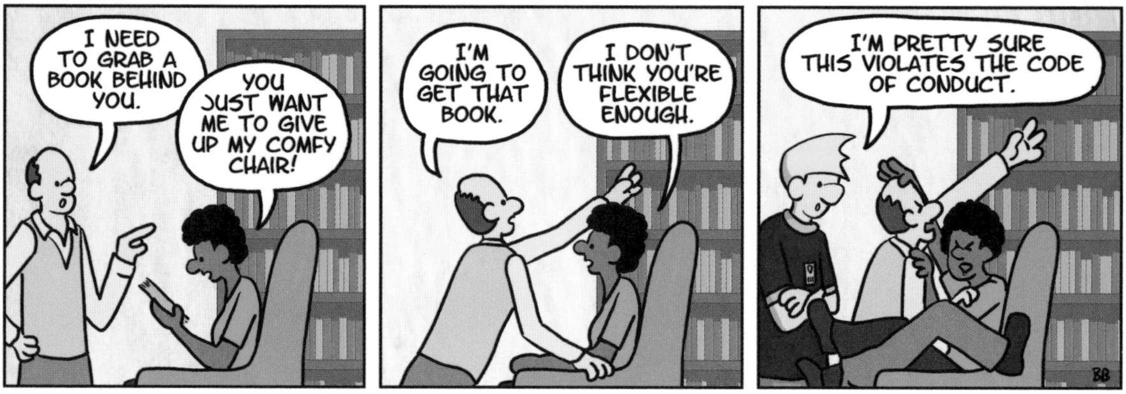
I NEED TO GRAB A BOOK BEHIND YOU.
YOU JUST WANT ME TO GIVE UP MY COMFY CHAIR!
I'M GOING TO GET THAT BOOK.
I DON'T THINK YOU'RE FLEXIBLE ENOUGH.
I'M PRETTY SURE THIS VIOLATES THE CODE OF CONDUCT.
BB

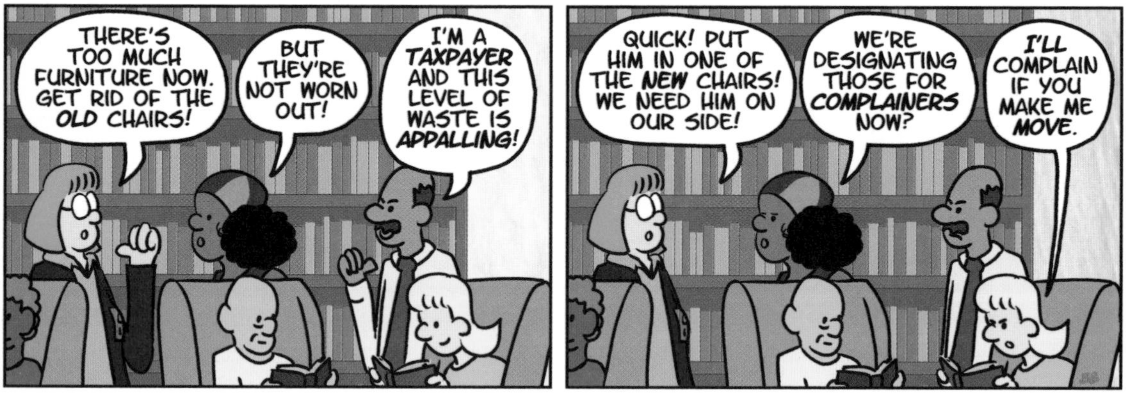
THERE'S TOO MUCH FURNITURE NOW. GET RID OF THE OLD CHAIRS!
BUT THEY'RE NOT WORN OUT!
I'M A TAXPAYER AND THIS LEVEL OF WASTE IS APPALLING!
QUICK! PUT HIM IN ONE OF THE NEW CHAIRS! WE NEED HIM ON OUR SIDE!
WE'RE DESIGNATING THOSE FOR COMPLAINERS NOW?
I'LL COMPLAIN IF YOU MAKE ME MOVE.

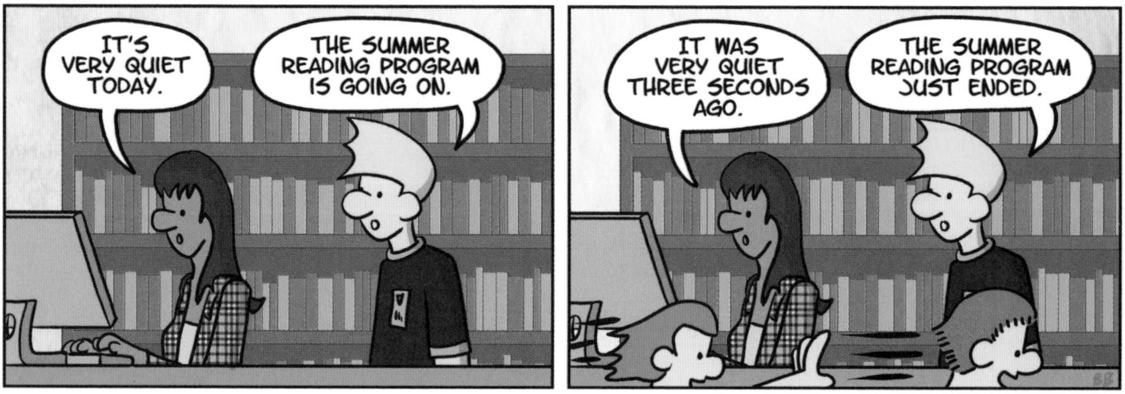
IT'S VERY QUIET TODAY.
THE SUMMER READING PROGRAM IS GOING ON.
IT WAS VERY QUIET THREE SECONDS AGO.
THE SUMMER READING PROGRAM JUST ENDED.

Reads Well With Others

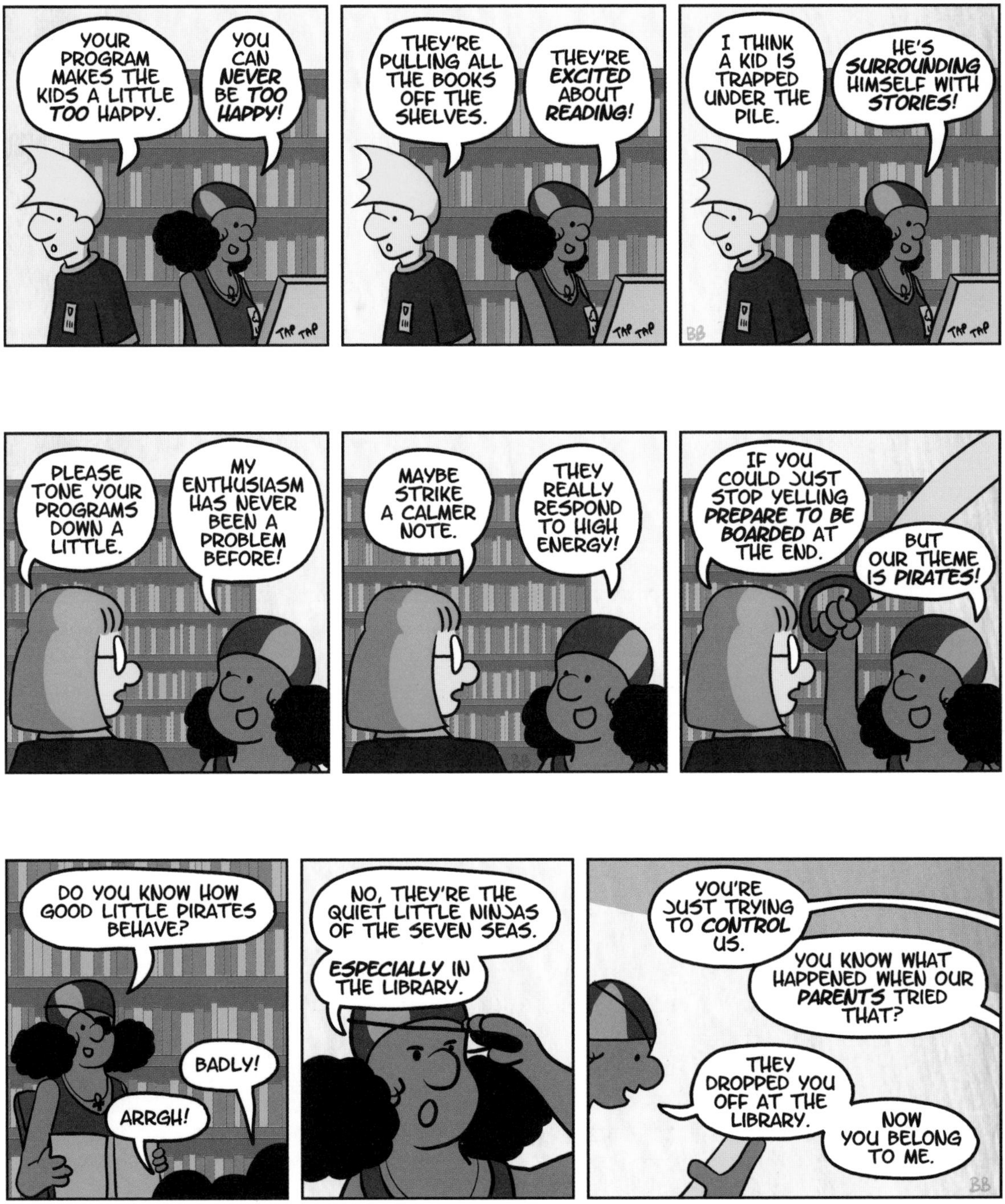

YOUR PROGRAM MAKES THE KIDS A LITTLE TOO HAPPY.
YOU CAN NEVER BE TOO HAPPY!
TAP TAP
THEY'RE PULLING ALL THE BOOKS OFF THE SHELVES.
THEY'RE EXCITED ABOUT READING!
TAP TAP
I THINK A KID IS TRAPPED UNDER THE PILE.
HE'S SURROUNDING HIMSELF WITH STORIES!
TAP TAP
BB
PLEASE TONE YOUR PROGRAMS DOWN A LITTLE.
MY ENTHUSIASM HAS NEVER BEEN A PROBLEM BEFORE!
MAYBE STRIKE A CALMER NOTE.
THEY REALLY RESPOND TO HIGH ENERGY!
BB
IF YOU COULD JUST STOP YELLING PREPARE TO BE BOARDED AT THE END.
BUT OUR THEME IS PIRATES!
DO YOU KNOW HOW GOOD LITTLE PIRATES BEHAVE?
BADLY!
ARRGH!
NO, THEY'RE THE QUIET LITTLE NINJAS OF THE SEVEN SEAS.
ESPECIALLY IN THE LIBRARY.
YOU'RE JUST TRYING TO CONTROL US.
YOU KNOW WHAT HAPPENED WHEN OUR PARENTS TRIED THAT?
THEY DROPPED YOU OFF AT THE LIBRARY.
NOW YOU BELONG TO ME.
BB

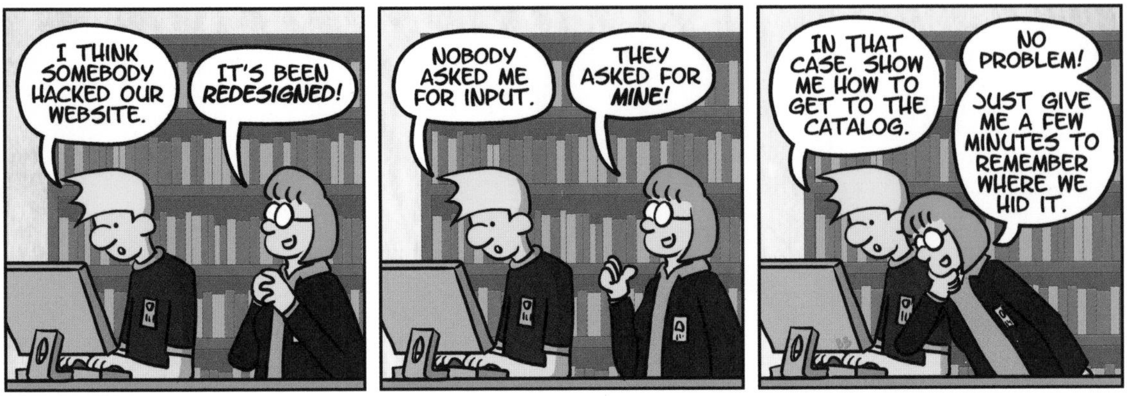
I THINK SOMEBODY HACKED OUR WEBSITE.
IT'S BEEN *REDESIGNED*!
NOBODY ASKED ME FOR INPUT.
THEY ASKED FOR *MINE*!
IN THAT CASE, SHOW ME HOW TO GET TO THE CATALOG.
NO PROBLEM!
JUST GIVE ME A FEW MINUTES TO REMEMBER WHERE WE HID IT.
BB

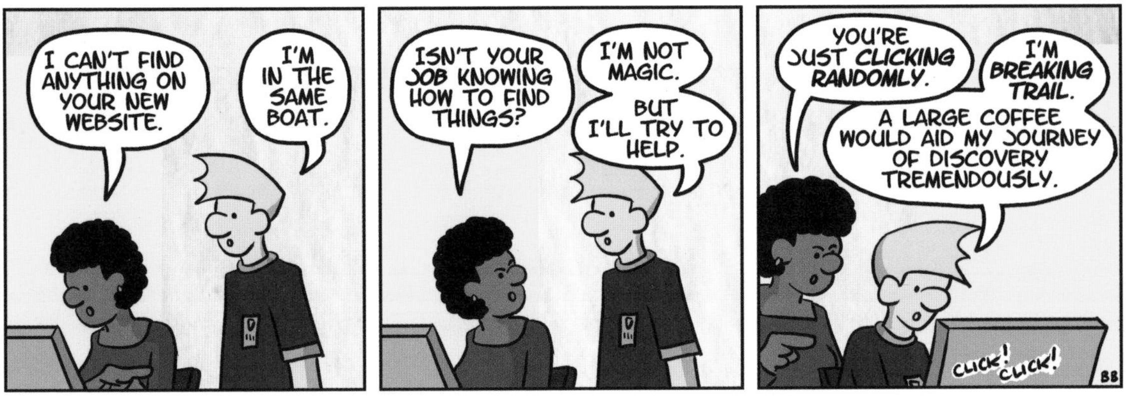
I CAN'T FIND ANYTHING ON YOUR NEW WEBSITE.
I'M IN THE SAME BOAT.
ISN'T YOUR JOB KNOWING HOW TO FIND THINGS?
I'M NOT MAGIC.
BUT I'LL TRY TO HELP.
YOU'RE JUST *CLICKING RANDOMLY*.
I'M *BREAKING TRAIL*.
A LARGE COFFEE WOULD AID MY JOURNEY OF DISCOVERY TREMENDOUSLY.
CLICK! CLICK!
BB

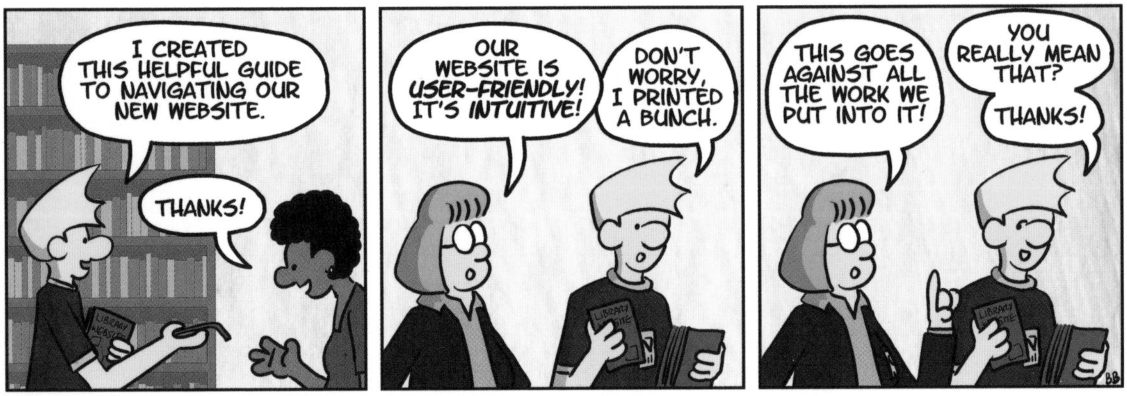
I CREATED THIS HELPFUL GUIDE TO NAVIGATING OUR NEW WEBSITE.
THANKS!
OUR WEBSITE IS *USER-FRIENDLY*! IT'S *INTUITIVE*!
DON'T WORRY, I PRINTED A BUNCH.
THIS GOES AGAINST ALL THE WORK WE PUT INTO IT!
YOU REALLY MEAN THAT?
THANKS!
BB

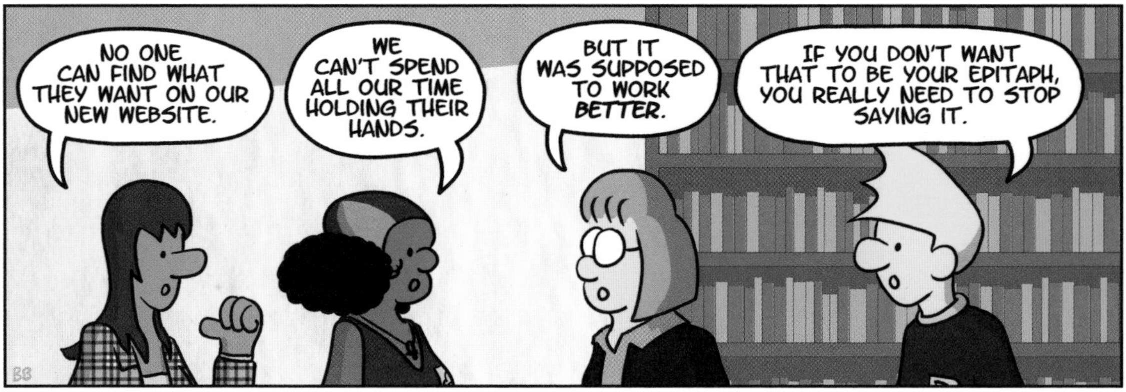
NO ONE CAN FIND WHAT THEY WANT ON OUR NEW WEBSITE.
WE CAN'T SPEND ALL OUR TIME HOLDING THEIR HANDS.
BUT IT WAS SUPPOSED TO WORK BETTER.
IF YOU DON'T WANT THAT TO BE YOUR EPITAPH, YOU REALLY NEED TO STOP SAYING IT.
BB

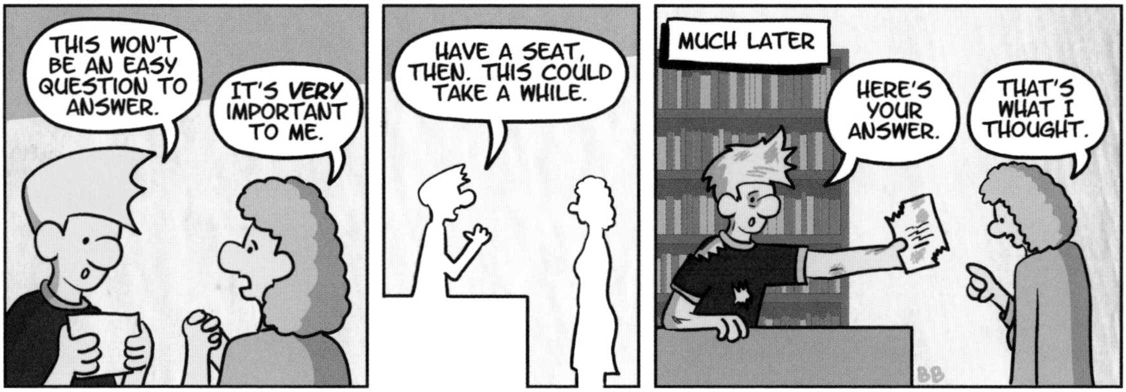
THIS WON'T BE AN EASY QUESTION TO ANSWER.
IT'S VERY IMPORTANT TO ME.
HAVE A SEAT, THEN. THIS COULD TAKE A WHILE.
MUCH LATER
HERE'S YOUR ANSWER.
THAT'S WHAT I THOUGHT.
BB

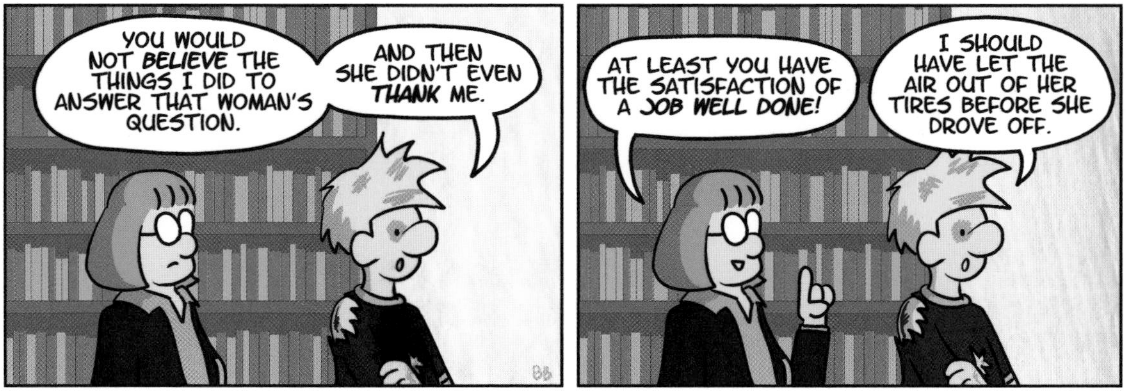
YOU WOULD NOT BELIEVE THE THINGS I DID TO ANSWER THAT WOMAN'S QUESTION.
AND THEN SHE DIDN'T EVEN THANK ME.
BB
AT LEAST YOU HAVE THE SATISFACTION OF A JOB WELL DONE!
I SHOULD HAVE LET THE AIR OUT OF HER TIRES BEFORE SHE DROVE OFF.

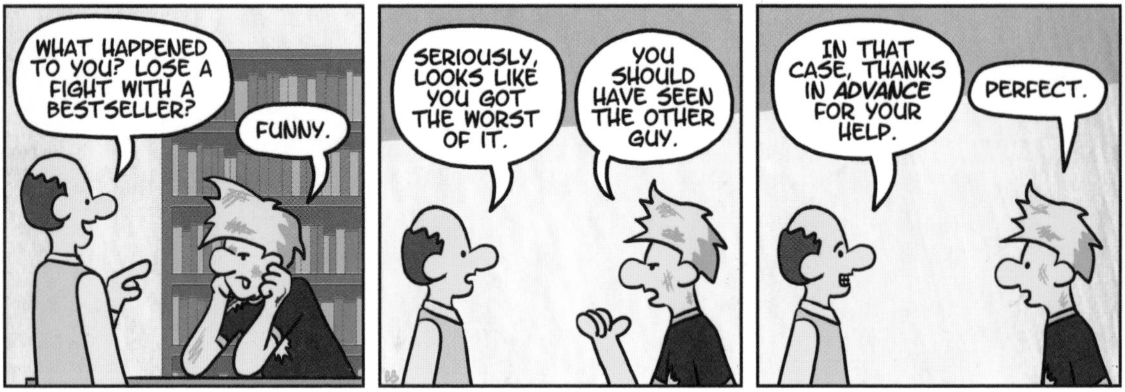
WHAT HAPPENED TO YOU? LOSE A FIGHT WITH A BESTSELLER?
FUNNY.
SERIOUSLY, LOOKS LIKE YOU GOT THE WORST OF IT.
YOU SHOULD HAVE SEEN THE OTHER GUY.
IN THAT CASE, THANKS IN ADVANCE FOR YOUR HELP.
PERFECT.

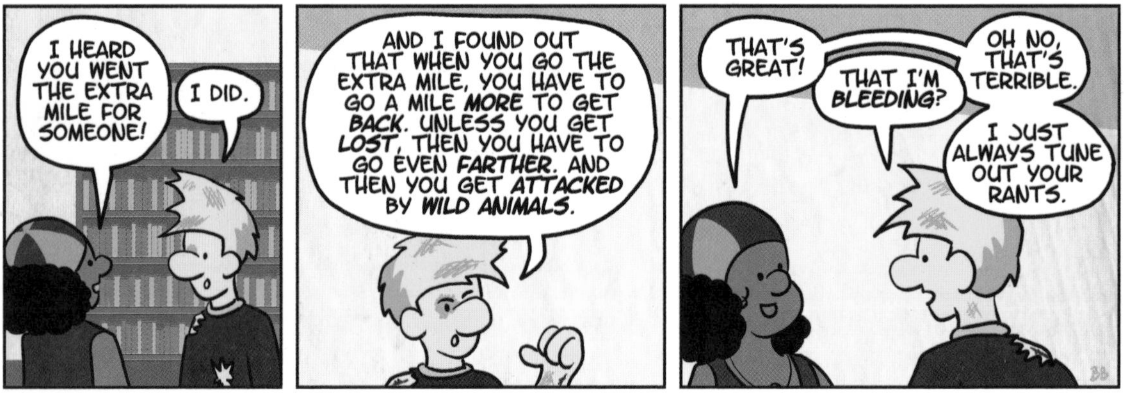
I HEARD YOU WENT THE EXTRA MILE FOR SOMEONE!
I DID.
AND I FOUND OUT THAT WHEN YOU GO THE EXTRA MILE, YOU HAVE TO GO A MILE MORE TO GET BACK. UNLESS YOU GET LOST, THEN YOU HAVE TO GO EVEN FARTHER. AND THEN YOU GET ATTACKED BY WILD ANIMALS.
THAT'S GREAT!
THAT I'M BLEEDING?
OH NO, THAT'S TERRIBLE.
I JUST ALWAYS TUNE OUT YOUR RANTS.

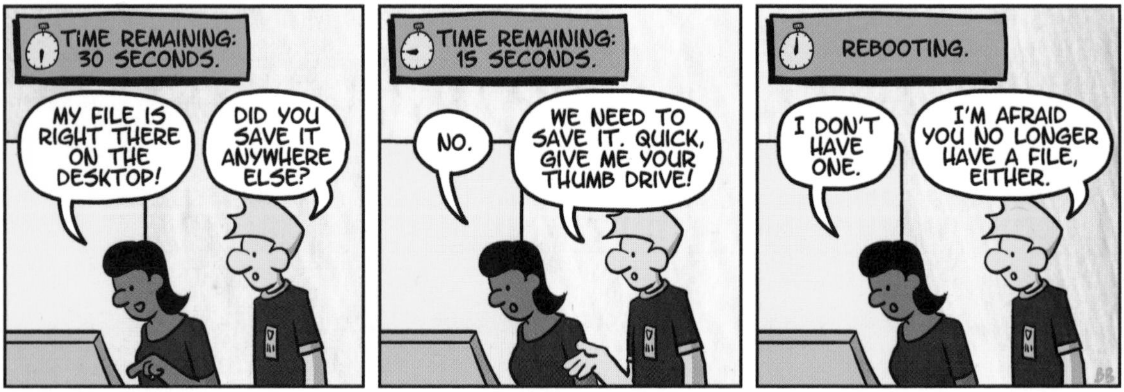
TIME REMAINING: 30 SECONDS.
MY FILE IS RIGHT THERE ON THE DESKTOP!
DID YOU SAVE IT ANYWHERE ELSE?
TIME REMAINING: 15 SECONDS.
NO.
WE NEED TO SAVE IT. QUICK, GIVE ME YOUR THUMB DRIVE!
REBOOTING.
I DON'T HAVE ONE.
I'M AFRAID YOU NO LONGER HAVE A FILE, EITHER.

Reads Well With Others

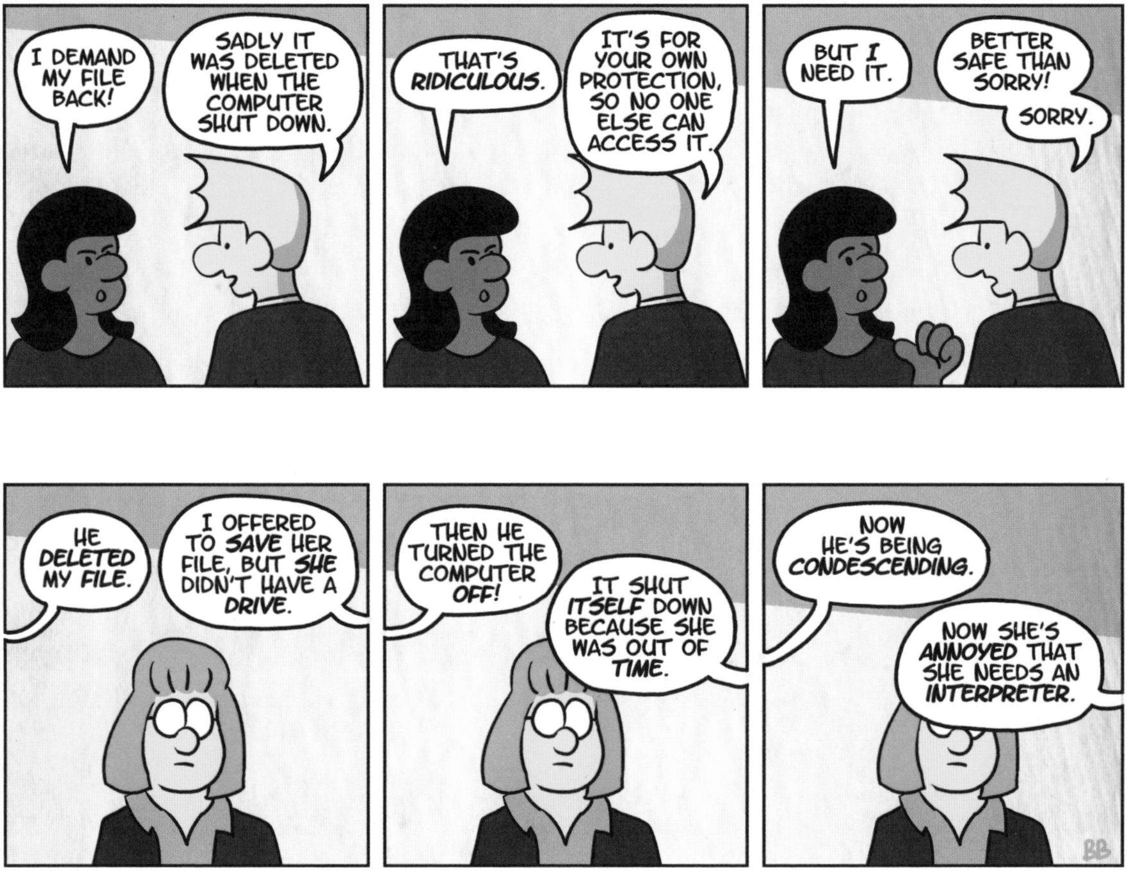

I DEMAND MY FILE BACK!
SADLY IT WAS DELETED WHEN THE COMPUTER SHUT DOWN.
THAT'S RIDICULOUS.
IT'S FOR YOUR OWN PROTECTION, SO NO ONE ELSE CAN ACCESS IT.
BUT I NEED IT.
BETTER SAFE THAN SORRY!
SORRY.
HE DELETED MY FILE.
I OFFERED TO SAVE HER FILE, BUT SHE DIDN'T HAVE A DRIVE.
THEN HE TURNED THE COMPUTER OFF!
IT SHUT ITSELF DOWN BECAUSE SHE WAS OUT OF TIME.
NOW HE'S BEING CONDESCENDING.
NOW SHE'S ANNOYED THAT SHE NEEDS AN INTERPRETER.

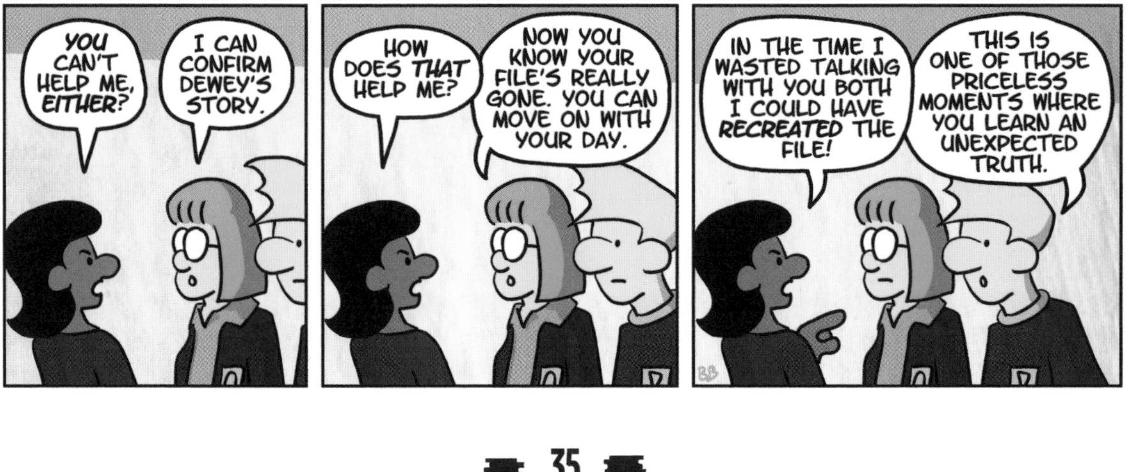

YOU CAN'T HELP ME, EITHER?
I CAN CONFIRM DEWEY'S STORY.
HOW DOES THAT HELP ME?
NOW YOU KNOW YOUR FILE'S REALLY GONE. YOU CAN MOVE ON WITH YOUR DAY.
IN THE TIME I WASTED TALKING WITH YOU BOTH I COULD HAVE RECREATED THE FILE!
THIS IS ONE OF THOSE PRICELESS MOMENTS WHERE YOU LEARN AN UNEXPECTED TRUTH.

About once a month we can be found keynoting library conferences and staff days, book festivals, and comic conventions all over the US and Canada. Once in a while we do something special. Prior to the event, attendees send us true library stories they have personally experienced. We pick several to turn into strips, and Bill draws our favorite the old-fashioned way, with pencil and ink on paper. As you can see, it's a very different look than the rest of our strips, which are drawn directly onto a computer. But when the apocalypse comes and electricity is just a memory, it's good to know that Bill will have a trade to fall back on.

I'M RETURNING THIS.
FIFTY SHADES OF GREY?
THAT'S RIGHT.
HOW... HOW DID YOU LIKE IT?
I DIDN'T LEARN ANYTHING NEW FROM IT.
BB

I WANT THE FREE STUFF.
EVERYTHING'S FREE HERE.
UNLESS YOU BRING IT BACK LATE.
BB
THE FREE STUFF! WEE FEE!
I'M NOT SURE WHAT YOU MEAN.
IF YOU THINK YOU'RE MAD NOW, WAIT UNTIL I EXPLAIN WHAT THAT IS.
FREE WI-FI

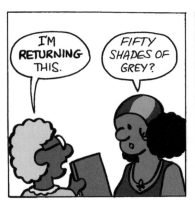

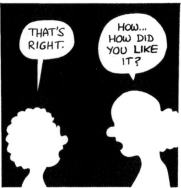

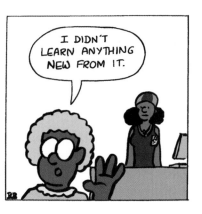

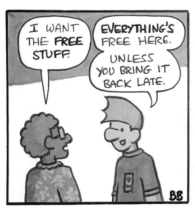

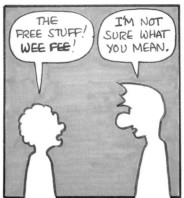

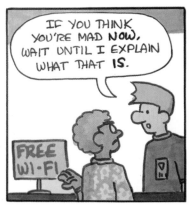

Reads Well With Others

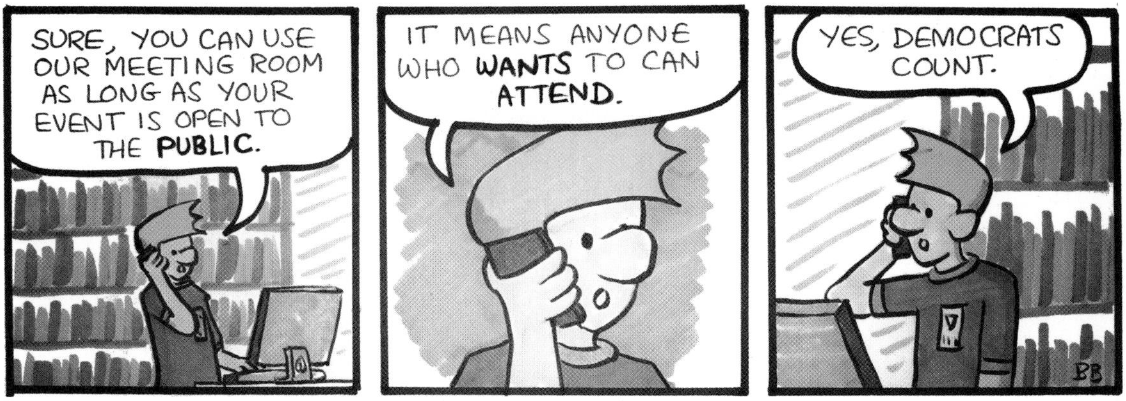
SURE, YOU CAN USE OUR MEETING ROOM AS LONG AS YOUR EVENT IS OPEN TO THE **PUBLIC**.
IT MEANS ANYONE WHO **WANTS** TO CAN **ATTEND**.
YES, DEMOCRATS COUNT.
BB

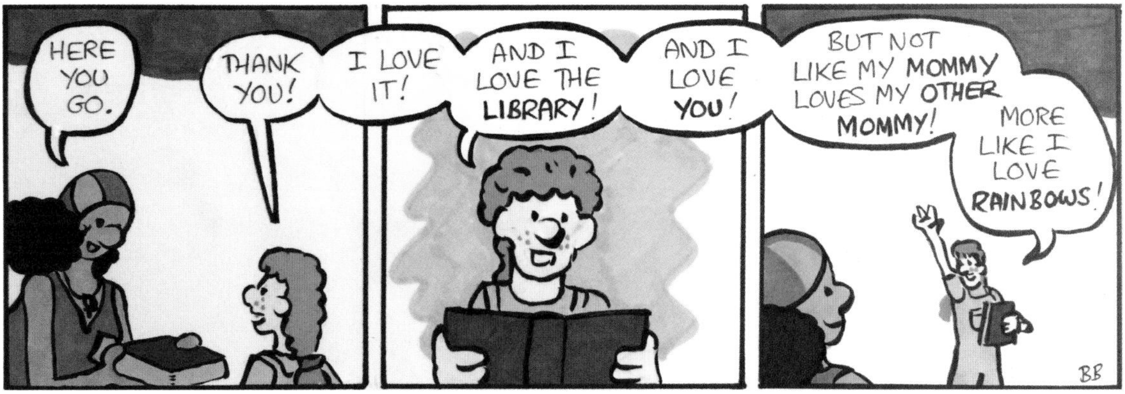
HERE YOU GO.
THANK YOU!
I LOVE IT!
AND I LOVE THE **LIBRARY**!
AND I LOVE **YOU**!
BUT NOT LIKE MY **MOMMY** LOVES MY **OTHER MOMMY**!
MORE LIKE I LOVE **RAINBOWS**!
BB

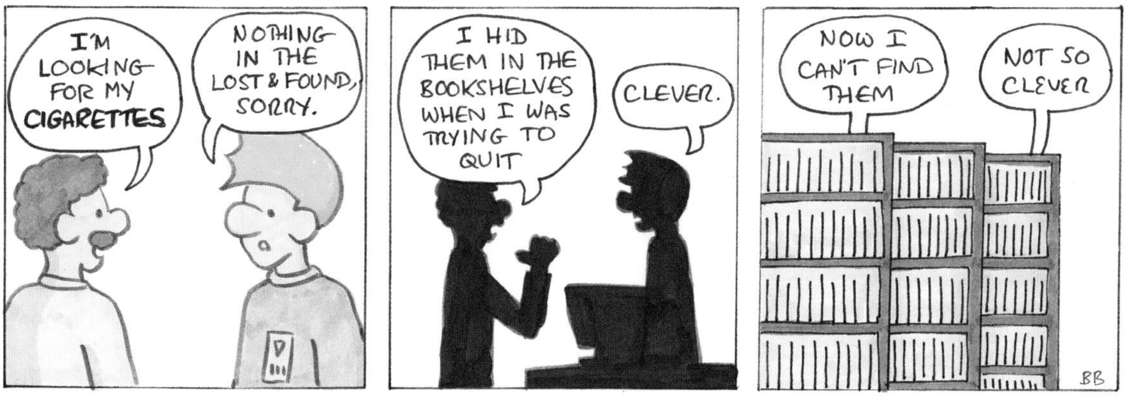
I'M LOOKING FOR MY **CIGARETTES**
NOTHING IN THE LOST & FOUND, SORRY.
I HID THEM IN THE BOOKSHELVES WHEN I WAS TRYING TO QUIT
CLEVER.
NOW I CAN'T FIND THEM
NOT SO CLEVER
BB

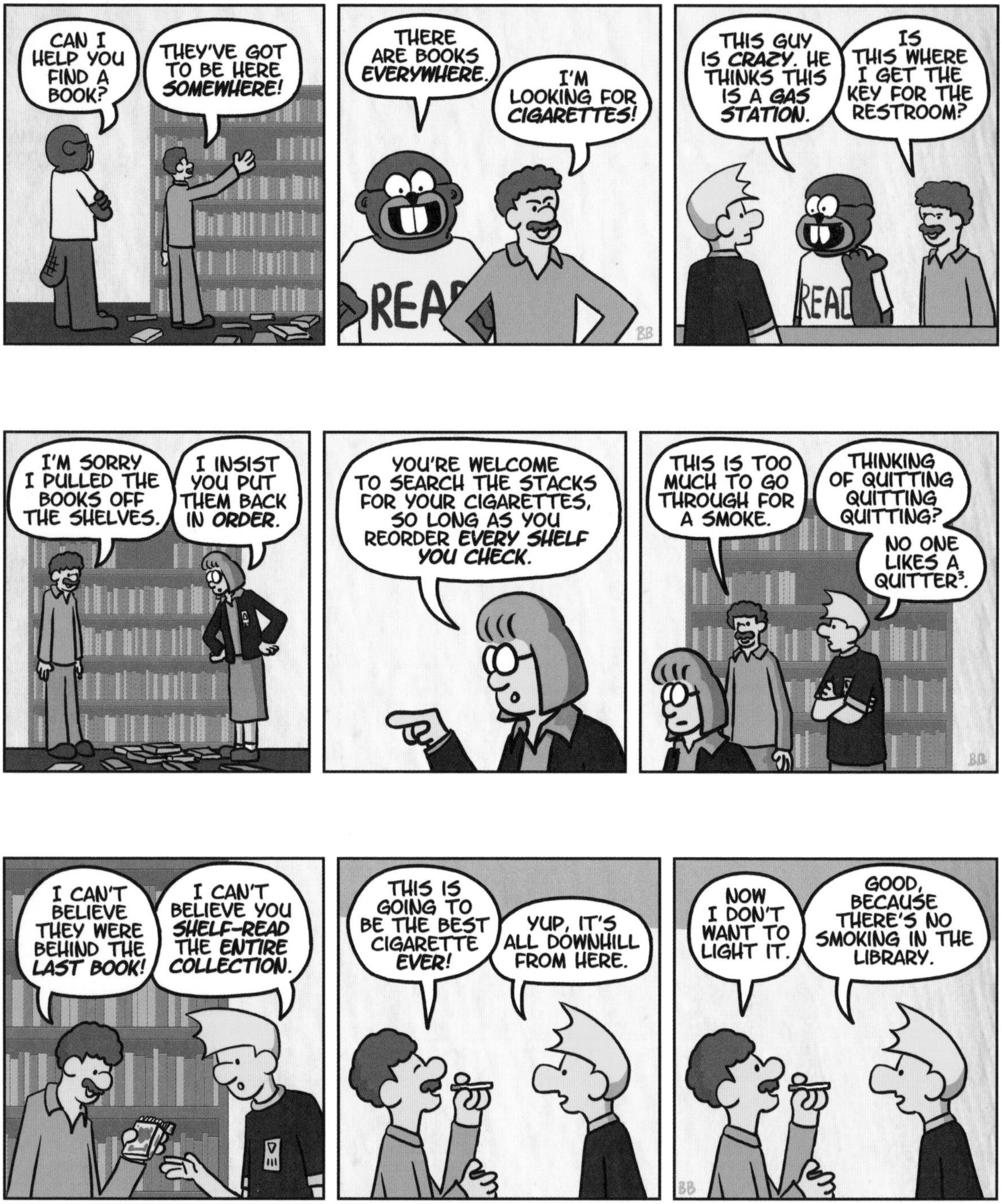
CAN I HELP YOU FIND A BOOK?
THEY'VE GOT TO BE HERE SOMEWHERE!
THERE ARE BOOKS EVERYWHERE.
I'M LOOKING FOR CIGARETTES!
READ
BB
THIS GUY IS CRAZY. HE THINKS THIS IS A GAS STATION.
IS THIS WHERE I GET THE KEY FOR THE RESTROOM?
READ
I'M SORRY I PULLED THE BOOKS OFF THE SHELVES.
I INSIST YOU PUT THEM BACK IN ORDER.
YOU'RE WELCOME TO SEARCH THE STACKS FOR YOUR CIGARETTES, SO LONG AS YOU REORDER EVERY SHELF YOU CHECK.
THIS IS TOO MUCH TO GO THROUGH FOR A SMOKE.
THINKING OF QUITTING QUITTING QUITTING?
NO ONE LIKES A QUITTER[3].
BB
I CAN'T BELIEVE THEY WERE BEHIND THE LAST BOOK!
I CAN'T BELIEVE YOU SHELF-READ THE ENTIRE COLLECTION.
THIS IS GOING TO BE THE BEST CIGARETTE EVER!
YUP, IT'S ALL DOWNHILL FROM HERE.
BB
NOW I DON'T WANT TO LIGHT IT.
GOOD, BECAUSE THERE'S NO SMOKING IN THE LIBRARY.

Reads Well With Others

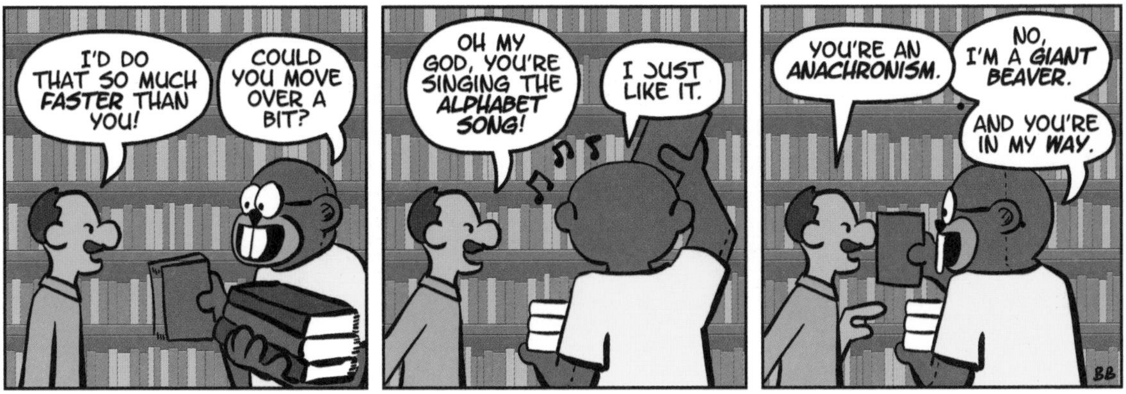

I'D DO THAT SO MUCH FASTER THAN YOU!
COULD YOU MOVE OVER A BIT?
OH MY GOD, YOU'RE SINGING THE ALPHABET SONG!
I JUST LIKE IT.
YOU'RE AN ANACHRONISM.
NO, I'M A GIANT BEAVER.
AND YOU'RE IN MY WAY.
BB

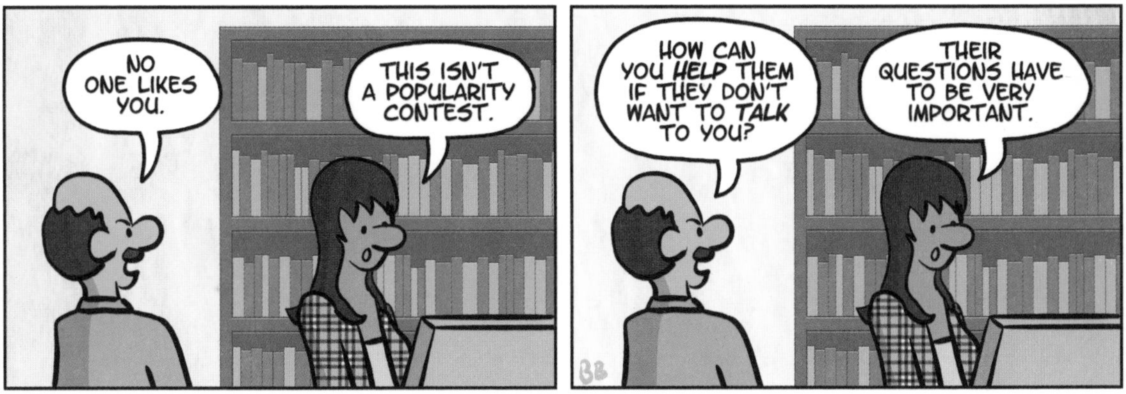

NO ONE LIKES YOU.
THIS ISN'T A POPULARITY CONTEST.
HOW CAN YOU HELP THEM IF THEY DON'T WANT TO TALK TO YOU?
THEIR QUESTIONS HAVE TO BE VERY IMPORTANT.
BB

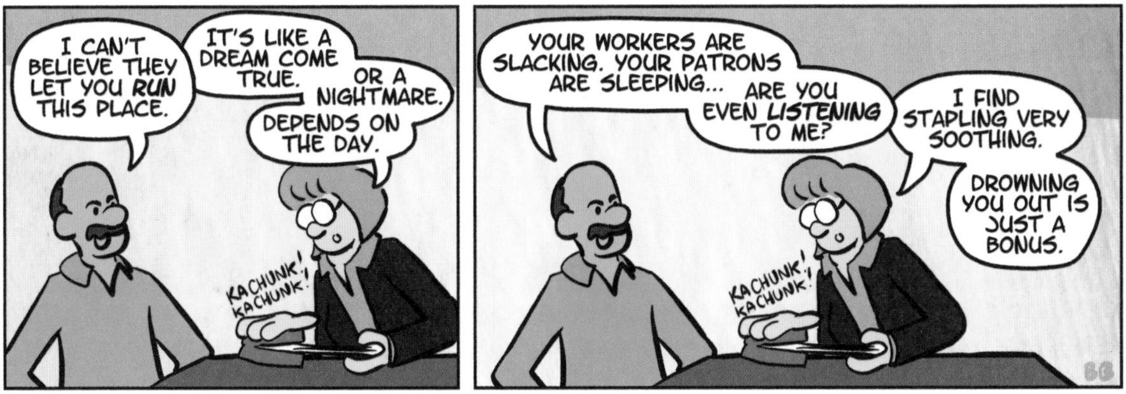

I CAN'T BELIEVE THEY LET YOU RUN THIS PLACE.
IT'S LIKE A DREAM COME TRUE.
OR A NIGHTMARE.
DEPENDS ON THE DAY.
KACHUNK! KACHUNK!
YOUR WORKERS ARE SLACKING. YOUR PATRONS ARE SLEEPING...
ARE YOU EVEN LISTENING TO ME?
I FIND STAPLING VERY SOOTHING.
DROWNING YOU OUT IS JUST A BONUS.
KACHUNK! KACHUNK!
BB

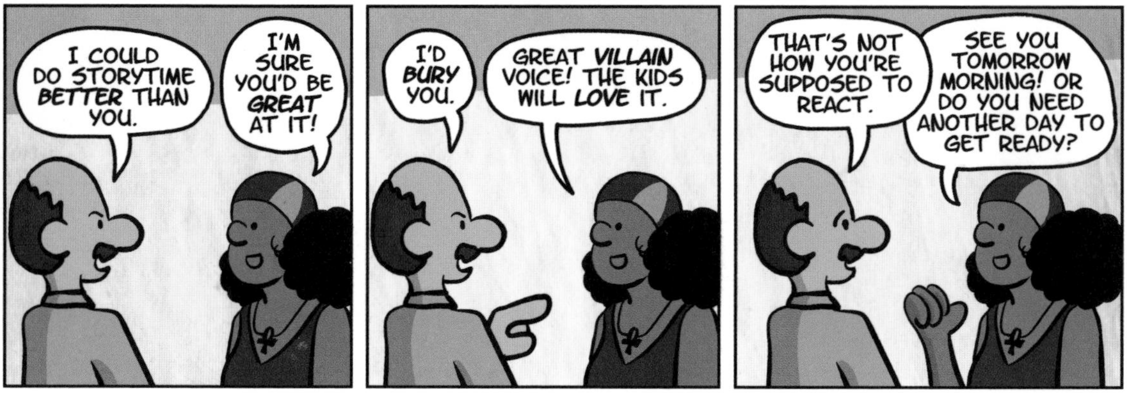
I COULD DO STORYTIME BETTER THAN YOU.
I'M SURE YOU'D BE GREAT AT IT!
I'D BURY YOU.
GREAT VILLAIN VOICE! THE KIDS WILL LOVE IT.
THAT'S NOT HOW YOU'RE SUPPOSED TO REACT.
SEE YOU TOMORROW MORNING! OR DO YOU NEED ANOTHER DAY TO GET READY?

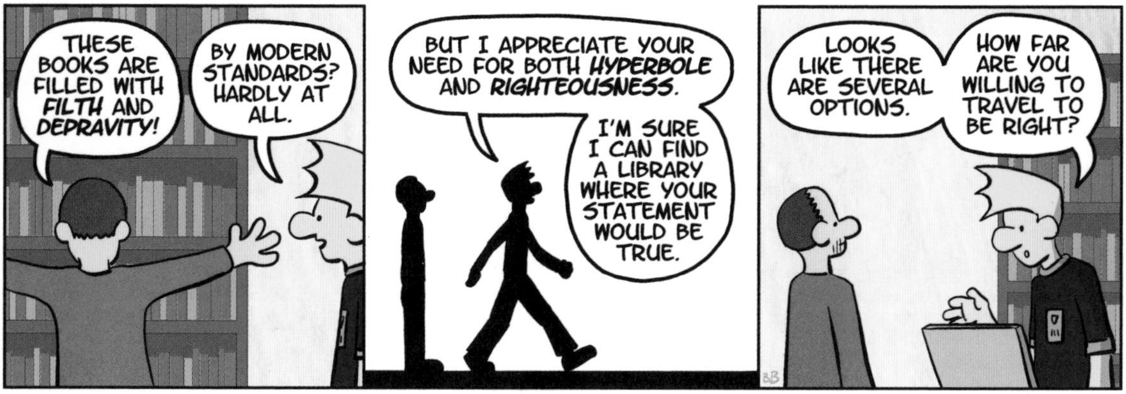
THESE BOOKS ARE FILLED WITH FILTH AND DEPRAVITY!
BY MODERN STANDARDS? HARDLY AT ALL.
BUT I APPRECIATE YOUR NEED FOR BOTH HYPERBOLE AND RIGHTEOUSNESS.
I'M SURE I CAN FIND A LIBRARY WHERE YOUR STATEMENT WOULD BE TRUE.
LOOKS LIKE THERE ARE SEVERAL OPTIONS.
HOW FAR ARE YOU WILLING TO TRAVEL TO BE RIGHT?
BB

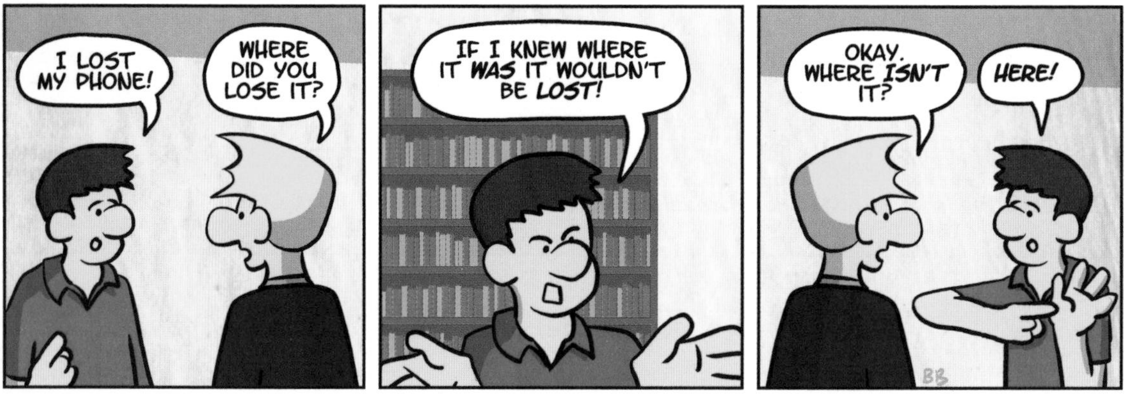
I LOST MY PHONE!
WHERE DID YOU LOSE IT?
IF I KNEW WHERE IT WAS IT WOULDN'T BE LOST!
OKAY. WHERE ISN'T IT?
HERE!
BB

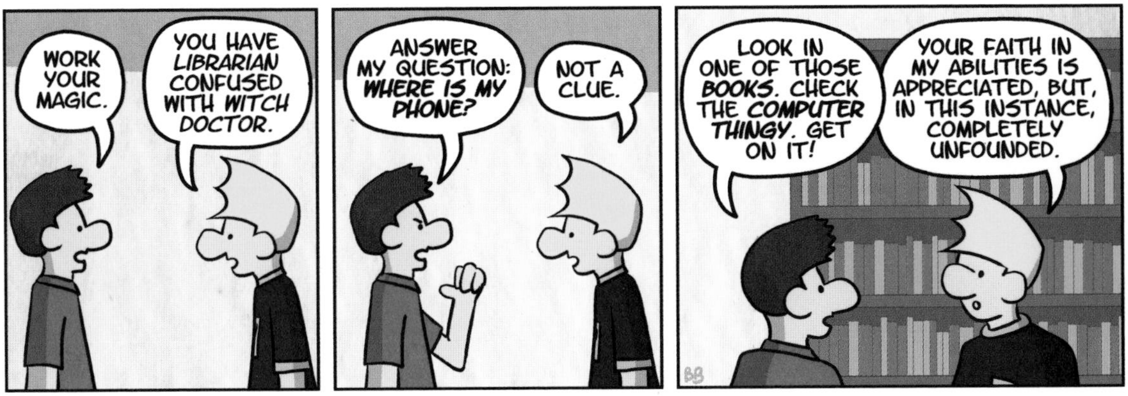
WORK YOUR MAGIC.
YOU HAVE LIBRARIAN CONFUSED WITH WITCH DOCTOR.
ANSWER MY QUESTION: WHERE IS MY PHONE?
NOT A CLUE.
LOOK IN ONE OF THOSE BOOKS. CHECK THE COMPUTER THINGY. GET ON IT!
YOUR FAITH IN MY ABILITIES IS APPRECIATED, BUT, IN THIS INSTANCE, COMPLETELY UNFOUNDED.
BB

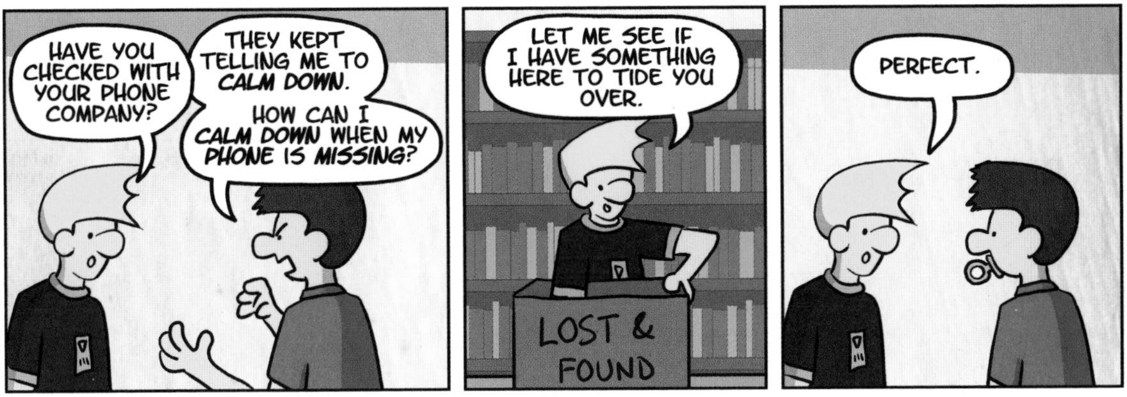
HAVE YOU CHECKED WITH YOUR PHONE COMPANY?
THEY KEPT TELLING ME TO CALM DOWN.
HOW CAN I CALM DOWN WHEN MY PHONE IS MISSING?
LET ME SEE IF I HAVE SOMETHING HERE TO TIDE YOU OVER.
LOST & FOUND
PERFECT.

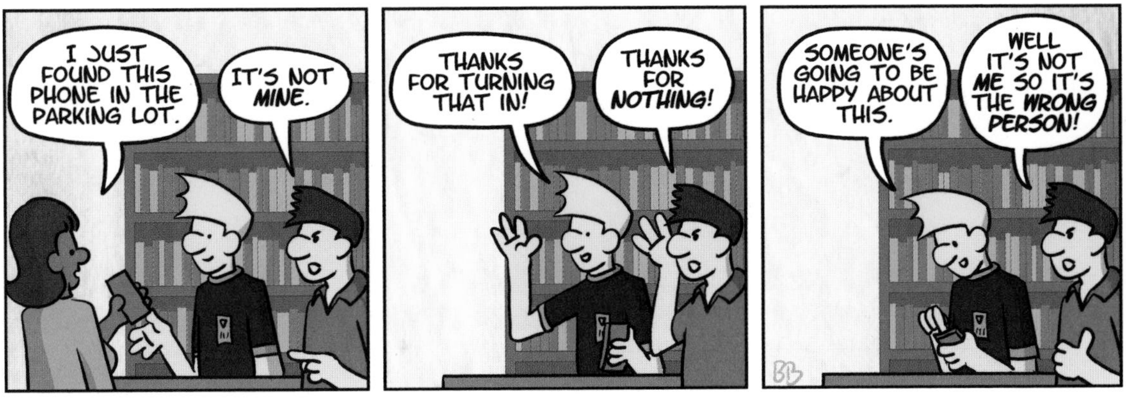
I JUST FOUND THIS PHONE IN THE PARKING LOT.
IT'S NOT MINE.
THANKS FOR TURNING THAT IN!
THANKS FOR NOTHING!
SOMEONE'S GOING TO BE HAPPY ABOUT THIS.
WELL IT'S NOT ME SO IT'S THE WRONG PERSON!
BB

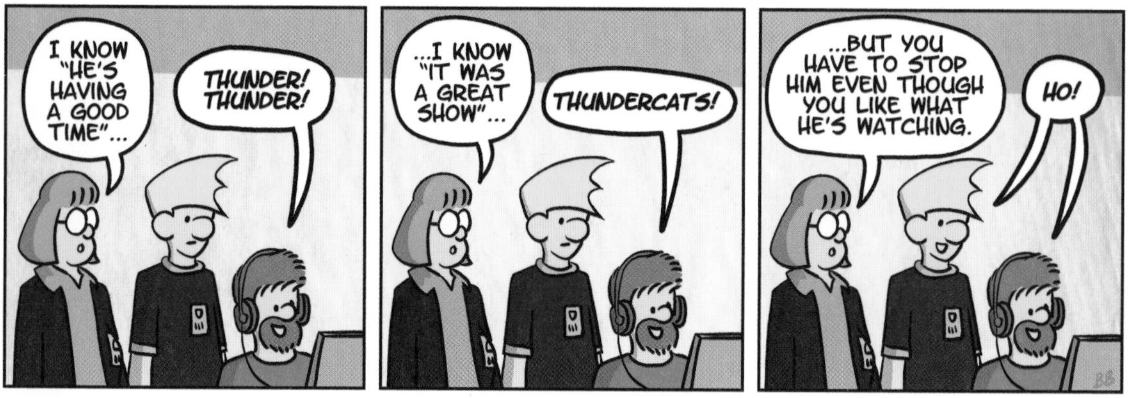
I KNOW "HE'S HAVING A GOOD TIME"...
THUNDER! THUNDER!
...I KNOW "IT WAS A GREAT SHOW"...
THUNDERCATS!
...BUT YOU HAVE TO STOP HIM EVEN THOUGH YOU LIKE WHAT HE'S WATCHING.
HO!

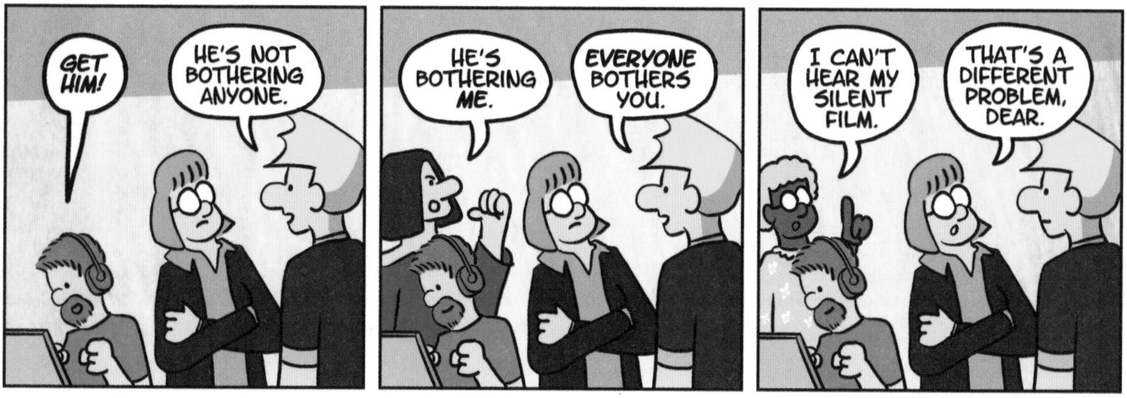
GET HIM!
HE'S NOT BOTHERING ANYONE.
HE'S BOTHERING ME.
EVERYONE BOTHERS YOU.
I CAN'T HEAR MY SILENT FILM.
THAT'S A DIFFERENT PROBLEM, DEAR.

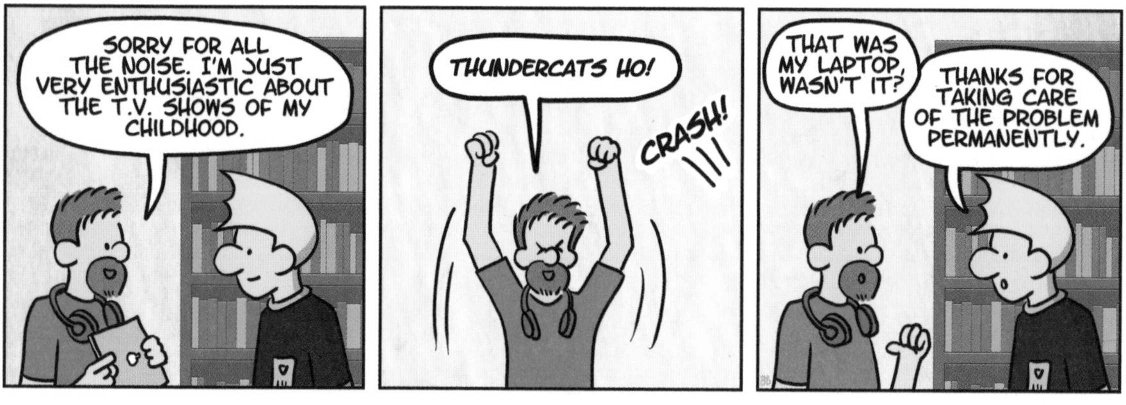
SORRY FOR ALL THE NOISE. I'M JUST VERY ENTHUSIASTIC ABOUT THE T.V. SHOWS OF MY CHILDHOOD.
THUNDERCATS HO!
CRASH!
THAT WAS MY LAPTOP, WASN'T IT?
THANKS FOR TAKING CARE OF THE PROBLEM PERMANENTLY.

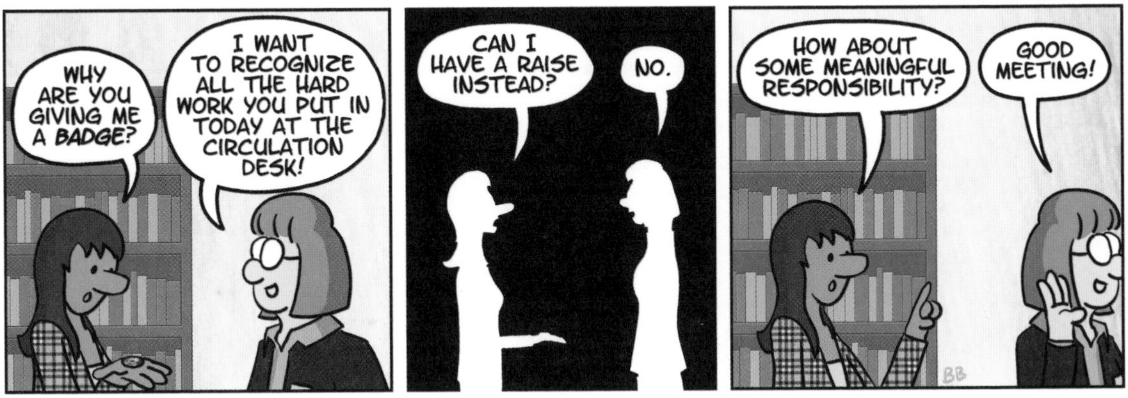
WHY ARE YOU GIVING ME A BADGE?
I WANT TO RECOGNIZE ALL THE HARD WORK YOU PUT IN TODAY AT THE CIRCULATION DESK!
CAN I HAVE A RAISE INSTEAD?
NO.
HOW ABOUT SOME MEANINGFUL RESPONSIBILITY?
GOOD MEETING!
BB

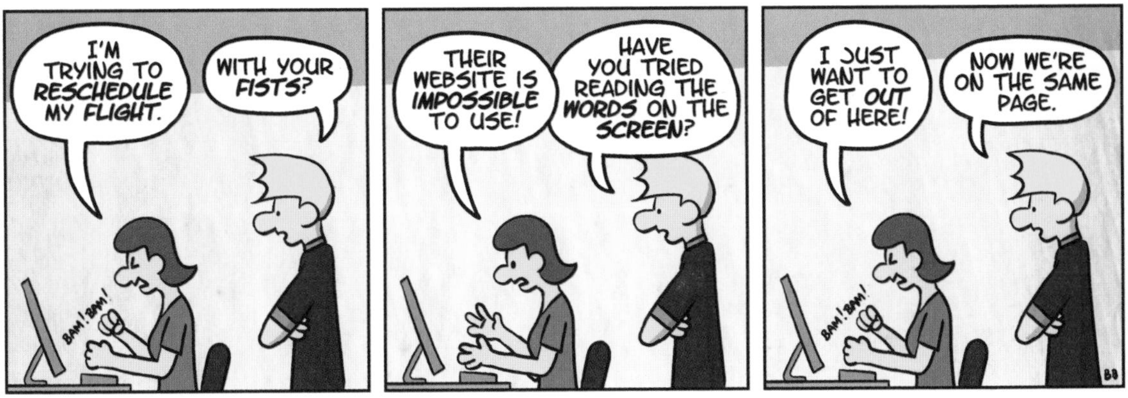
I'M TRYING TO RESCHEDULE MY FLIGHT.
WITH YOUR FISTS?
BAM! BAM!
THEIR WEBSITE IS IMPOSSIBLE TO USE!
HAVE YOU TRIED READING THE WORDS ON THE SCREEN?
I JUST WANT TO GET OUT OF HERE!
NOW WE'RE ON THE SAME PAGE.
BAM! BAM!
BB

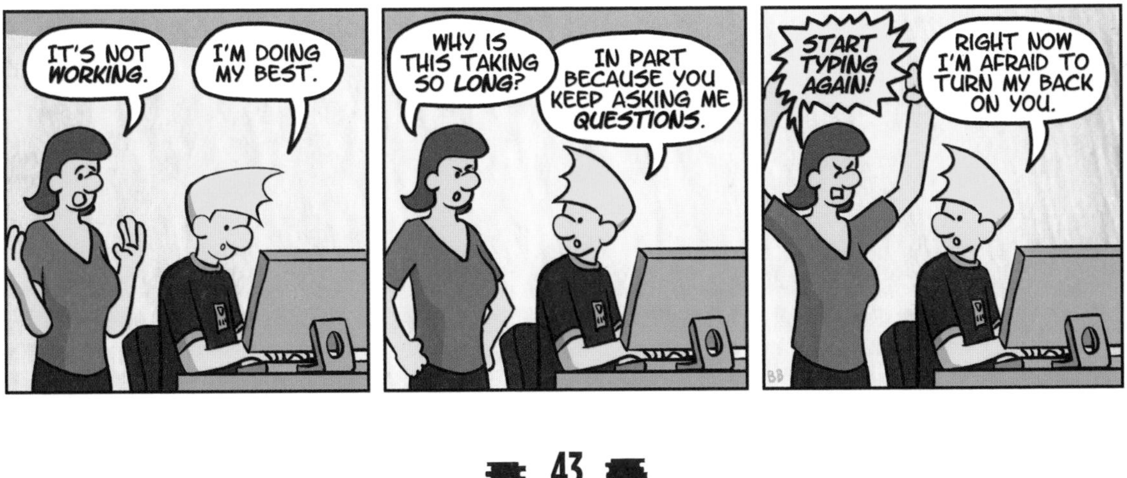
IT'S NOT WORKING.
I'M DOING MY BEST.
WHY IS THIS TAKING SO LONG?
IN PART BECAUSE YOU KEEP ASKING ME QUESTIONS.
START TYPING AGAIN!
RIGHT NOW I'M AFRAID TO TURN MY BACK ON YOU.
BB

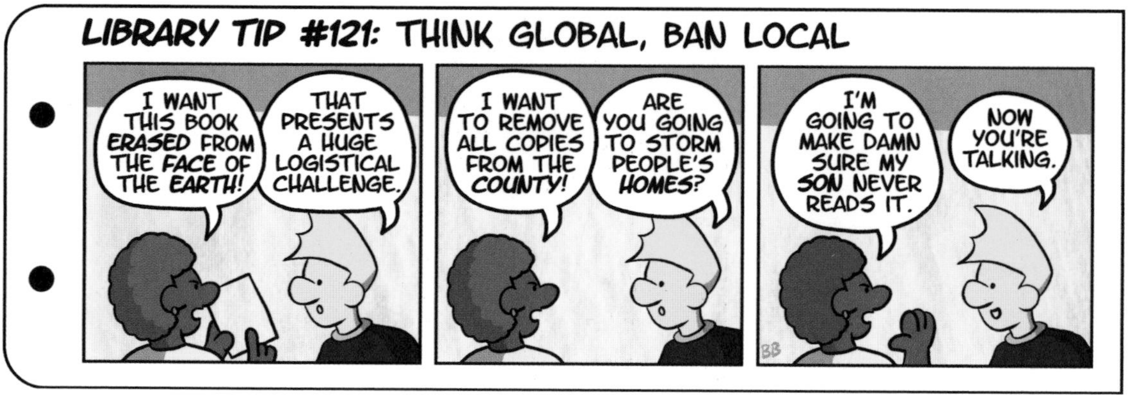
LIBRARY TIP #121: THINK GLOBAL, BAN LOCAL
I WANT THIS BOOK *ERASED* FROM THE *FACE* OF THE *EARTH*!
THAT PRESENTS A HUGE LOGISTICAL CHALLENGE.
I WANT TO REMOVE ALL COPIES FROM THE *COUNTY*!
ARE YOU GOING TO STORM PEOPLE'S *HOMES*?
I'M GOING TO MAKE DAMN SURE MY *SON* NEVER READS IT.
NOW YOU'RE TALKING.
BB

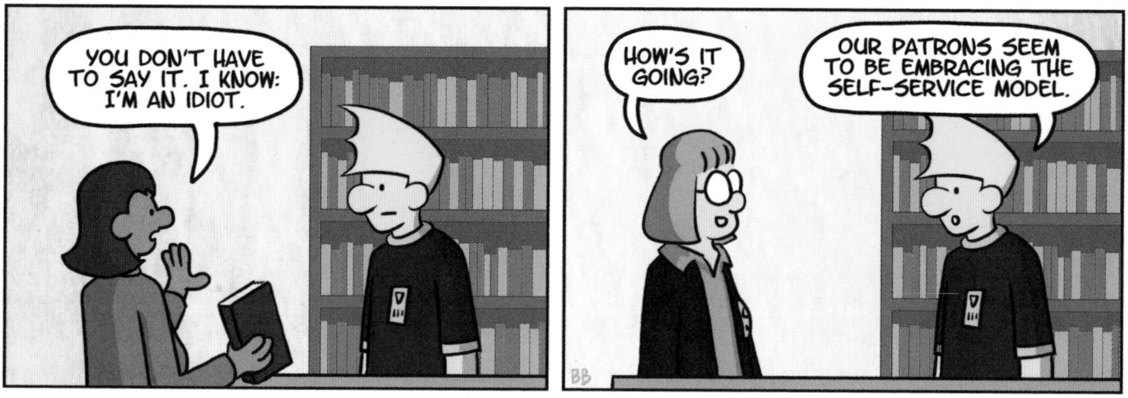
YOU DON'T HAVE TO SAY IT. I KNOW: I'M AN IDIOT.
HOW'S IT GOING?
OUR PATRONS SEEM TO BE EMBRACING THE SELF-SERVICE MODEL.
BB

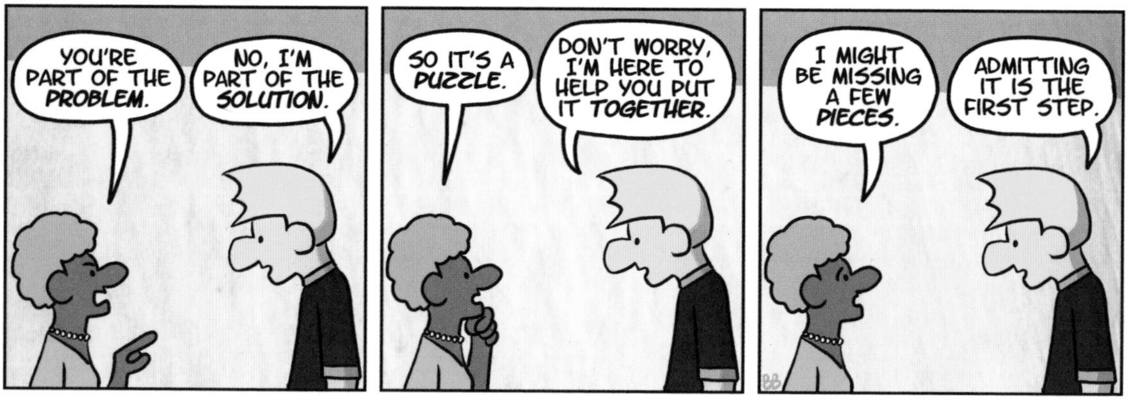
YOU'RE PART OF THE *PROBLEM*.
NO, I'M PART OF THE *SOLUTION*.
SO IT'S A *PUZZLE*.
DON'T WORRY, I'M HERE TO HELP YOU PUT IT *TOGETHER*.
I MIGHT BE MISSING A FEW *PIECES*.
ADMITTING IT IS THE FIRST STEP.
BB

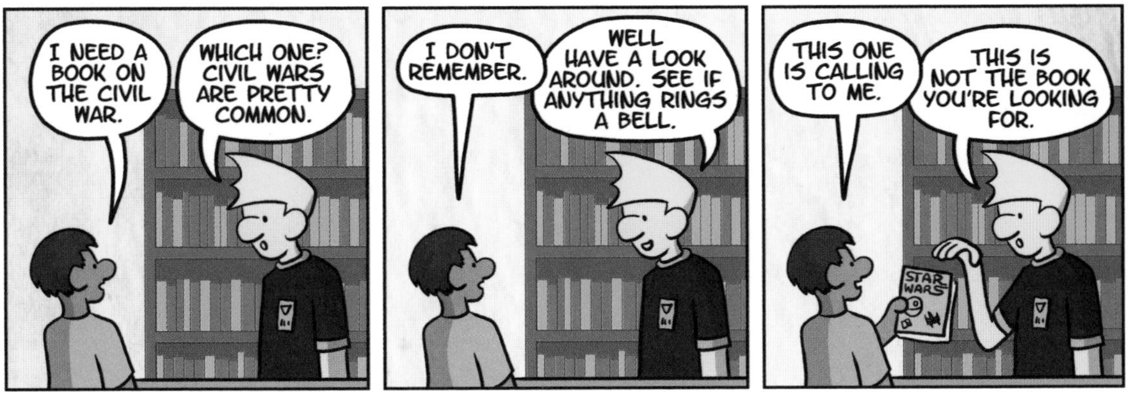
I NEED A BOOK ON THE CIVIL WAR.
WHICH ONE? CIVIL WARS ARE PRETTY COMMON.
I DON'T REMEMBER.
WELL HAVE A LOOK AROUND. SEE IF ANYTHING RINGS A BELL.
THIS ONE IS CALLING TO ME.
STAR WARS
THIS IS NOT THE BOOK YOU'RE LOOKING FOR.

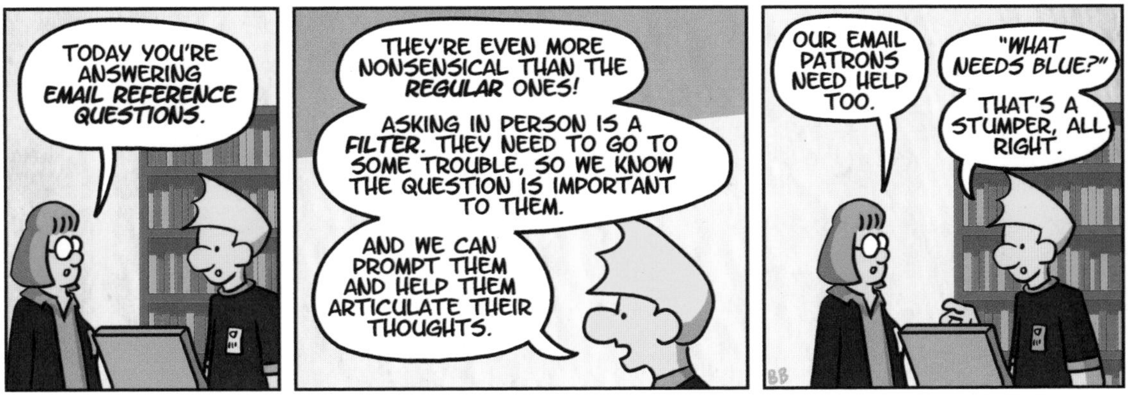
TODAY YOU'RE ANSWERING *EMAIL REFERENCE QUESTIONS*.
THEY'RE EVEN MORE NONSENSICAL THAN THE *REGULAR* ONES!
ASKING IN PERSON IS A *FILTER*. THEY NEED TO GO TO SOME TROUBLE, SO WE KNOW THE QUESTION IS IMPORTANT TO THEM.
AND WE CAN PROMPT THEM AND HELP THEM ARTICULATE THEIR THOUGHTS.
OUR EMAIL PATRONS NEED HELP TOO.
"WHAT NEEDS BLUE?"
THAT'S A STUMPER, ALL RIGHT.
BB

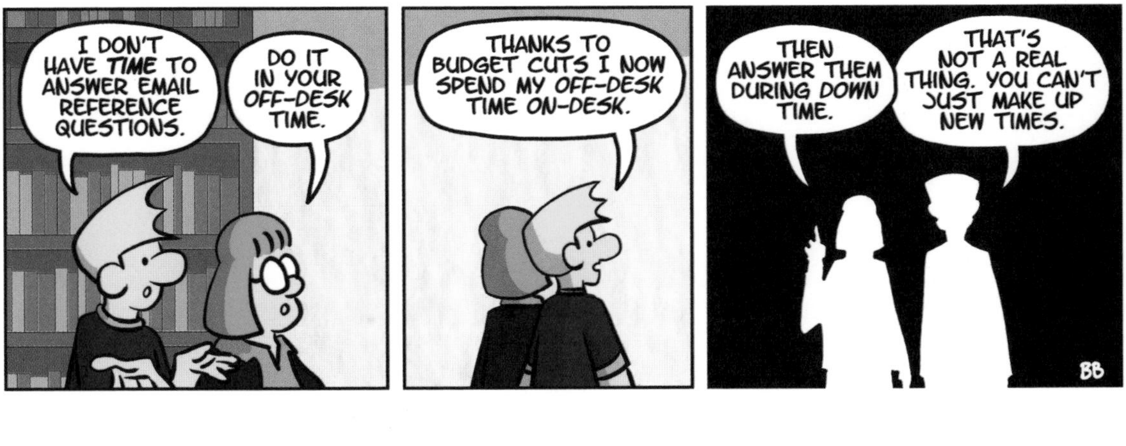
I DON'T HAVE *TIME* TO ANSWER EMAIL REFERENCE QUESTIONS.
DO IT IN YOUR *OFF-DESK* TIME.
THANKS TO BUDGET CUTS I NOW SPEND MY *OFF-DESK* TIME *ON-DESK*.
THEN ANSWER THEM DURING *DOWN* TIME.
THAT'S NOT A REAL THING. YOU CAN'T JUST MAKE UP NEW TIMES.
BB

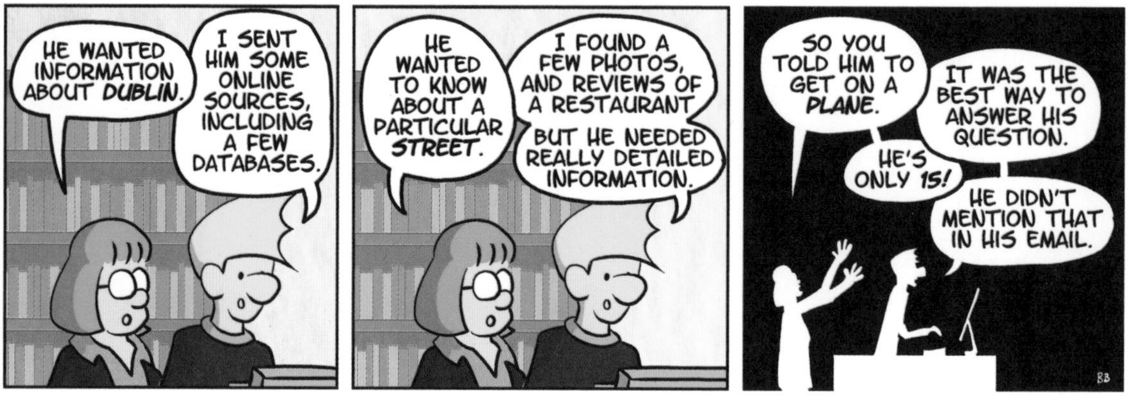
HE WANTED INFORMATION ABOUT DUBLIN.
I SENT HIM SOME ONLINE SOURCES, INCLUDING A FEW DATABASES.
HE WANTED TO KNOW ABOUT A PARTICULAR STREET.
I FOUND A FEW PHOTOS, AND REVIEWS OF A RESTAURANT
BUT HE NEEDED REALLY DETAILED INFORMATION.
SO YOU TOLD HIM TO GET ON A PLANE.
IT WAS THE BEST WAY TO ANSWER HIS QUESTION.
HE'S ONLY 15!
HE DIDN'T MENTION THAT IN HIS EMAIL.
BB

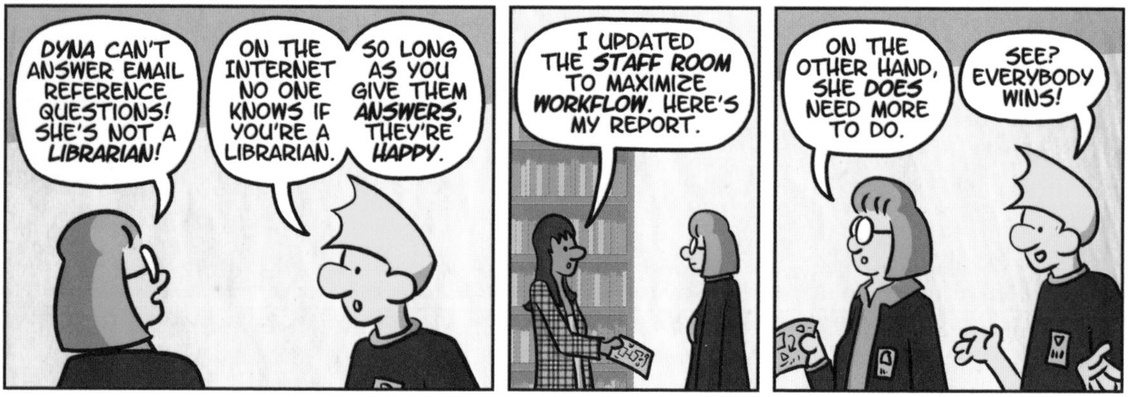
DYNA CAN'T ANSWER EMAIL REFERENCE QUESTIONS! SHE'S NOT A LIBRARIAN!
ON THE INTERNET NO ONE KNOWS IF YOU'RE A LIBRARIAN.
SO LONG AS YOU GIVE THEM ANSWERS, THEY'RE HAPPY.
I UPDATED THE STAFF ROOM TO MAXIMIZE WORKFLOW. HERE'S MY REPORT.
ON THE OTHER HAND, SHE DOES NEED MORE TO DO.
SEE? EVERYBODY WINS!

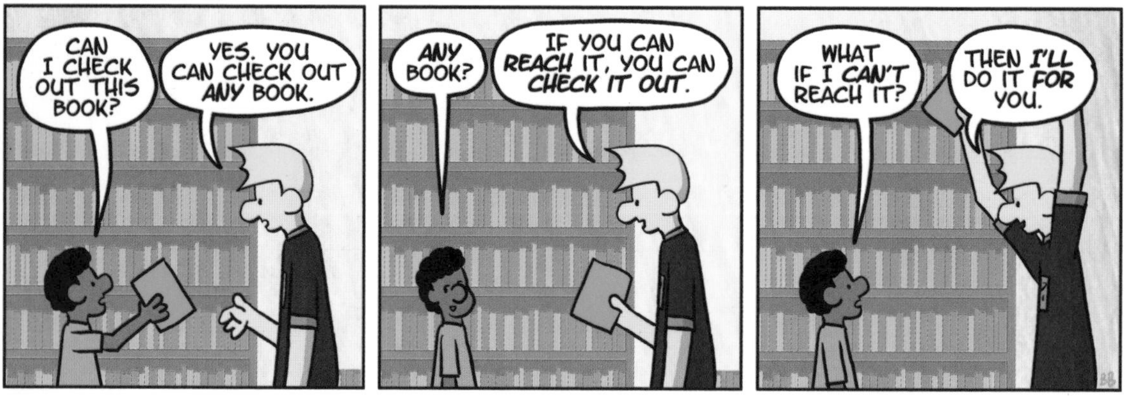
CAN I CHECK OUT THIS BOOK?
YES. YOU CAN CHECK OUT ANY BOOK.
ANY BOOK?
IF YOU CAN REACH IT, YOU CAN CHECK IT OUT.
WHAT IF I CAN'T REACH IT?
THEN I'LL DO IT FOR YOU.
BB

Reads Well With Others

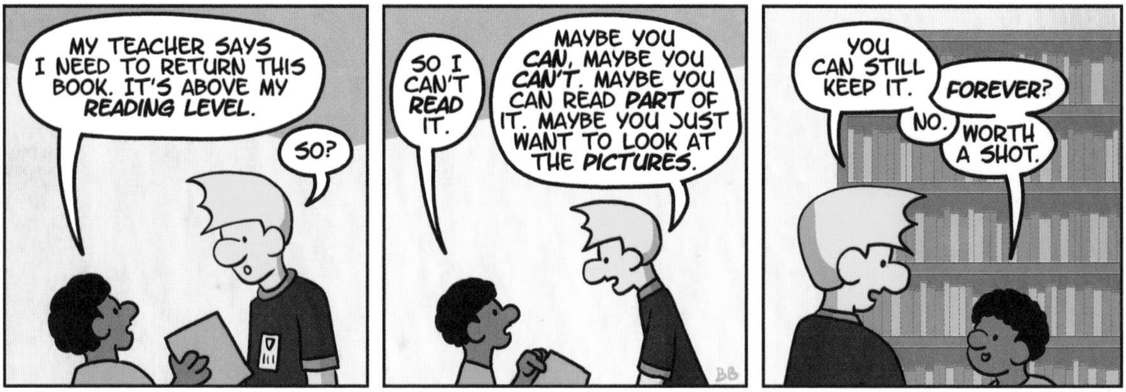
MY TEACHER SAYS I NEED TO RETURN THIS BOOK. IT'S ABOVE MY *READING LEVEL*.
SO?
SO I CAN'T *READ* IT.
MAYBE YOU *CAN*, MAYBE YOU *CAN'T*. MAYBE YOU CAN READ *PART* OF IT. MAYBE YOU JUST WANT TO LOOK AT THE *PICTURES*.
YOU CAN STILL KEEP IT.
FOREVER?
NO.
WORTH A SHOT.

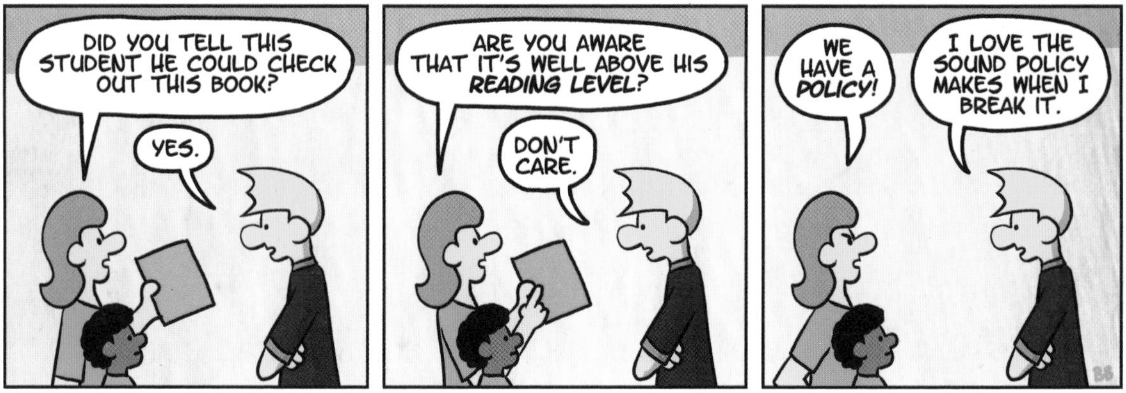
DID YOU TELL THIS STUDENT HE COULD CHECK OUT THIS BOOK?
YES.
ARE YOU AWARE THAT IT'S WELL ABOVE HIS *READING LEVEL*?
DON'T CARE.
WE HAVE A *POLICY*!
I LOVE THE SOUND POLICY MAKES WHEN I BREAK IT.

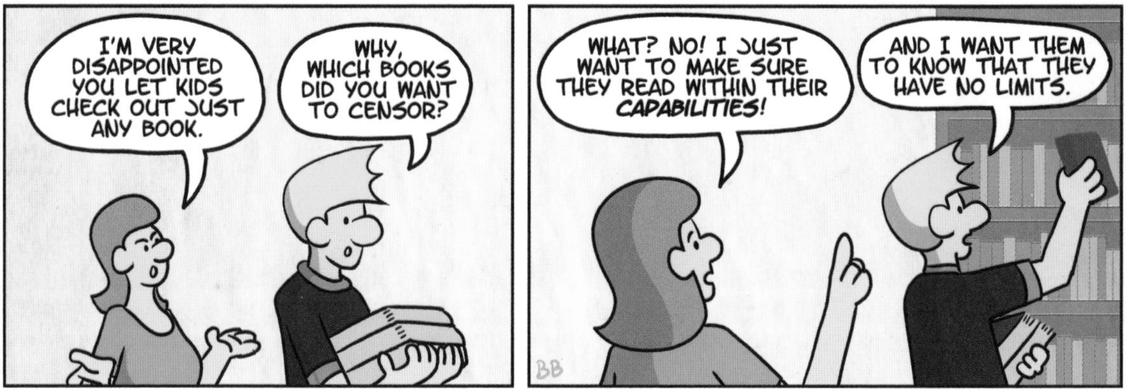
I'M VERY DISAPPOINTED YOU LET KIDS CHECK OUT JUST ANY BOOK.
WHY, WHICH BOOKS DID YOU WANT TO CENSOR?
WHAT? NO! I JUST WANT TO MAKE SURE THEY READ WITHIN THEIR *CAPABILITIES*!
AND I WANT THEM TO KNOW THAT THEY HAVE NO LIMITS.

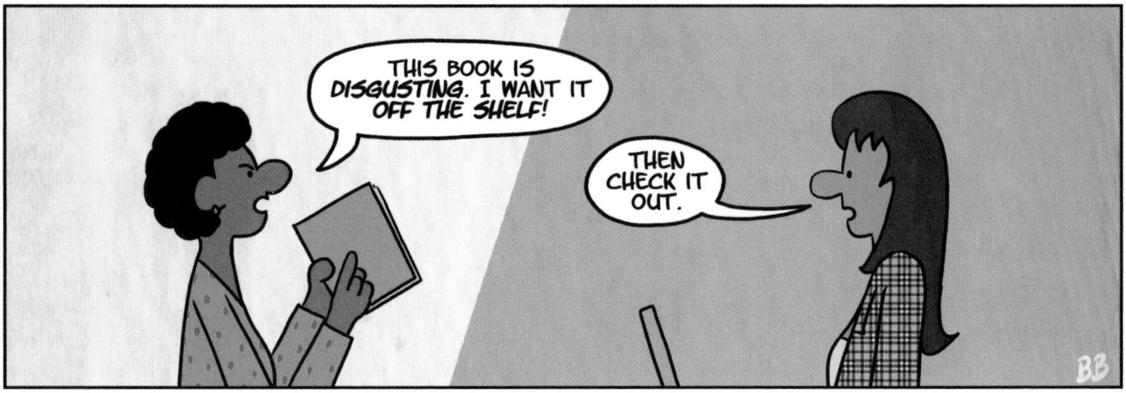
THIS BOOK IS DISGUSTING. I WANT IT OFF THE SHELF!
THEN CHECK IT OUT.
BB

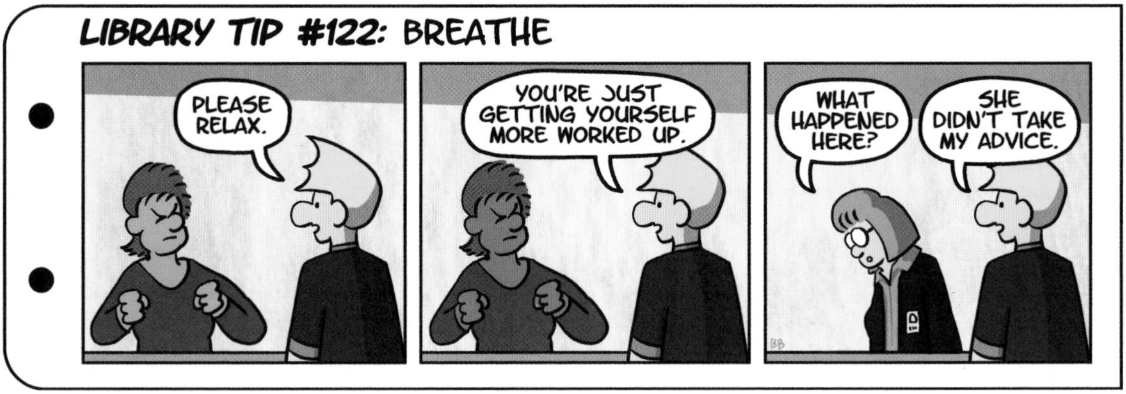
LIBRARY TIP #122: BREATHE
PLEASE RELAX.
YOU'RE JUST GETTING YOURSELF MORE WORKED UP.
WHAT HAPPENED HERE?
SHE DIDN'T TAKE MY ADVICE.
BB

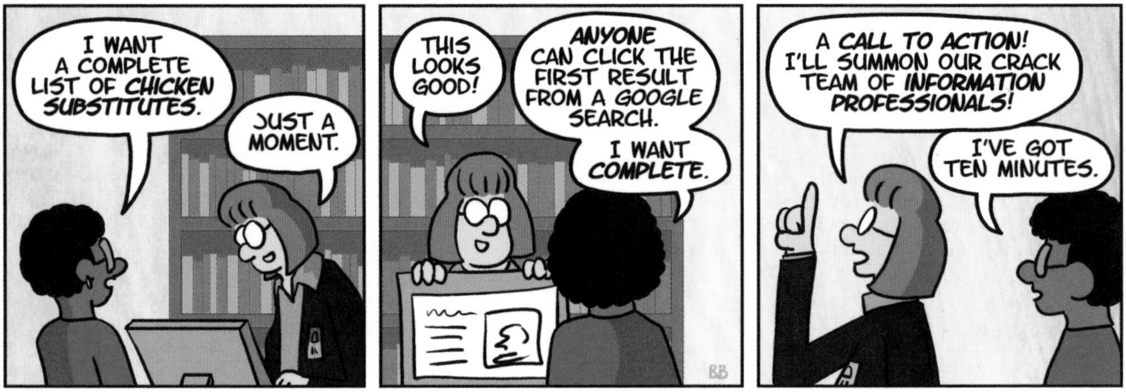
I WANT A COMPLETE LIST OF CHICKEN SUBSTITUTES.
JUST A MOMENT.
THIS LOOKS GOOD!
ANYONE CAN CLICK THE FIRST RESULT FROM A GOOGLE SEARCH.
I WANT COMPLETE.
A CALL TO ACTION! I'LL SUMMON OUR CRACK TEAM OF INFORMATION PROFESSIONALS!
I'VE GOT TEN MINUTES.
BB

Reads Well With Others

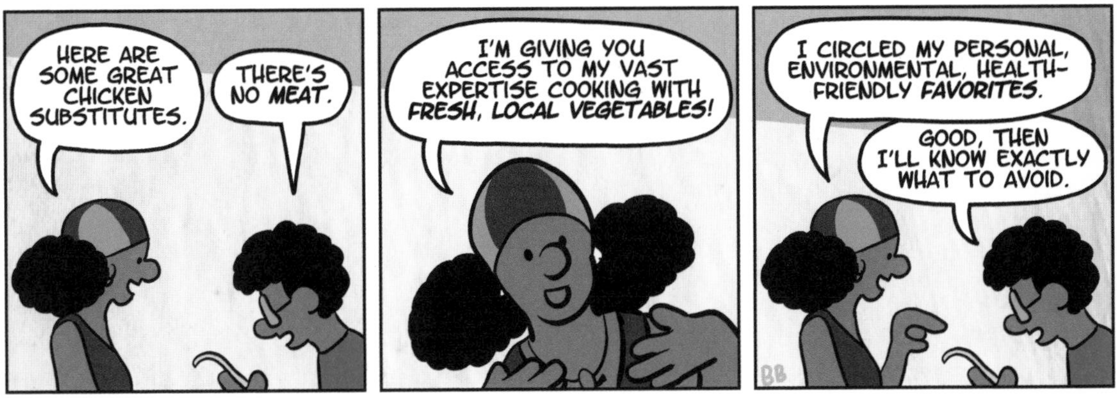
HERE ARE SOME GREAT CHICKEN SUBSTITUTES.
THERE'S NO MEAT.
I'M GIVING YOU ACCESS TO MY VAST EXPERTISE COOKING WITH FRESH, LOCAL VEGETABLES!
I CIRCLED MY PERSONAL, ENVIRONMENTAL, HEALTH-FRIENDLY FAVORITES.
GOOD, THEN I'LL KNOW EXACTLY WHAT TO AVOID.
BB

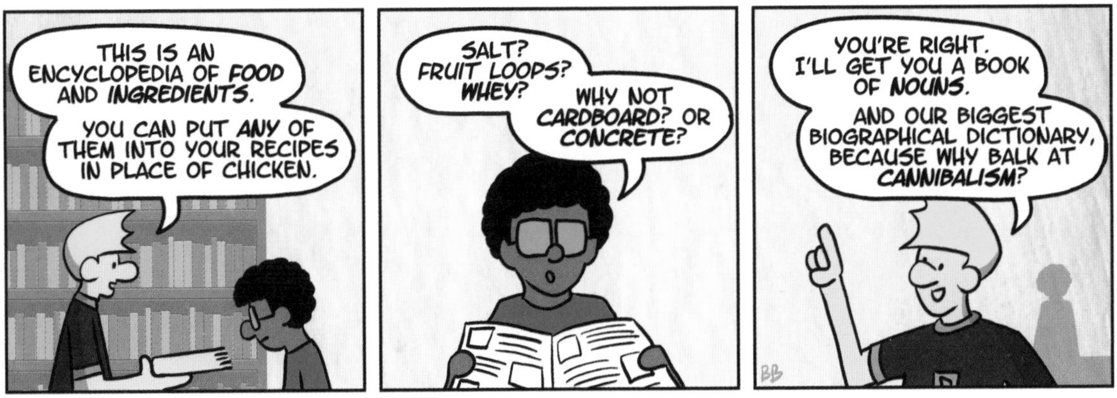
THIS IS AN ENCYCLOPEDIA OF FOOD AND INGREDIENTS.
YOU CAN PUT ANY OF THEM INTO YOUR RECIPES IN PLACE OF CHICKEN.
SALT? FRUIT LOOPS? WHEY?
WHY NOT CARDBOARD? OR CONCRETE?
YOU'RE RIGHT. I'LL GET YOU A BOOK OF NOUNS.
AND OUR BIGGEST BIOGRAPHICAL DICTIONARY, BECAUSE WHY BALK AT CANNIBALISM?
BB

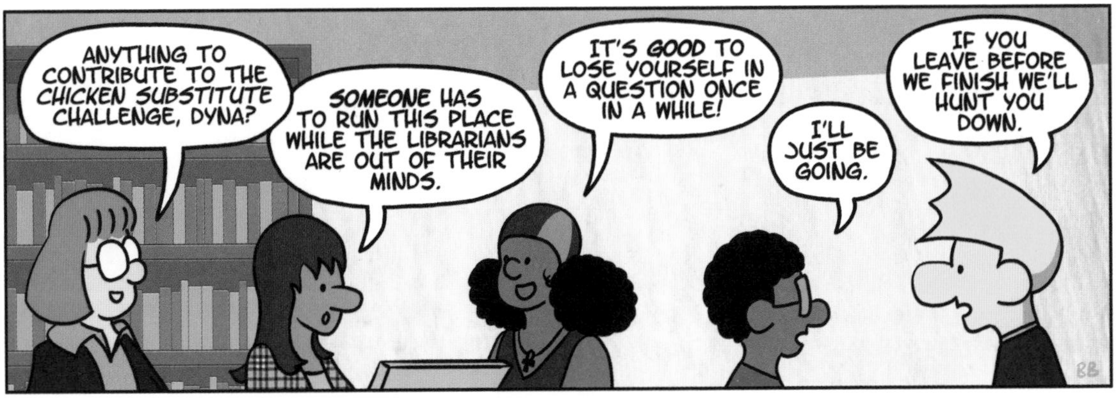
ANYTHING TO CONTRIBUTE TO THE CHICKEN SUBSTITUTE CHALLENGE, DYNA?
SOMEONE HAS TO RUN THIS PLACE WHILE THE LIBRARIANS ARE OUT OF THEIR MINDS.
IT'S GOOD TO LOSE YOURSELF IN A QUESTION ONCE IN A WHILE!
I'LL JUST BE GOING.
IF YOU LEAVE BEFORE WE FINISH WE'LL HUNT YOU DOWN.
BB

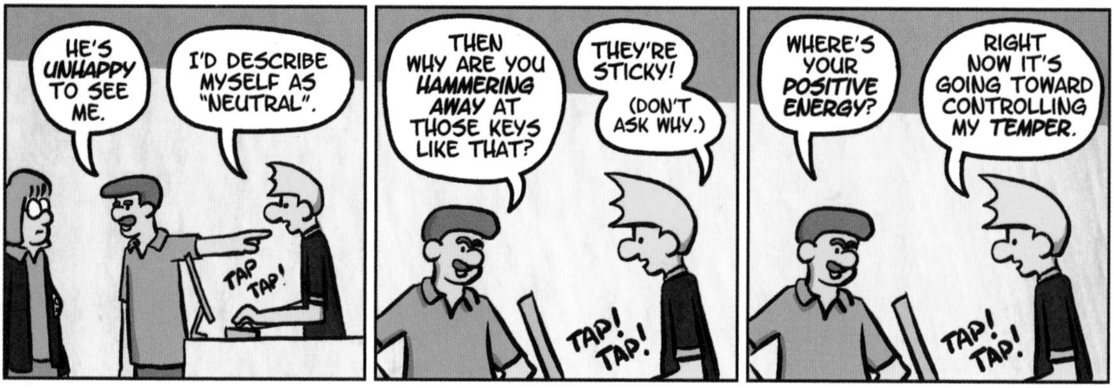
HE'S UNHAPPY TO SEE ME.
I'D DESCRIBE MYSELF AS "NEUTRAL".
TAP TAP!
THEN WHY ARE YOU HAMMERING AWAY AT THOSE KEYS LIKE THAT?
THEY'RE STICKY!
(DON'T ASK WHY.)
TAP! TAP!
WHERE'S YOUR POSITIVE ENERGY?
RIGHT NOW IT'S GOING TOWARD CONTROLLING MY TEMPER.
TAP! TAP!

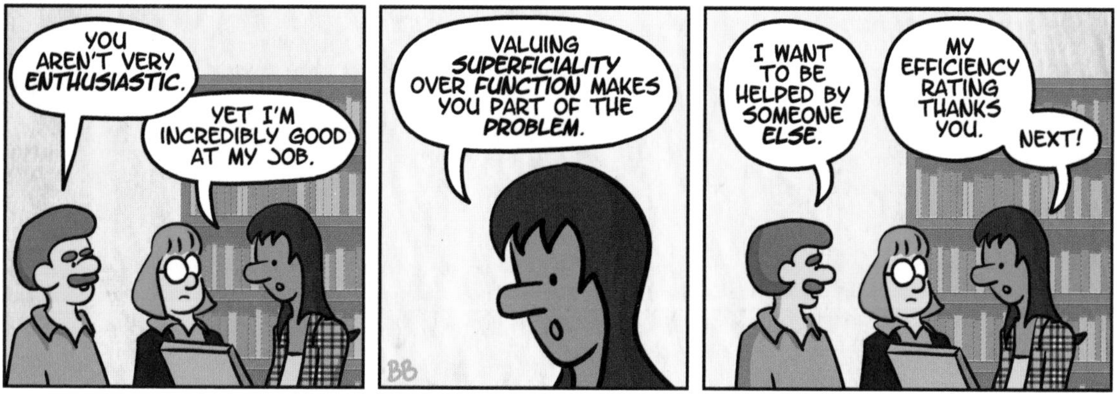
YOU AREN'T VERY ENTHUSIASTIC.
YET I'M INCREDIBLY GOOD AT MY JOB.
VALUING SUPERFICIALITY OVER FUNCTION MAKES YOU PART OF THE PROBLEM.
BB
I WANT TO BE HELPED BY SOMEONE ELSE.
MY EFFICIENCY RATING THANKS YOU.
NEXT!

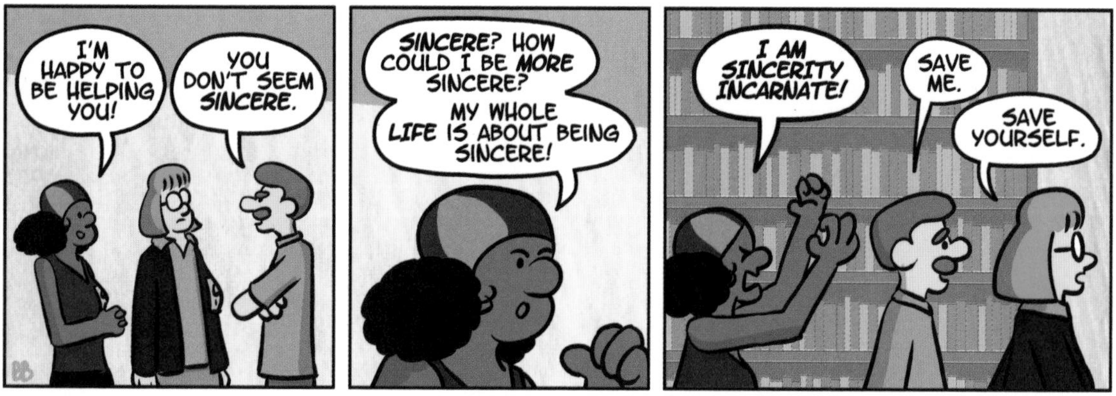
I'M HAPPY TO BE HELPING YOU!
YOU DON'T SEEM SINCERE.
BB
SINCERE? HOW COULD I BE MORE SINCERE?
MY WHOLE LIFE IS ABOUT BEING SINCERE!
I AM SINCERITY INCARNATE!
SAVE ME.
SAVE YOURSELF.

Reads Well With Others

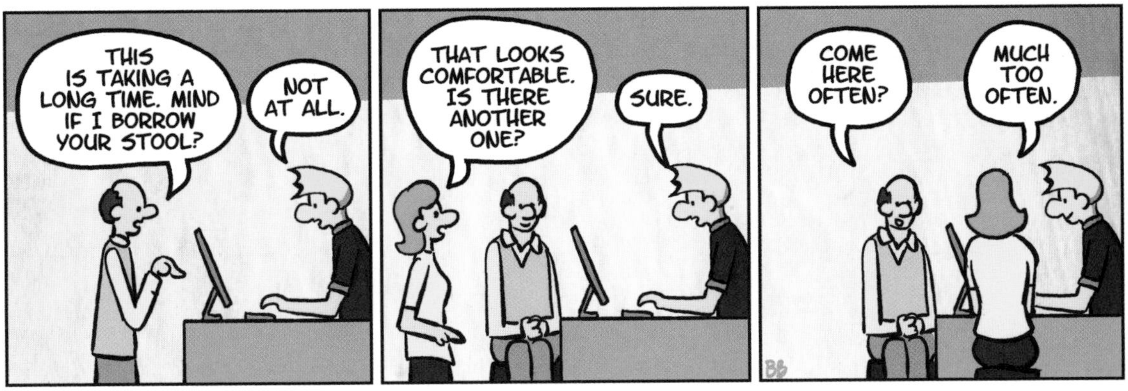
THIS IS TAKING A LONG TIME. MIND IF I BORROW YOUR STOOL?
NOT AT ALL.
THAT LOOKS COMFORTABLE. IS THERE ANOTHER ONE?
SURE.
COME HERE OFTEN?
MUCH TOO OFTEN.
BB

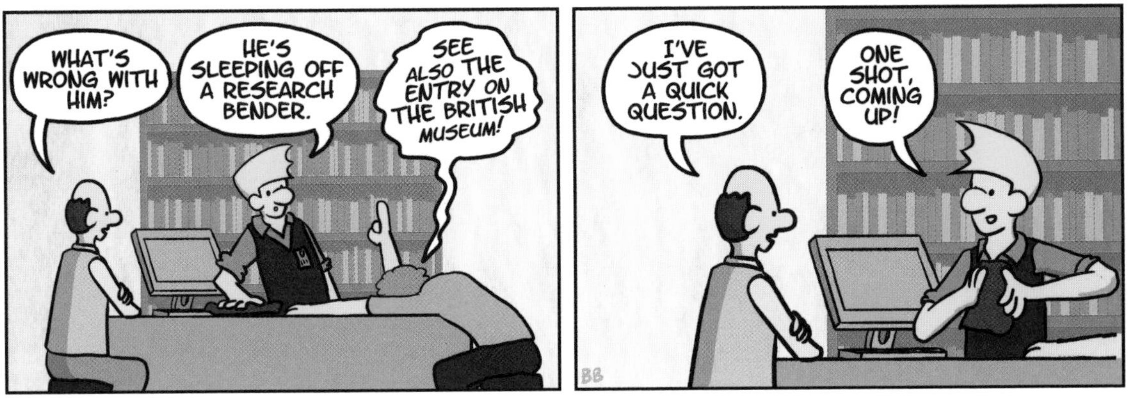
WHAT'S WRONG WITH HIM?
HE'S SLEEPING OFF A RESEARCH BENDER.
SEE ALSO THE ENTRY ON THE BRITISH MUSEUM!
I'VE JUST GOT A QUICK QUESTION.
ONE SHOT, COMING UP!
BB

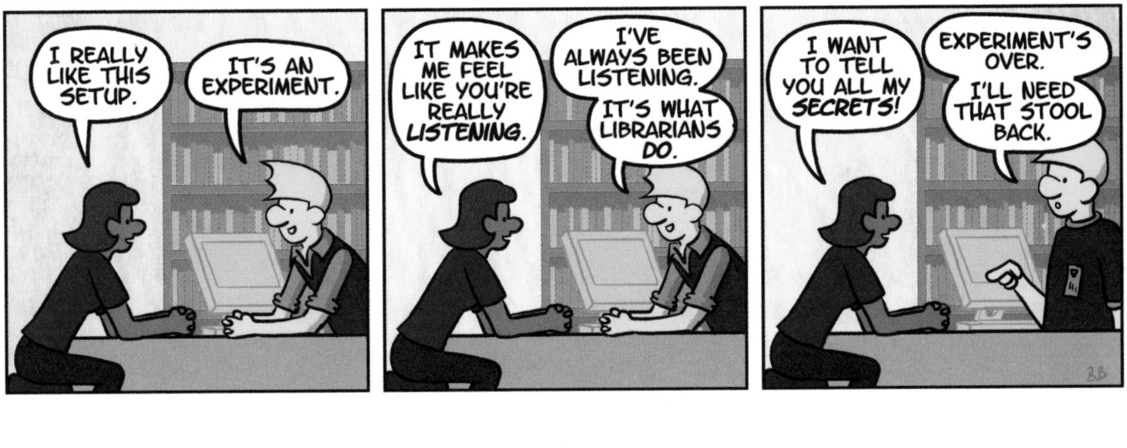
I REALLY LIKE THIS SETUP.
IT'S AN EXPERIMENT.
IT MAKES ME FEEL LIKE YOU'RE REALLY LISTENING.
I'VE ALWAYS BEEN LISTENING.
IT'S WHAT LIBRARIANS DO.
I WANT TO TELL YOU ALL MY SECRETS!
EXPERIMENT'S OVER.
I'LL NEED THAT STOOL BACK.
BB

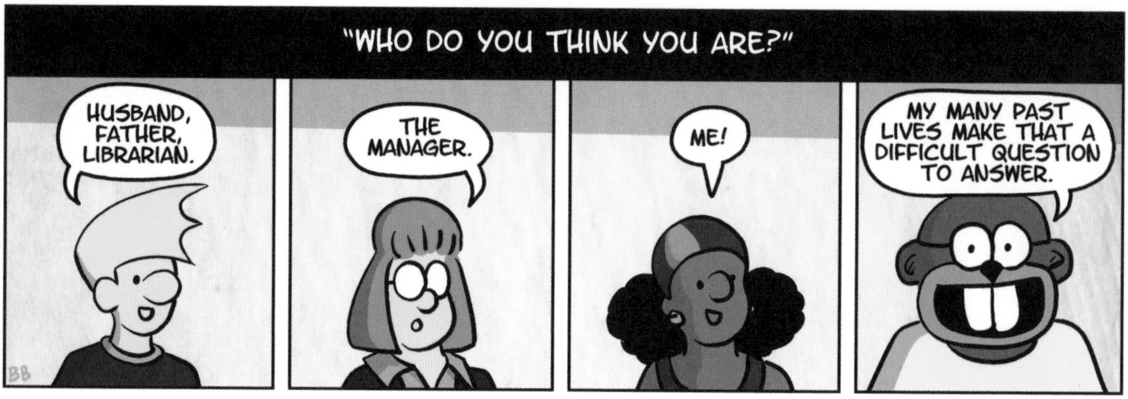
"WHO DO YOU THINK YOU ARE?"
HUSBAND, FATHER, LIBRARIAN.
THE MANAGER.
ME!
MY MANY PAST LIVES MAKE THAT A DIFFICULT QUESTION TO ANSWER.
BB

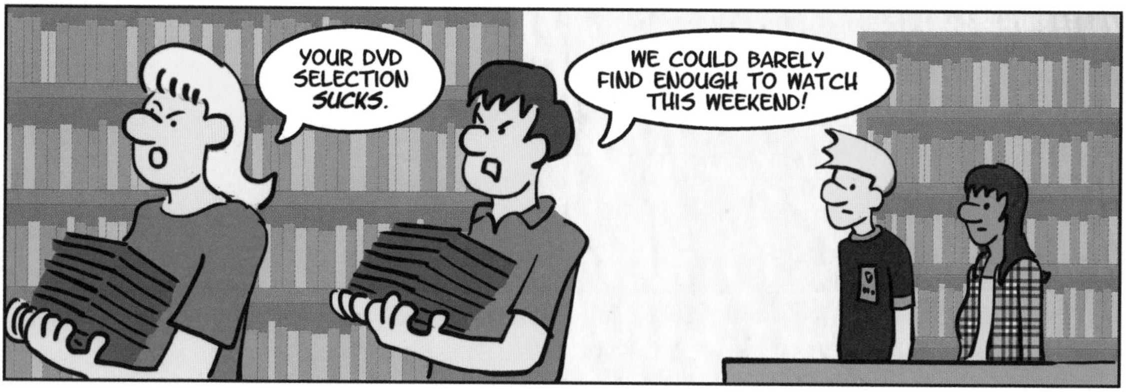
YOUR DVD SELECTION SUCKS.
WE COULD BARELY FIND ENOUGH TO WATCH THIS WEEKEND!

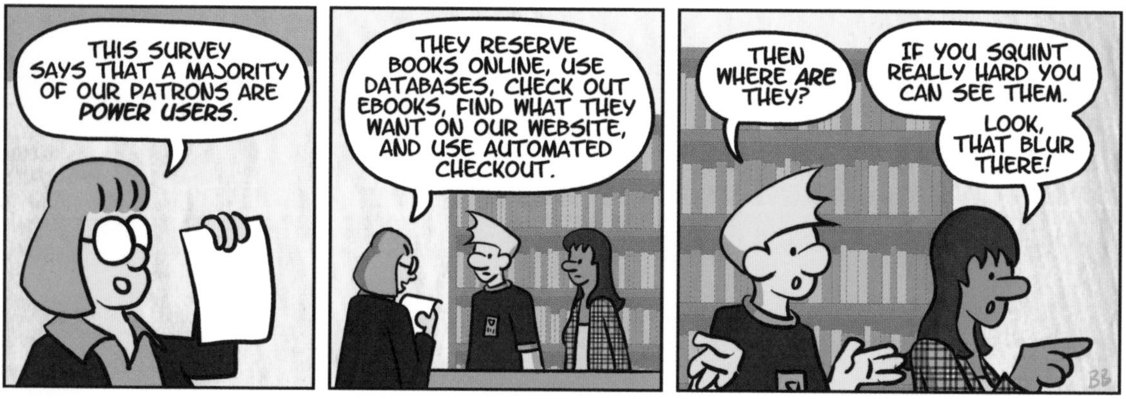
THIS SURVEY SAYS THAT A MAJORITY OF OUR PATRONS ARE POWER USERS.
THEY RESERVE BOOKS ONLINE, USE DATABASES, CHECK OUT EBOOKS, FIND WHAT THEY WANT ON OUR WEBSITE, AND USE AUTOMATED CHECKOUT.
THEN WHERE ARE THEY?
IF YOU SQUINT REALLY HARD YOU CAN SEE THEM.
LOOK, THAT BLUR THERE!
BB

Reads Well With Others

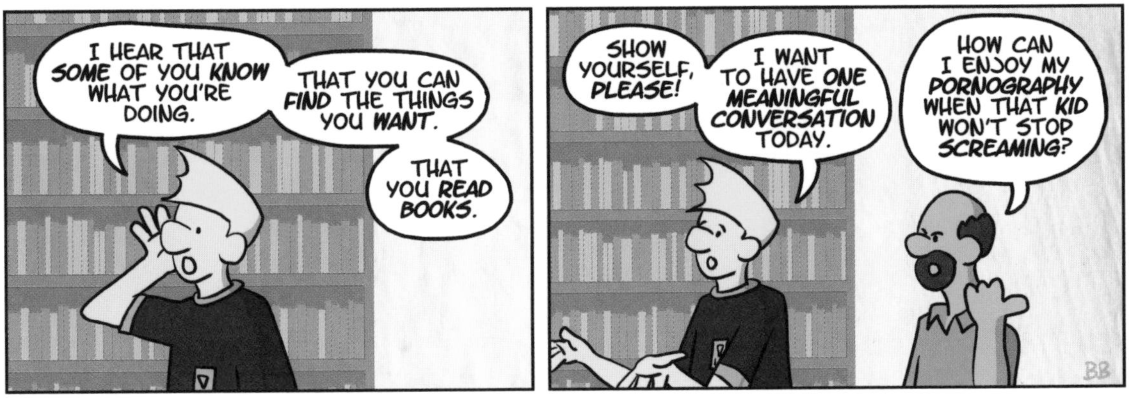

I HEAR THAT SOME OF YOU KNOW WHAT YOU'RE DOING.
THAT YOU CAN FIND THE THINGS YOU WANT.
THAT YOU READ BOOKS.
SHOW YOURSELF, PLEASE!
I WANT TO HAVE ONE MEANINGFUL CONVERSATION TODAY.
HOW CAN I ENJOY MY PORNOGRAPHY WHEN THAT KID WON'T STOP SCREAMING?
BB

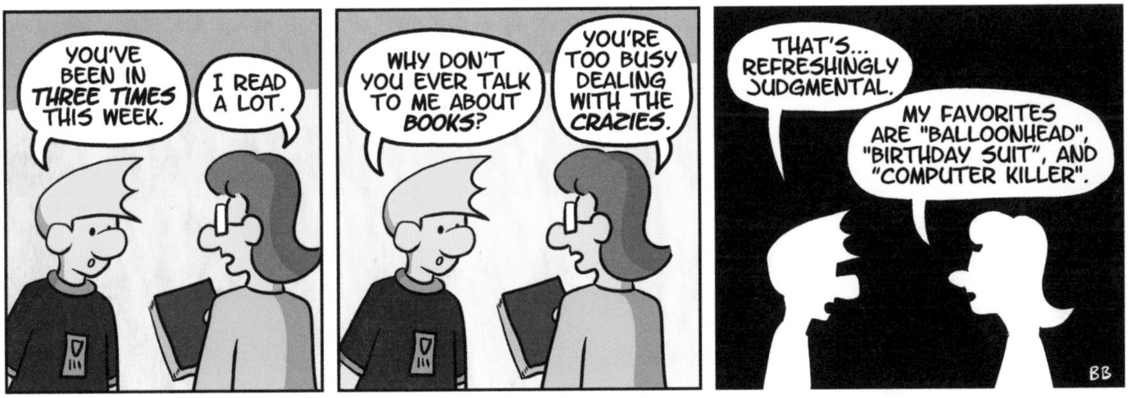

YOU'VE BEEN IN THREE TIMES THIS WEEK.
I READ A LOT.
WHY DON'T YOU EVER TALK TO ME ABOUT BOOKS?
YOU'RE TOO BUSY DEALING WITH THE CRAZIES.
THAT'S... REFRESHINGLY JUDGMENTAL.
MY FAVORITES ARE "BALLOONHEAD", "BIRTHDAY SUIT", AND "COMPUTER KILLER".
BB

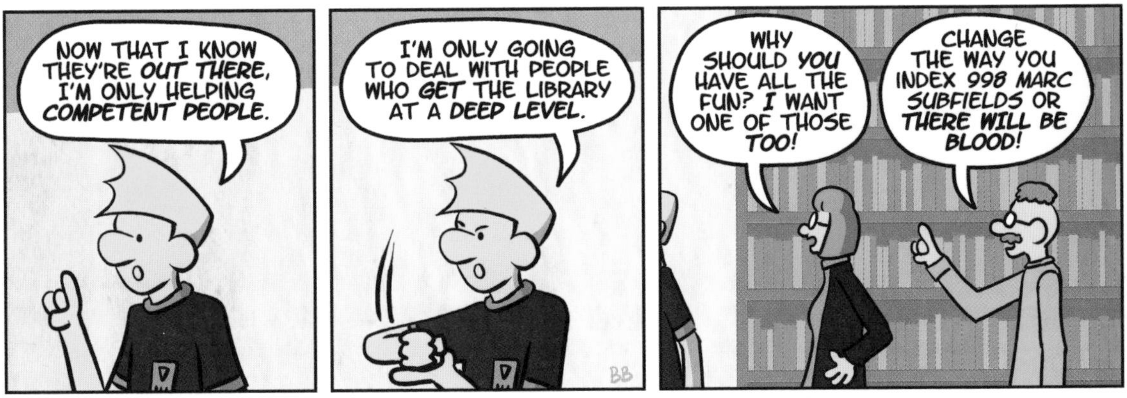

NOW THAT I KNOW THEY'RE OUT THERE, I'M ONLY HELPING COMPETENT PEOPLE.
I'M ONLY GOING TO DEAL WITH PEOPLE WHO GET THE LIBRARY AT A DEEP LEVEL.
BB
WHY SHOULD YOU HAVE ALL THE FUN? I WANT ONE OF THOSE TOO!
CHANGE THE WAY YOU INDEX 998 MARC SUBFIELDS OR THERE WILL BE BLOOD!

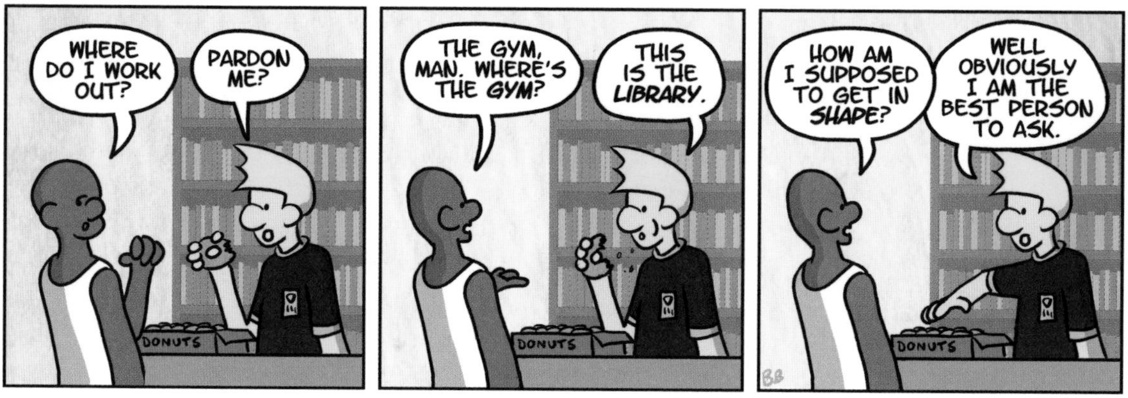
WHERE DO I WORK OUT?
PARDON ME?
THE GYM, MAN. WHERE'S THE GYM?
THIS IS THE LIBRARY.
HOW AM I SUPPOSED TO GET IN SHAPE?
WELL OBVIOUSLY I AM THE BEST PERSON TO ASK.
DONUTS
BB

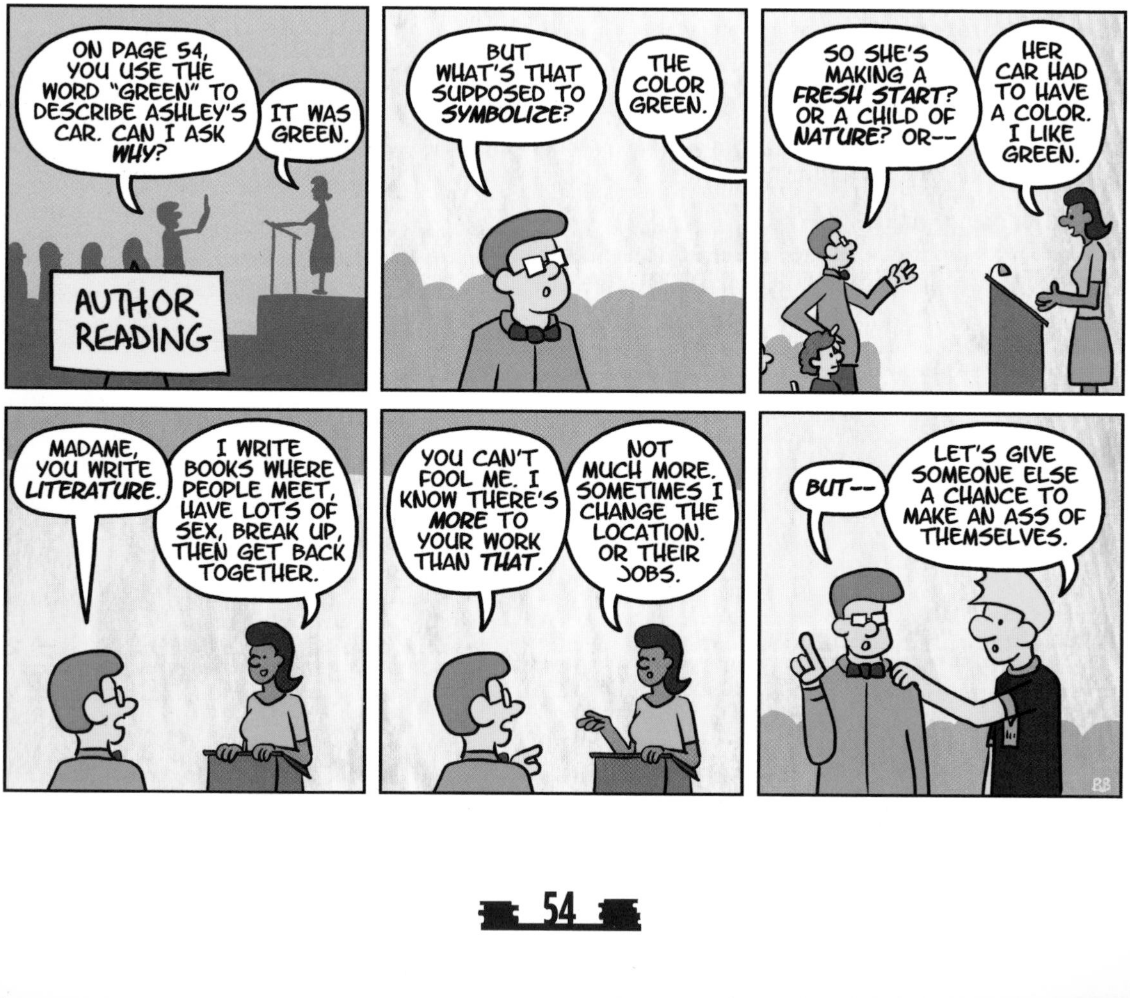
ON PAGE 54, YOU USE THE WORD "GREEN" TO DESCRIBE ASHLEY'S CAR. CAN I ASK WHY?
IT WAS GREEN.
AUTHOR READING
BUT WHAT'S THAT SUPPOSED TO SYMBOLIZE?
THE COLOR GREEN.
SO SHE'S MAKING A FRESH START? OR A CHILD OF NATURE? OR--
HER CAR HAD TO HAVE A COLOR. I LIKE GREEN.
MADAME, YOU WRITE LITERATURE.
I WRITE BOOKS WHERE PEOPLE MEET, HAVE LOTS OF SEX, BREAK UP, THEN GET BACK TOGETHER.
YOU CAN'T FOOL ME. I KNOW THERE'S MORE TO YOUR WORK THAN THAT.
NOT MUCH MORE. SOMETIMES I CHANGE THE LOCATION. OR THEIR JOBS.
BUT--
LET'S GIVE SOMEONE ELSE A CHANCE TO MAKE AN ASS OF THEMSELVES.
BB

Reads Well With Others

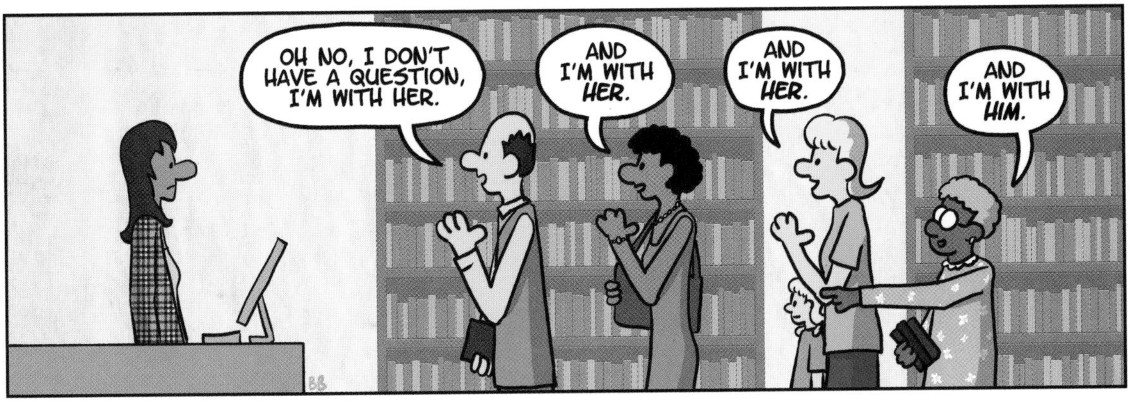

OH NO, I DON'T HAVE A QUESTION, I'M WITH HER.
AND I'M WITH HER.
AND I'M WITH HER.
AND I'M WITH HIM.
BB

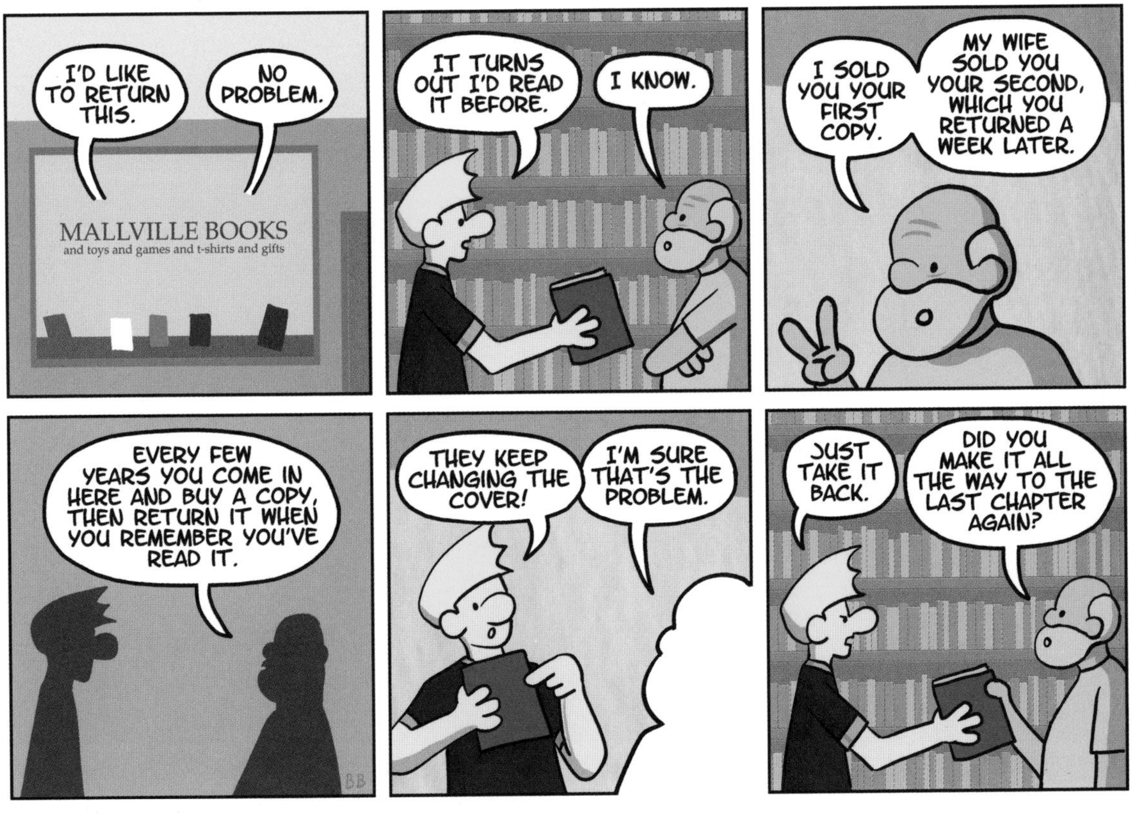

I'D LIKE TO RETURN THIS.
NO PROBLEM.
MALLVILLE BOOKS
and toys and games and t-shirts and gifts
IT TURNS OUT I'D READ IT BEFORE.
I KNOW.
I SOLD YOU YOUR FIRST COPY.
MY WIFE SOLD YOU YOUR SECOND, WHICH YOU RETURNED A WEEK LATER.
EVERY FEW YEARS YOU COME IN HERE AND BUY A COPY, THEN RETURN IT WHEN YOU REMEMBER YOU'VE READ IT.
BB
THEY KEEP CHANGING THE COVER!
I'M SURE THAT'S THE PROBLEM.
JUST TAKE IT BACK.
DID YOU MAKE IT ALL THE WAY TO THE LAST CHAPTER AGAIN?

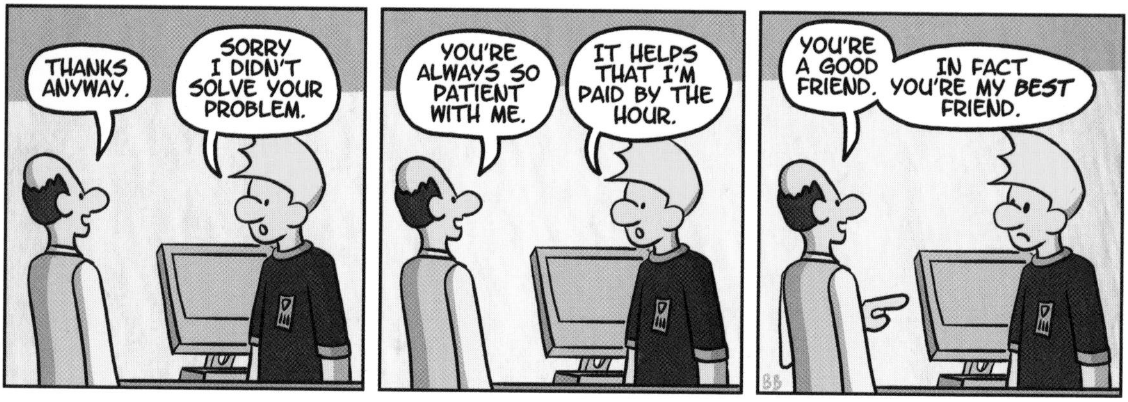
THANKS ANYWAY.
SORRY I DIDN'T SOLVE YOUR PROBLEM.
YOU'RE ALWAYS SO PATIENT WITH ME.
IT HELPS THAT I'M PAID BY THE HOUR.
YOU'RE A GOOD FRIEND.
IN FACT YOU'RE MY BEST FRIEND.
BB

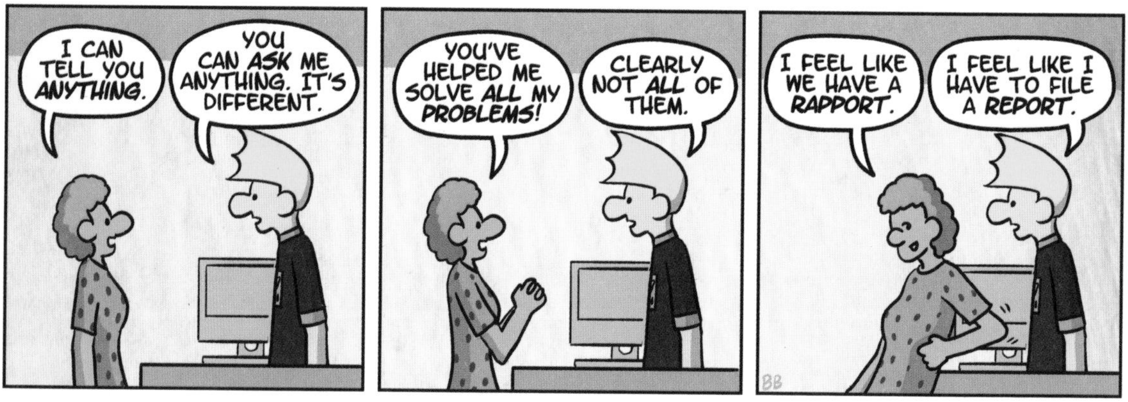
I CAN TELL YOU ANYTHING.
YOU CAN ASK ME ANYTHING. IT'S DIFFERENT.
YOU'VE HELPED ME SOLVE ALL MY PROBLEMS!
CLEARLY NOT ALL OF THEM.
I FEEL LIKE WE HAVE A RAPPORT.
I FEEL LIKE I HAVE TO FILE A REPORT.
BB

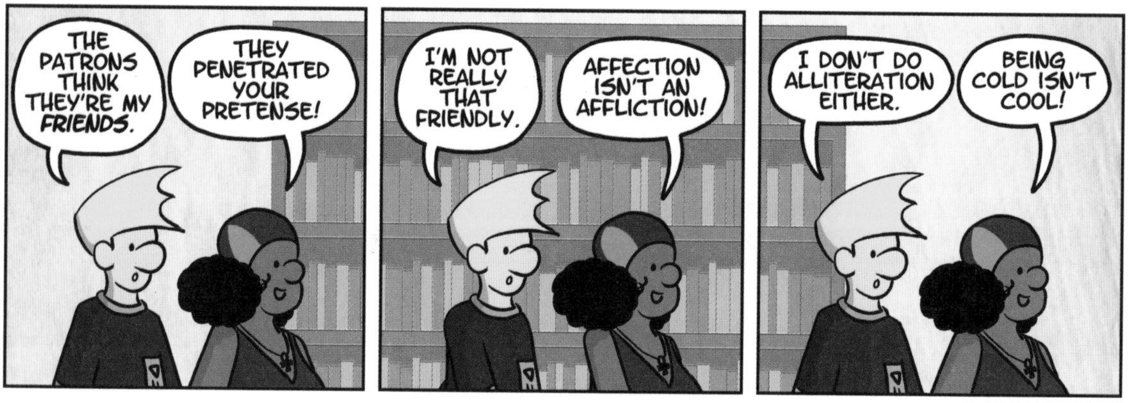
THE PATRONS THINK THEY'RE MY FRIENDS.
THEY PENETRATED YOUR PRETENSE!
I'M NOT REALLY THAT FRIENDLY.
AFFECTION ISN'T AN AFFLICTION!
I DON'T DO ALLITERATION EITHER.
BEING COLD ISN'T COOL!

Reads Well With Others

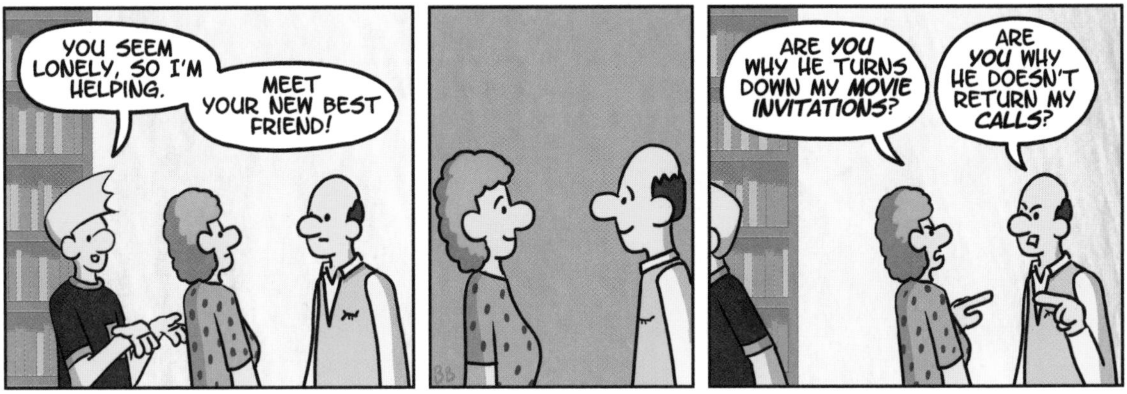

YOU SEEM LONELY, SO I'M HELPING.
MEET YOUR NEW BEST FRIEND!
ARE YOU WHY HE TURNS DOWN MY MOVIE INVITATIONS?
ARE YOU WHY HE DOESN'T RETURN MY CALLS?

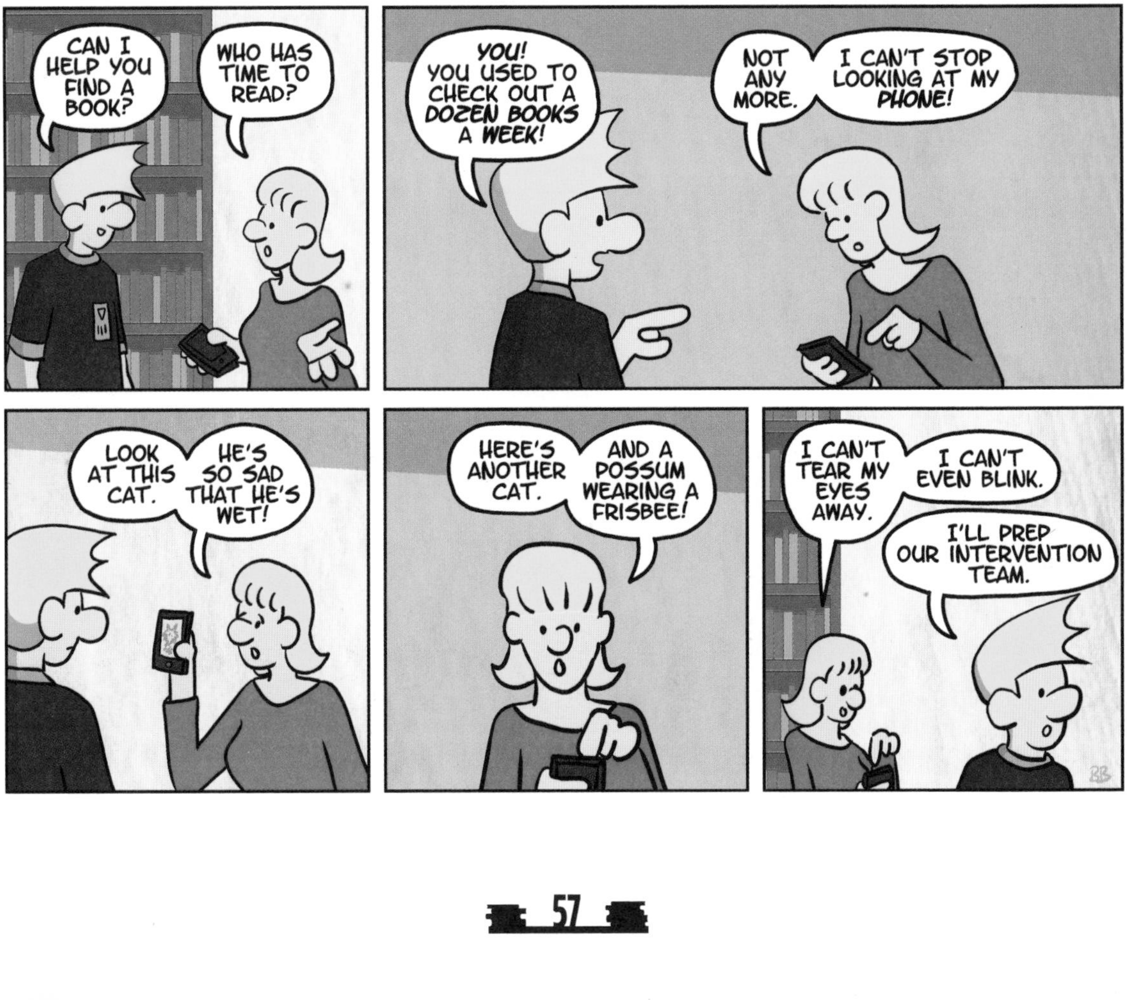

CAN I HELP YOU FIND A BOOK?
WHO HAS TIME TO READ?
YOU! YOU USED TO CHECK OUT A DOZEN BOOKS A WEEK!
NOT ANY MORE.
I CAN'T STOP LOOKING AT MY PHONE!
LOOK AT THIS CAT.
HE'S SO SAD THAT HE'S WET!
HERE'S ANOTHER CAT.
AND A POSSUM WEARING A FRISBEE!
I CAN'T TEAR MY EYES AWAY.
I CAN'T EVEN BLINK.
I'LL PREP OUR INTERVENTION TEAM.

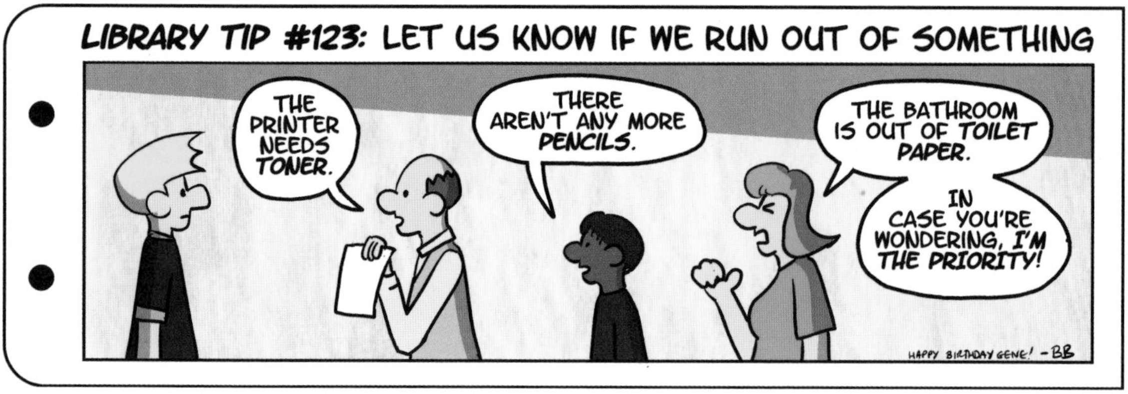
LIBRARY TIP #123: LET US KNOW IF WE RUN OUT OF SOMETHING
THE PRINTER NEEDS TONER.
THERE AREN'T ANY MORE PENCILS.
THE BATHROOM IS OUT OF TOILET PAPER.
IN CASE YOU'RE WONDERING, I'M THE PRIORITY!
HAPPY BIRTHDAY GENE! -BB

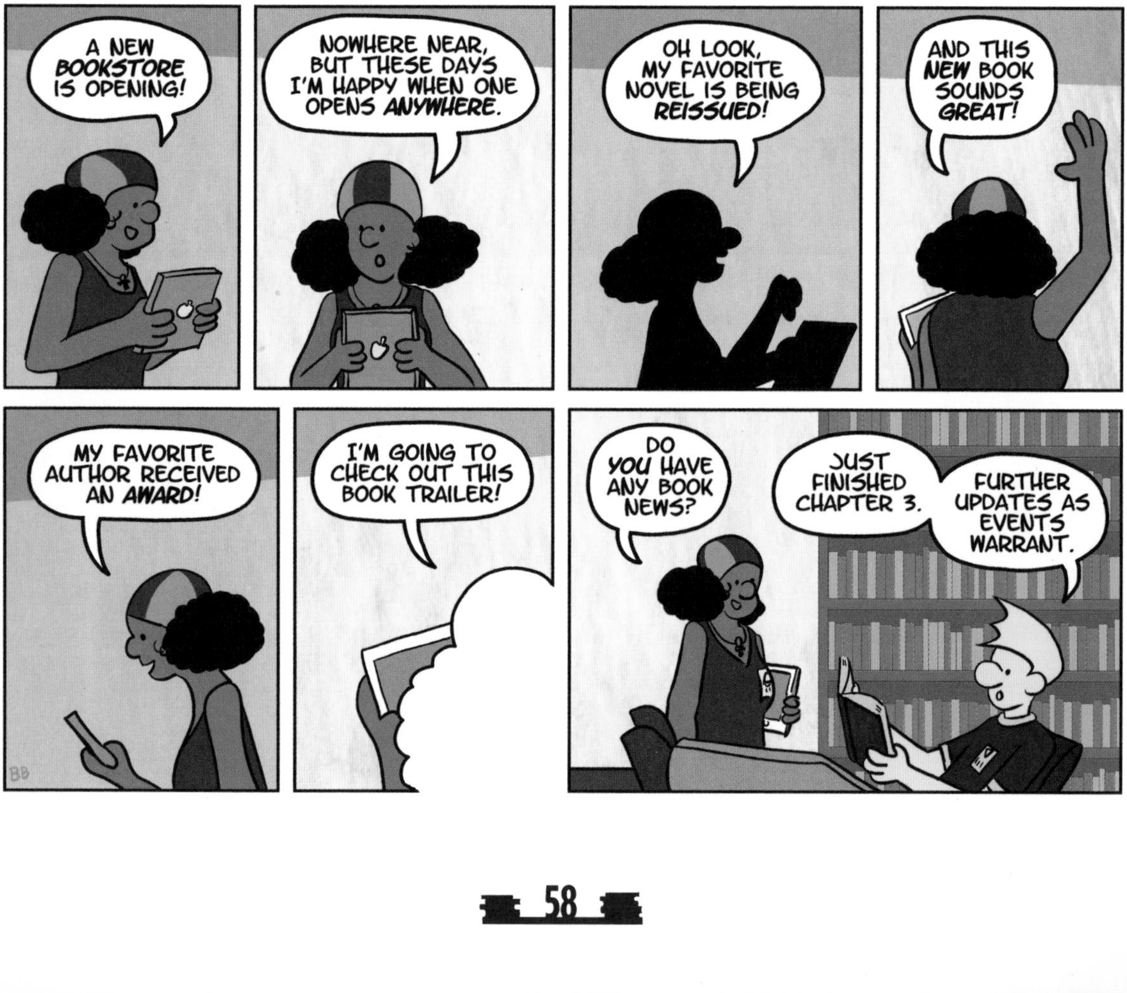
A NEW BOOKSTORE IS OPENING!
NOWHERE NEAR, BUT THESE DAYS I'M HAPPY WHEN ONE OPENS ANYWHERE.
OH LOOK, MY FAVORITE NOVEL IS BEING REISSUED!
AND THIS NEW BOOK SOUNDS GREAT!
MY FAVORITE AUTHOR RECEIVED AN AWARD!
I'M GOING TO CHECK OUT THIS BOOK TRAILER!
DO YOU HAVE ANY BOOK NEWS?
JUST FINISHED CHAPTER 3.
FURTHER UPDATES AS EVENTS WARRANT.
BB

Reads Well With Others

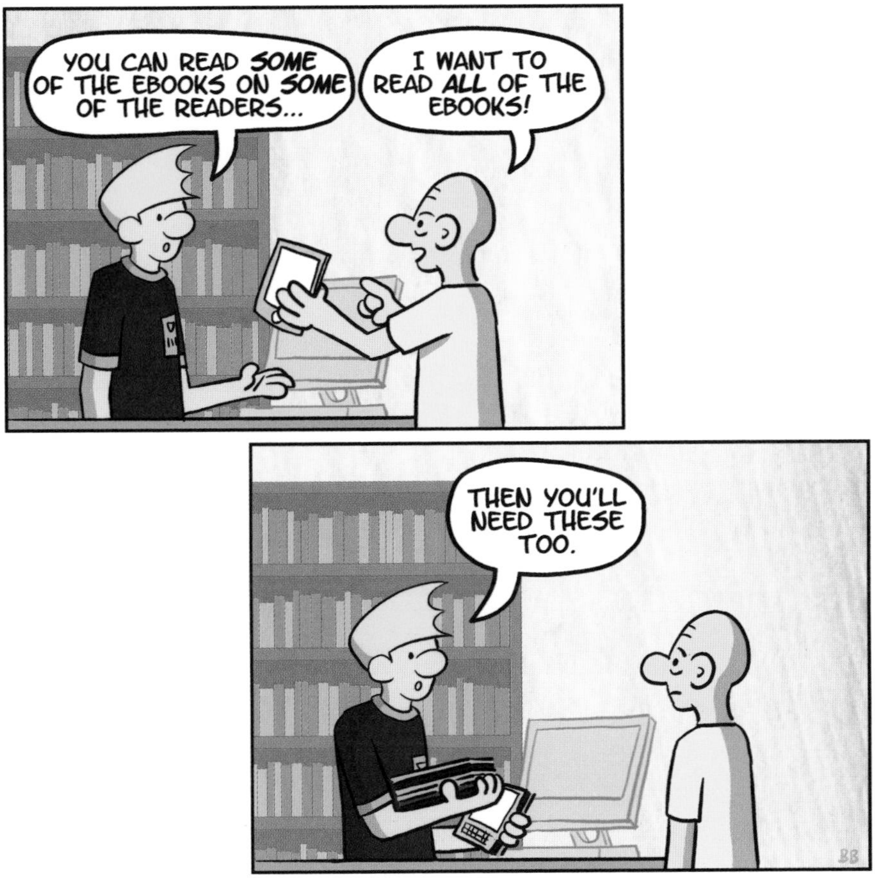
YOU CAN READ SOME OF THE EBOOKS ON SOME OF THE READERS...
I WANT TO READ ALL OF THE EBOOKS!
THEN YOU'LL NEED THESE TOO.
BB

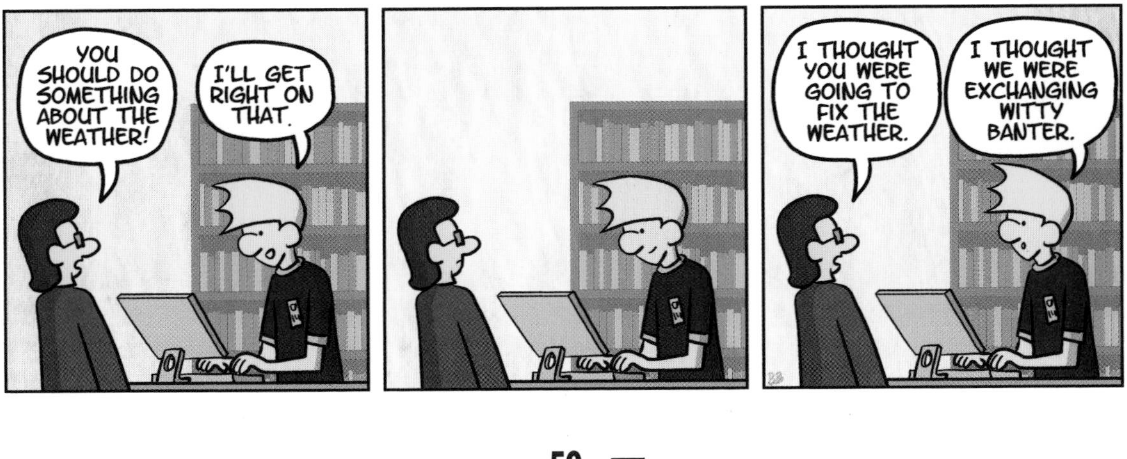
YOU SHOULD DO SOMETHING ABOUT THE WEATHER!
I'LL GET RIGHT ON THAT.
I THOUGHT YOU WERE GOING TO FIX THE WEATHER.
I THOUGHT WE WERE EXCHANGING WITTY BANTER.
BB

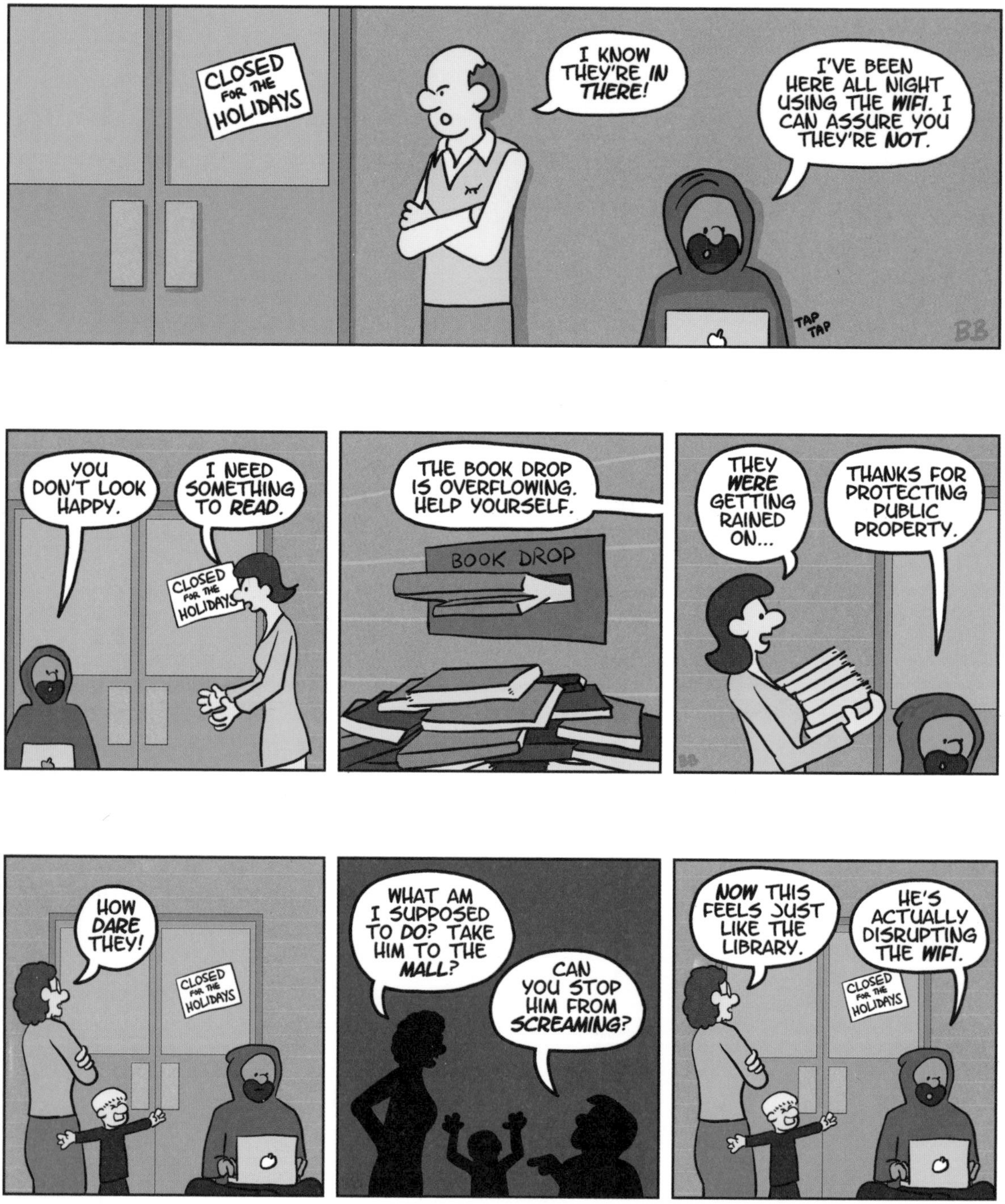
CLOSED FOR THE HOLIDAYS
I KNOW THEY'RE IN THERE!
I'VE BEEN HERE ALL NIGHT USING THE WIFI. I CAN ASSURE YOU THEY'RE NOT.
TAP TAP
YOU DON'T LOOK HAPPY.
I NEED SOMETHING TO READ.
CLOSED FOR THE HOLIDAYS
THE BOOK DROP IS OVERFLOWING. HELP YOURSELF.
BOOK DROP
THEY WERE GETTING RAINED ON...
THANKS FOR PROTECTING PUBLIC PROPERTY.
HOW DARE THEY!
CLOSED FOR THE HOLIDAYS
WHAT AM I SUPPOSED TO DO? TAKE HIM TO THE MALL?
CAN YOU STOP HIM FROM SCREAMING?
NOW THIS FEELS JUST LIKE THE LIBRARY.
HE'S ACTUALLY DISRUPTING THE WIFI.
CLOSED FOR THE HOLIDAYS

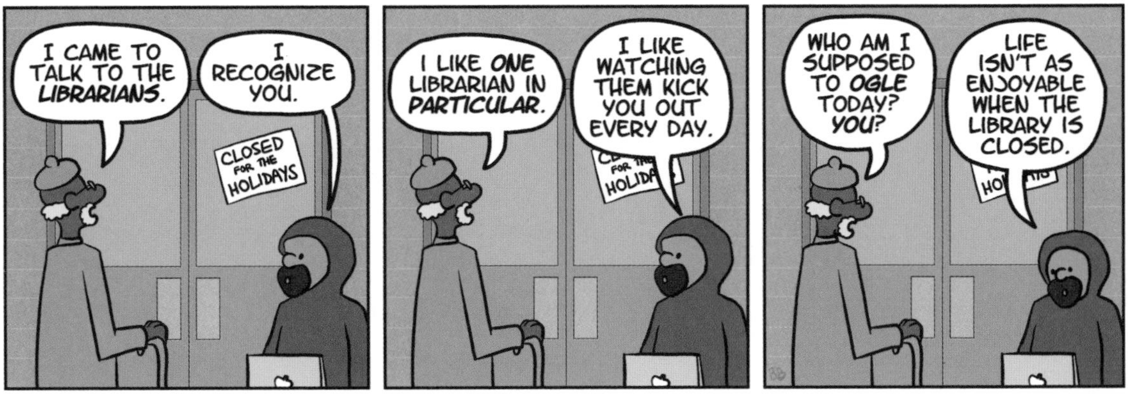
I CAME TO TALK TO THE LIBRARIANS.
I RECOGNIZE YOU.
CLOSED FOR THE HOLIDAYS
I LIKE ONE LIBRARIAN IN PARTICULAR.
I LIKE WATCHING THEM KICK YOU OUT EVERY DAY.
WHO AM I SUPPOSED TO OGLE TODAY? YOU?
LIFE ISN'T AS ENJOYABLE WHEN THE LIBRARY IS CLOSED.
BB

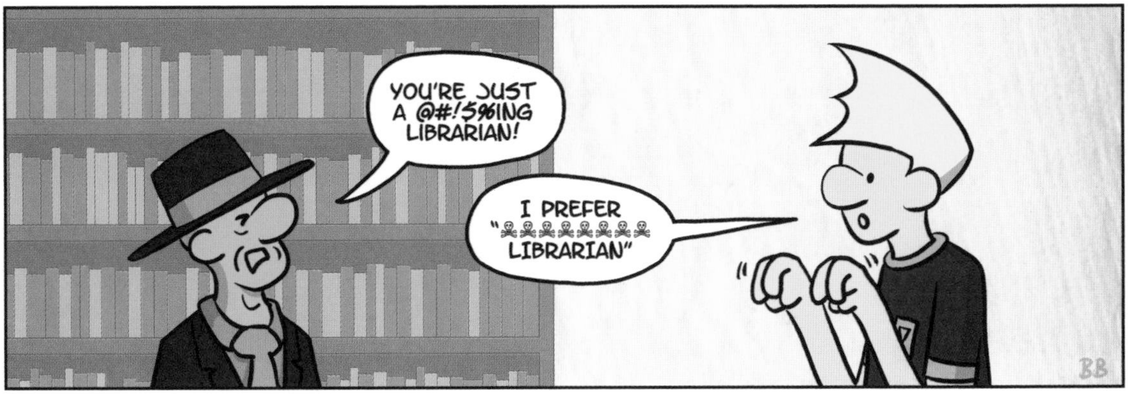
YOU'RE JUST A @#!$%ING LIBRARIAN!
I PREFER "☠☠☠☠☠☠☠☠ LIBRARIAN"
BB

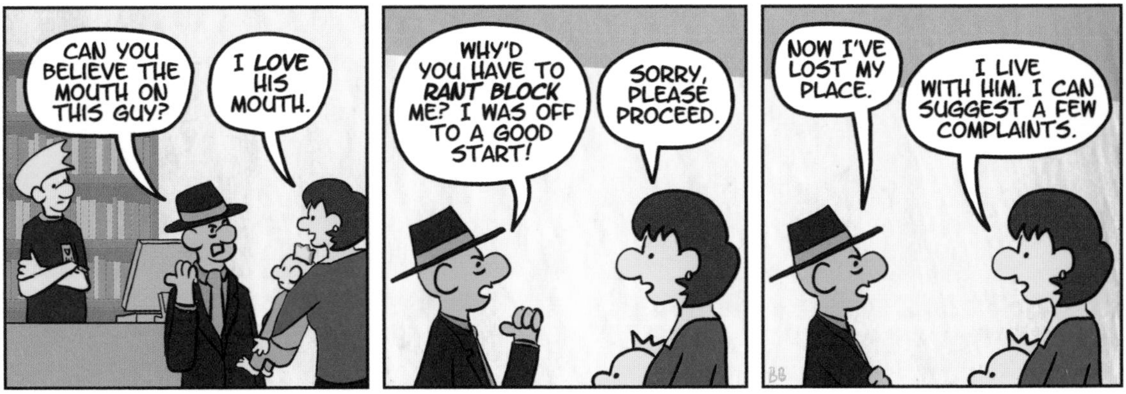
CAN YOU BELIEVE THE MOUTH ON THIS GUY?
I LOVE HIS MOUTH.
WHY'D YOU HAVE TO RANT BLOCK ME? I WAS OFF TO A GOOD START!
SORRY, PLEASE PROCEED.
NOW I'VE LOST MY PLACE.
I LIVE WITH HIM. I CAN SUGGEST A FEW COMPLAINTS.
BB

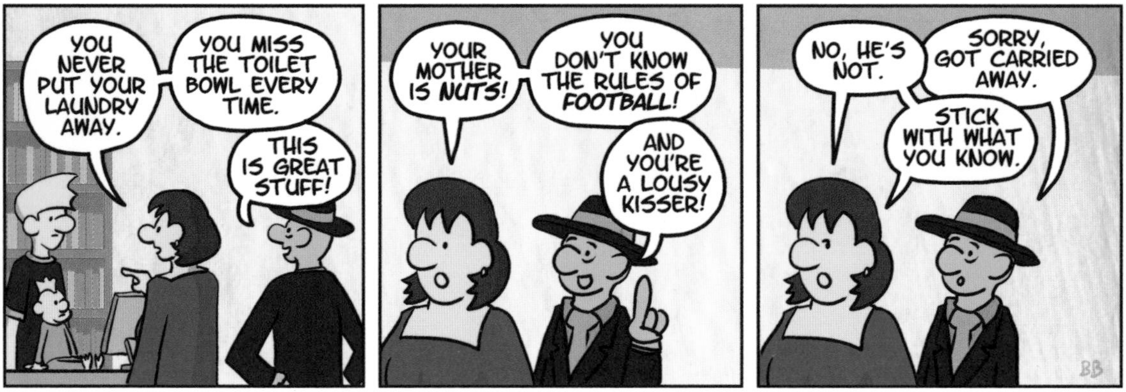
YOU NEVER PUT YOUR LAUNDRY AWAY.
YOU MISS THE TOILET BOWL EVERY TIME.
THIS IS GREAT STUFF!
YOUR MOTHER IS NUTS!
YOU DON'T KNOW THE RULES OF FOOTBALL!
AND YOU'RE A LOUSY KISSER!
NO, HE'S NOT.
SORRY, GOT CARRIED AWAY.
STICK WITH WHAT YOU KNOW.
BB

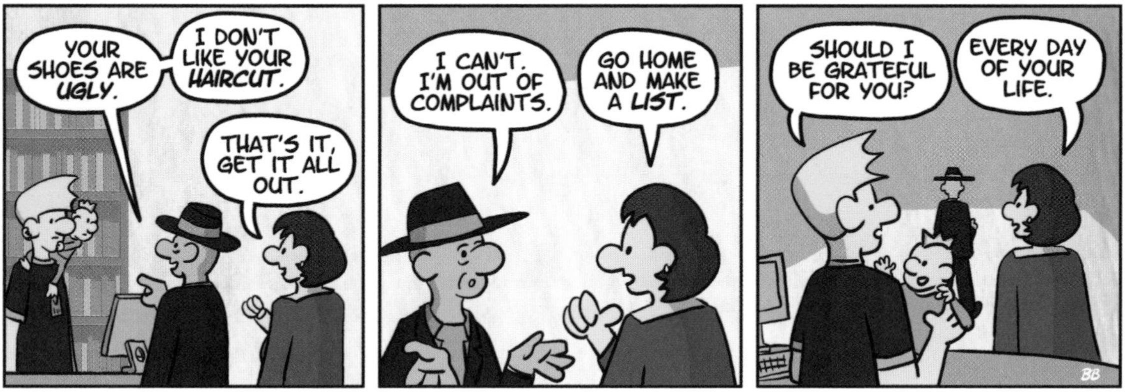
YOUR SHOES ARE UGLY.
I DON'T LIKE YOUR HAIRCUT.
THAT'S IT, GET IT ALL OUT.
I CAN'T. I'M OUT OF COMPLAINTS.
GO HOME AND MAKE A LIST.
SHOULD I BE GRATEFUL FOR YOU?
EVERY DAY OF YOUR LIFE.
BB

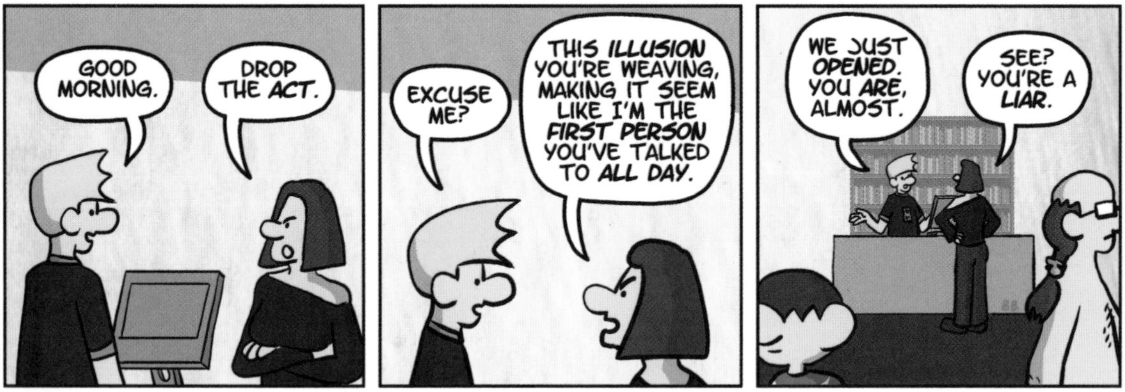
GOOD MORNING.
DROP THE ACT.
EXCUSE ME?
THIS ILLUSION YOU'RE WEAVING, MAKING IT SEEM LIKE I'M THE FIRST PERSON YOU'VE TALKED TO ALL DAY.
WE JUST OPENED. YOU ARE, ALMOST.
SEE? YOU'RE A LIAR.

Reads Well With Others

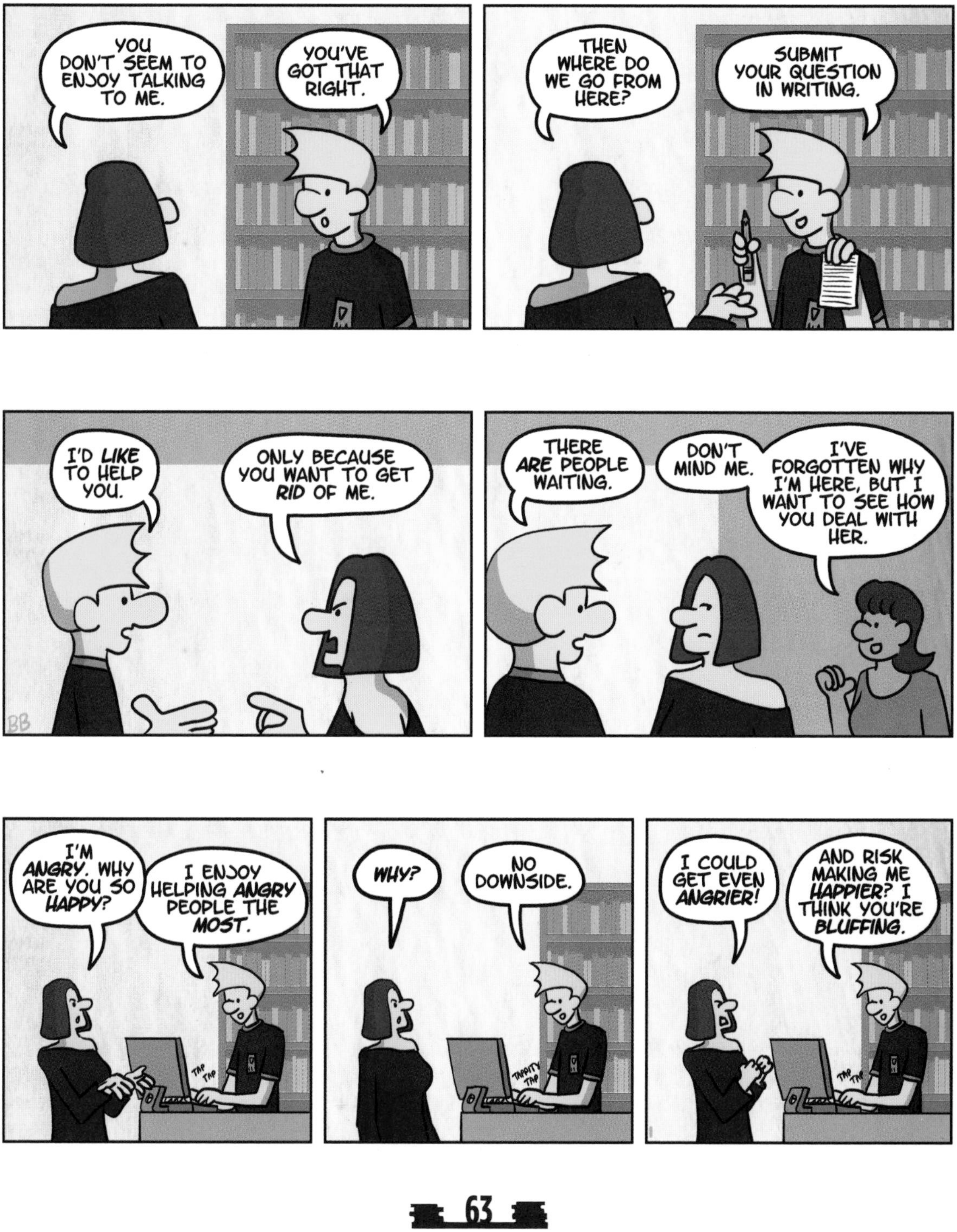
YOU DON'T SEEM TO ENJOY TALKING TO ME.
YOU'VE GOT THAT RIGHT.
THEN WHERE DO WE GO FROM HERE?
SUBMIT YOUR QUESTION IN WRITING.
I'D LIKE TO HELP YOU.
ONLY BECAUSE YOU WANT TO GET RID OF ME.
BB
THERE ARE PEOPLE WAITING.
DON'T MIND ME.
I'VE FORGOTTEN WHY I'M HERE, BUT I WANT TO SEE HOW YOU DEAL WITH HER.
I'M ANGRY. WHY ARE YOU SO HAPPY?
I ENJOY HELPING ANGRY PEOPLE THE MOST.
TAP TAP
WHY?
NO DOWNSIDE.
TAPPITY TAP
I COULD GET EVEN ANGRIER!
AND RISK MAKING ME HAPPIER? I THINK YOU'RE BLUFFING.
TAP TAP

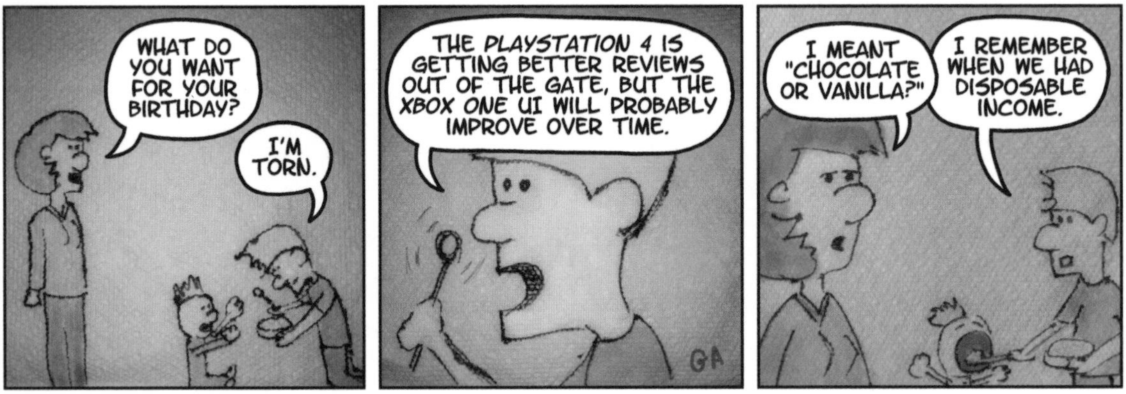
WHAT DO YOU WANT FOR YOUR BIRTHDAY?
I'M TORN.
THE PLAYSTATION 4 IS GETTING BETTER REVIEWS OUT OF THE GATE, BUT THE XBOX ONE UI WILL PROBABLY IMPROVE OVER TIME.
I MEANT "CHOCOLATE OR VANILLA?"
I REMEMBER WHEN WE HAD DISPOSABLE INCOME.

Every year Gene celebrates Bill's birthday by drawing the strip, this one on a napkin.

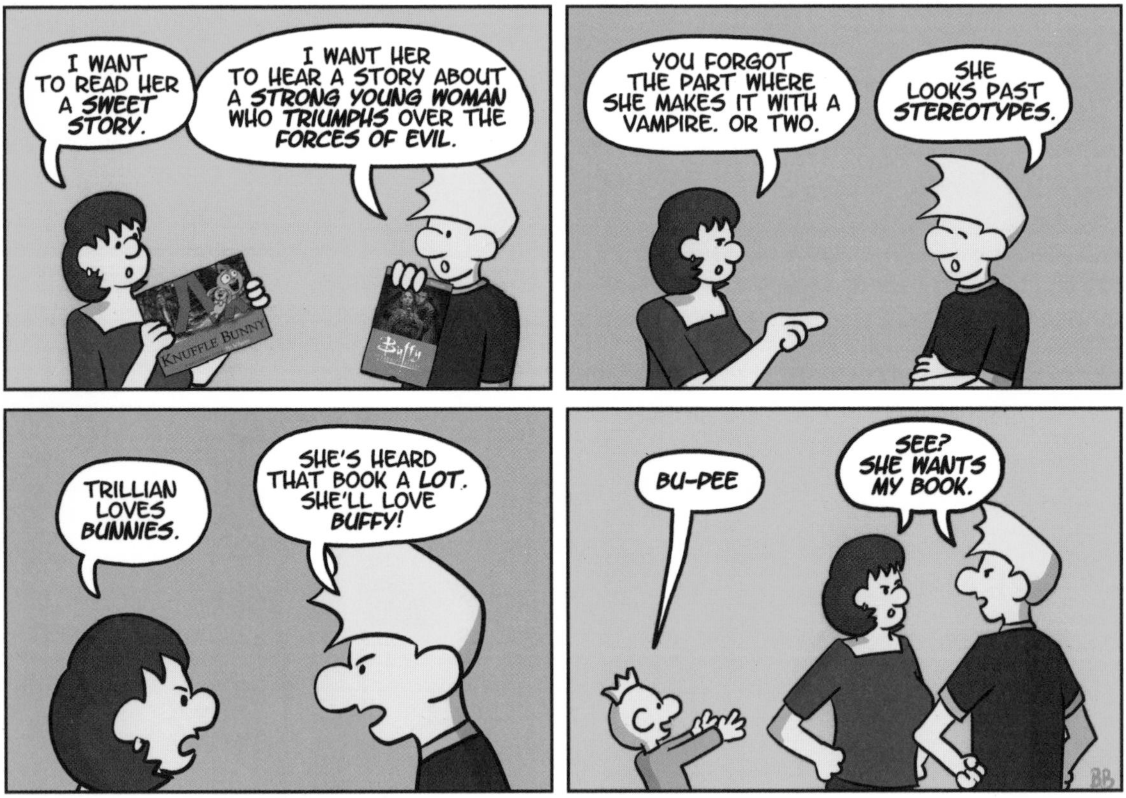
I WANT TO READ HER A SWEET STORY.
I WANT HER TO HEAR A STORY ABOUT A STRONG YOUNG WOMAN WHO TRIUMPHS OVER THE FORCES OF EVIL.
KNUFFLE BUNNY
Buffy
YOU FORGOT THE PART WHERE SHE MAKES IT WITH A VAMPIRE. OR TWO.
SHE LOOKS PAST STEREOTYPES.
TRILLIAN LOVES BUNNIES.
SHE'S HEARD THAT BOOK A LOT. SHE'LL LOVE BUFFY!
BU-PEE
SEE? SHE WANTS MY BOOK.

Reads Well With Others

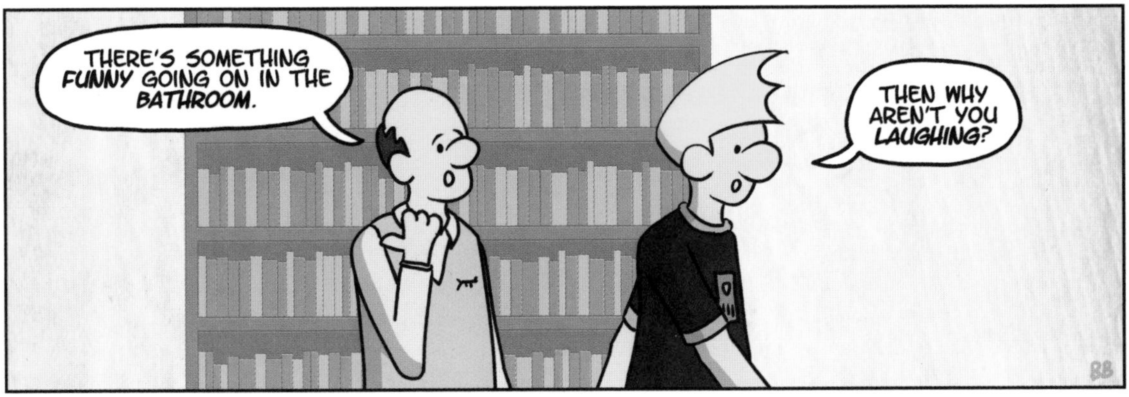
THERE'S SOMETHING FUNNY GOING ON IN THE BATHROOM.
THEN WHY AREN'T YOU LAUGHING?
BB

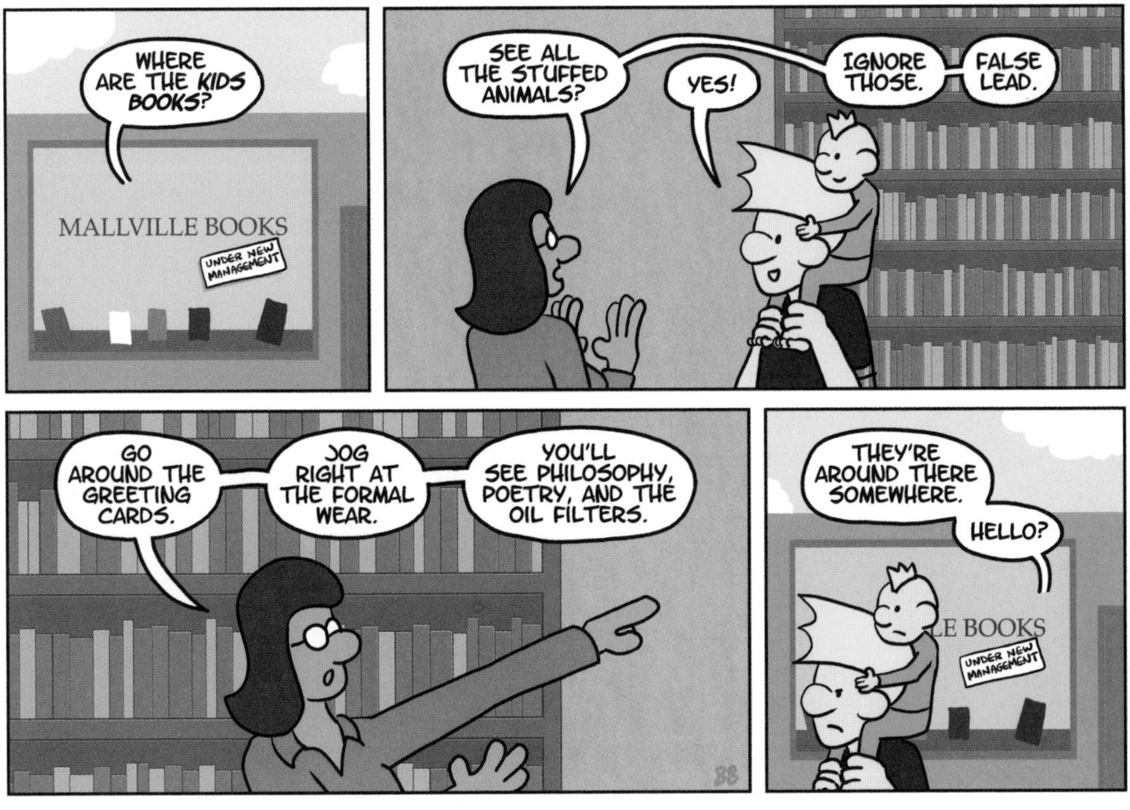
WHERE ARE THE KIDS BOOKS?
MALLVILLE BOOKS
UNDER NEW MANAGEMENT
SEE ALL THE STUFFED ANIMALS?
YES!
IGNORE THOSE.
FALSE LEAD.
GO AROUND THE GREETING CARDS.
JOG RIGHT AT THE FORMAL WEAR.
YOU'LL SEE PHILOSOPHY, POETRY, AND THE OIL FILTERS.
BB
THEY'RE AROUND THERE SOMEWHERE.
HELLO?
LE BOOKS
UNDER NEW MANAGEMENT

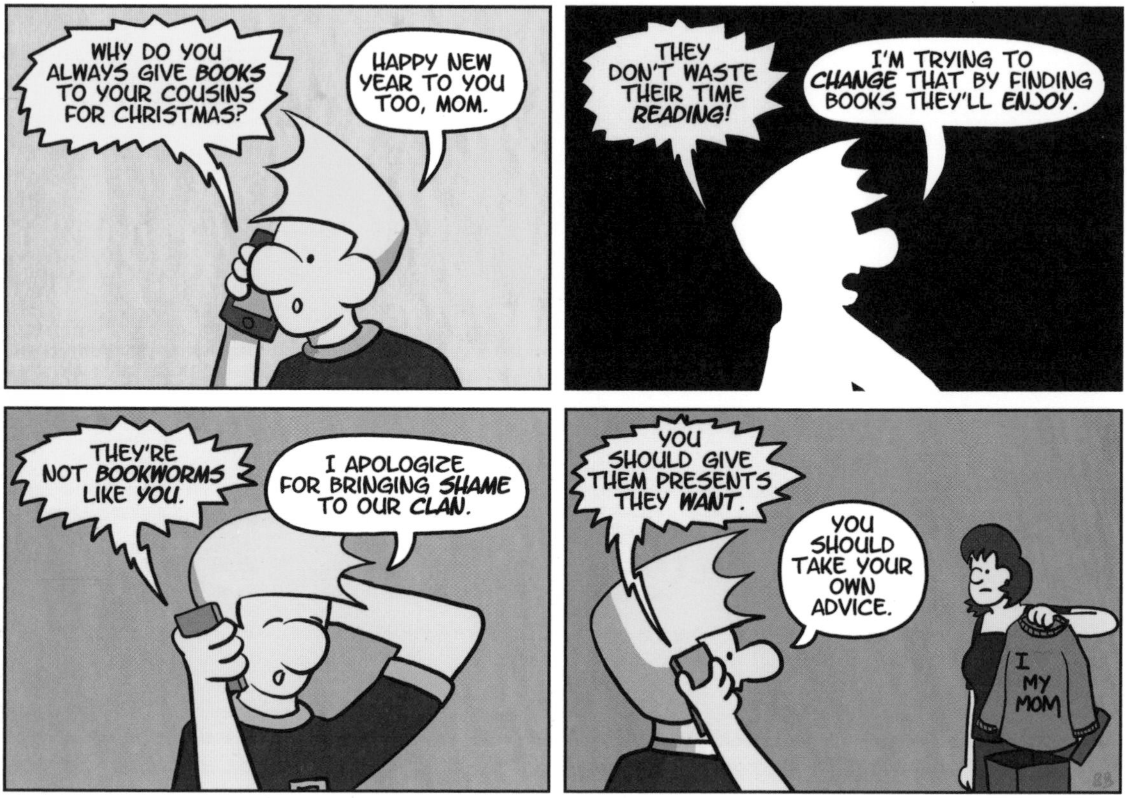
WHY DO YOU ALWAYS GIVE BOOKS TO YOUR COUSINS FOR CHRISTMAS?
HAPPY NEW YEAR TO YOU TOO, MOM.
THEY DON'T WASTE THEIR TIME READING!
I'M TRYING TO CHANGE THAT BY FINDING BOOKS THEY'LL ENJOY.
THEY'RE NOT BOOKWORMS LIKE YOU.
I APOLOGIZE FOR BRINGING SHAME TO OUR CLAN.
YOU SHOULD GIVE THEM PRESENTS THEY WANT.
YOU SHOULD TAKE YOUR OWN ADVICE.
I MY MOM

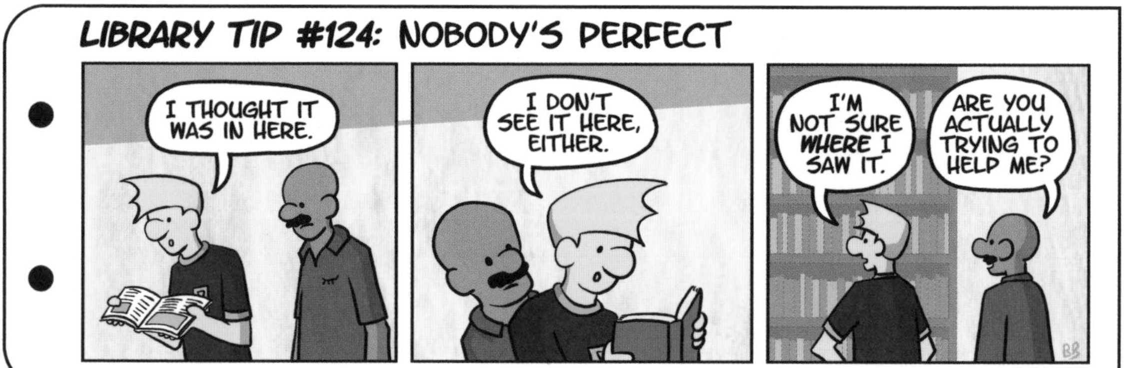
LIBRARY TIP #124: NOBODY'S PERFECT
I THOUGHT IT WAS IN HERE.
I DON'T SEE IT HERE, EITHER.
I'M NOT SURE WHERE I SAW IT.
ARE YOU ACTUALLY TRYING TO HELP ME?

Reads Well With Others

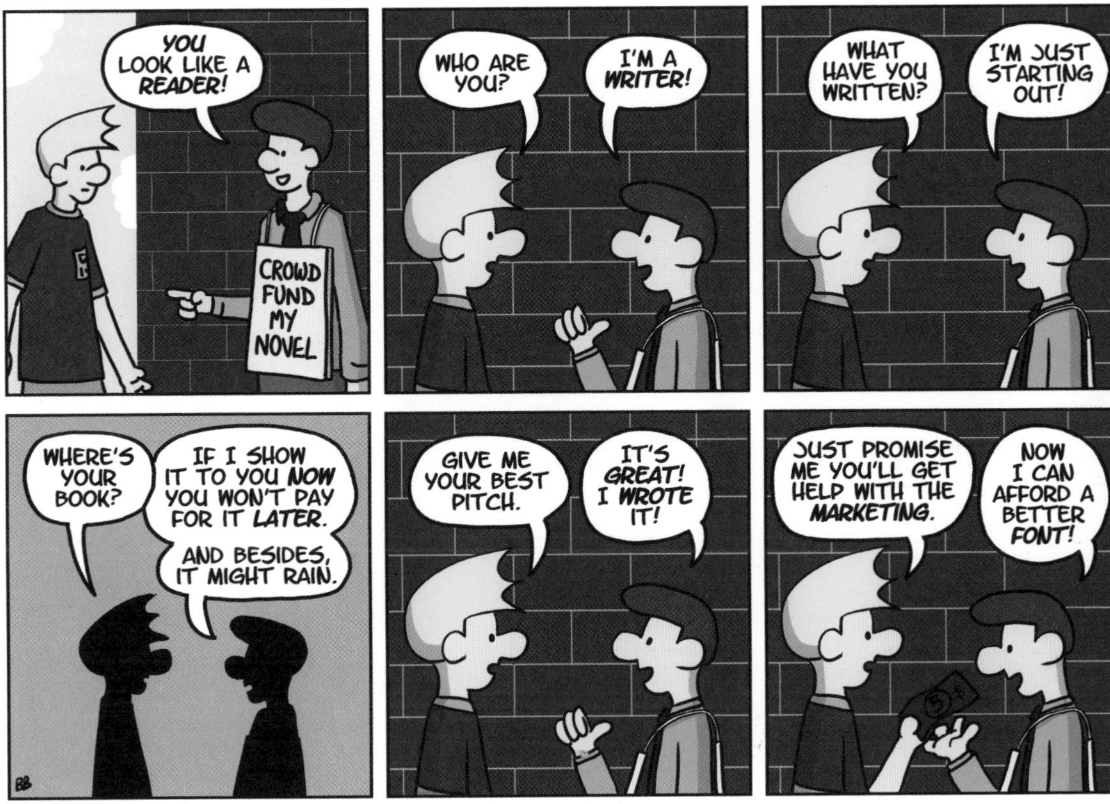
YOU LOOK LIKE A READER!
CROWD FUND MY NOVEL
WHO ARE YOU?
I'M A WRITER!
WHAT HAVE YOU WRITTEN?
I'M JUST STARTING OUT!
WHERE'S YOUR BOOK?
IF I SHOW IT TO YOU NOW YOU WON'T PAY FOR IT LATER.
AND BESIDES, IT MIGHT RAIN.
BB
GIVE ME YOUR BEST PITCH.
IT'S GREAT! I WROTE IT!
JUST PROMISE ME YOU'LL GET HELP WITH THE MARKETING.
NOW I CAN AFFORD A BETTER FONT!

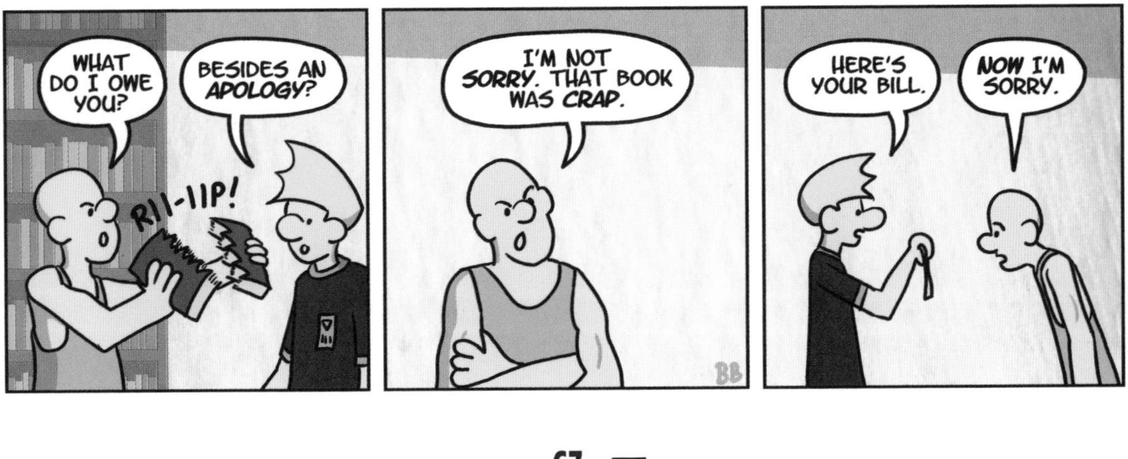
WHAT DO I OWE YOU?
BESIDES AN APOLOGY?
RII-IIP!
I'M NOT SORRY. THAT BOOK WAS CRAP.
BB
HERE'S YOUR BILL.
NOW I'M SORRY.

UNSHELVED

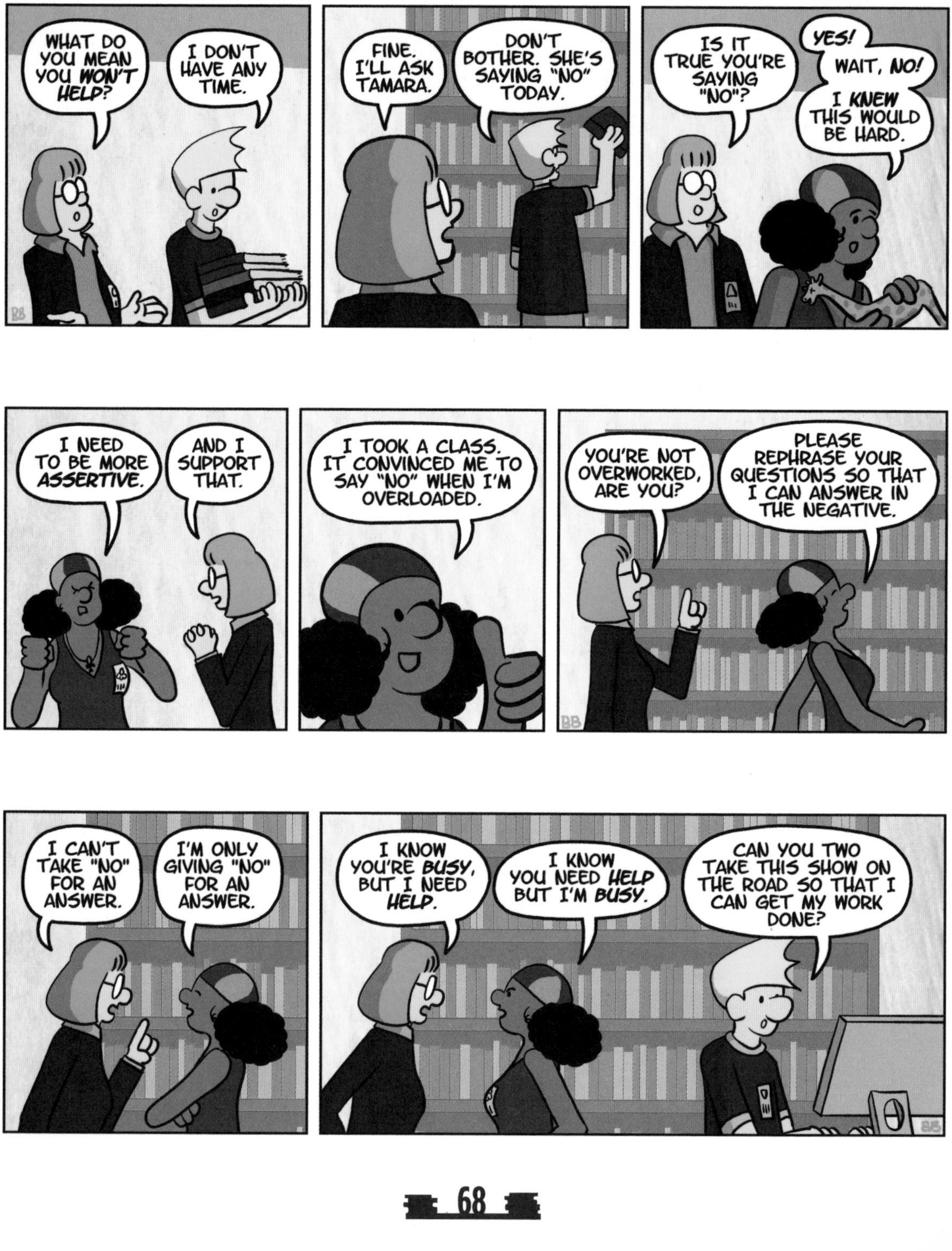
WHAT DO YOU MEAN YOU **WON'T HELP**?
I DON'T HAVE ANY TIME.
FINE. I'LL ASK TAMARA.
DON'T BOTHER. SHE'S SAYING "NO" TODAY.
IS IT TRUE YOU'RE SAYING "NO"?
YES!
WAIT, **NO!**
I **KNEW** THIS WOULD BE HARD.
I NEED TO BE MORE **ASSERTIVE**.
AND I SUPPORT THAT.
I TOOK A CLASS. IT CONVINCED ME TO SAY "NO" WHEN I'M OVERLOADED.
YOU'RE NOT OVERWORKED, ARE YOU?
PLEASE REPHRASE YOUR QUESTIONS SO THAT I CAN ANSWER IN THE NEGATIVE.
I CAN'T TAKE "NO" FOR AN ANSWER.
I'M ONLY GIVING "NO" FOR AN ANSWER.
I KNOW YOU'RE **BUSY**, BUT I NEED **HELP**.
I KNOW YOU NEED **HELP** BUT I'M **BUSY**.
CAN YOU TWO TAKE THIS SHOW ON THE ROAD SO THAT I CAN GET MY WORK DONE?

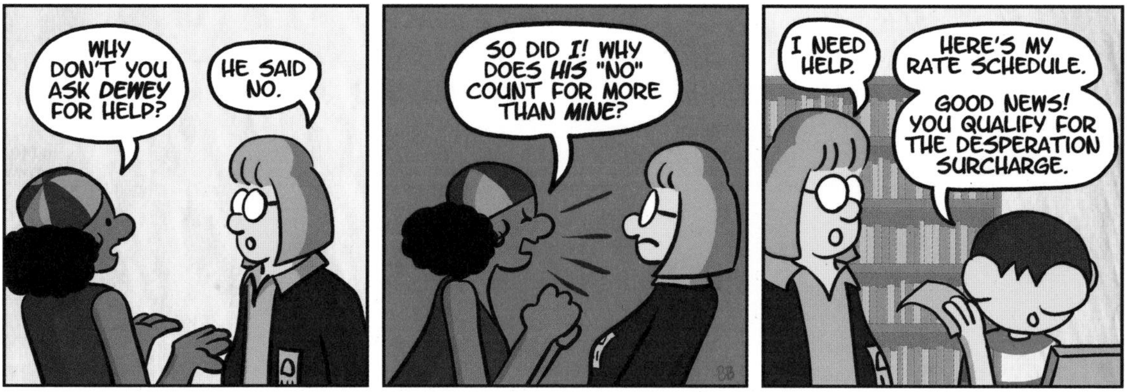
WHY DON'T YOU ASK DEWEY FOR HELP?
HE SAID NO.
SO DID I! WHY DOES HIS "NO" COUNT FOR MORE THAN MINE?
I NEED HELP.
HERE'S MY RATE SCHEDULE.
GOOD NEWS! YOU QUALIFY FOR THE DESPERATION SURCHARGE.

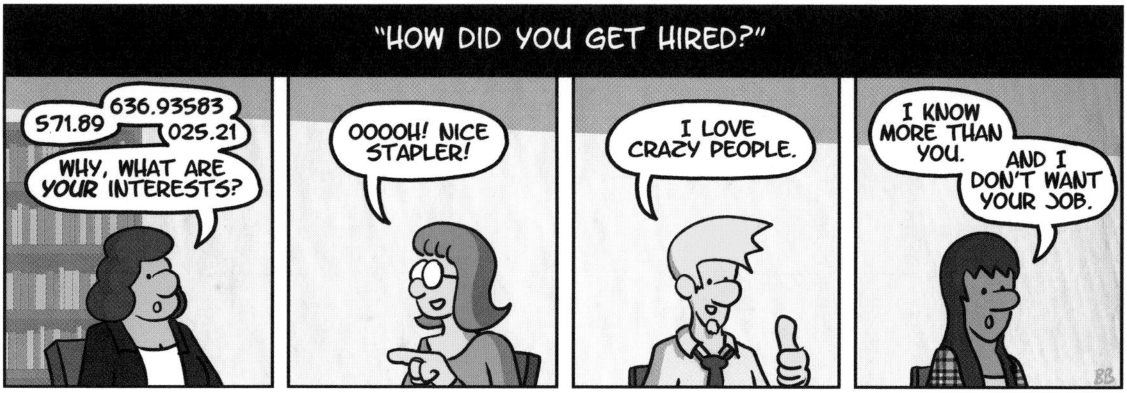
"HOW DID YOU GET HIRED?"
571.89
636.93583
025.21
WHY, WHAT ARE YOUR INTERESTS?
OOOOH! NICE STAPLER!
I LOVE CRAZY PEOPLE.
I KNOW MORE THAN YOU.
AND I DON'T WANT YOUR JOB.

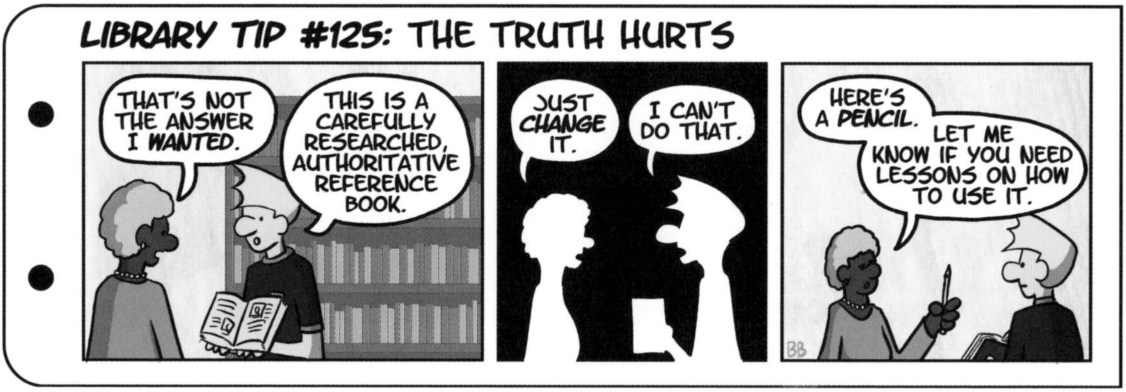
LIBRARY TIP #125: THE TRUTH HURTS
THAT'S NOT THE ANSWER I WANTED.
THIS IS A CAREFULLY RESEARCHED, AUTHORITATIVE REFERENCE BOOK.
JUST CHANGE IT.
I CAN'T DO THAT.
HERE'S A PENCIL.
LET ME KNOW IF YOU NEED LESSONS ON HOW TO USE IT.

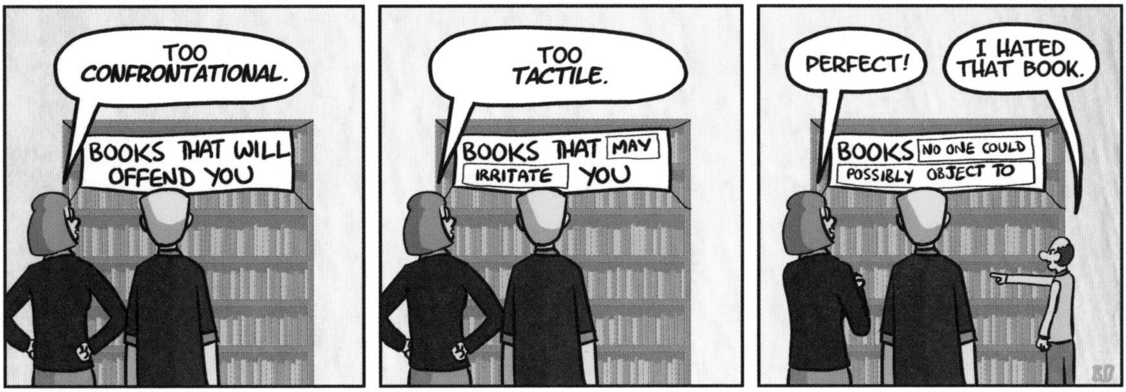
TOO CONFRONTATIONAL.
BOOKS THAT WILL OFFEND YOU
TOO TACTILE.
BOOKS THAT MAY IRRITATE YOU
PERFECT!
I HATED THAT BOOK.
BOOKS NO ONE COULD POSSIBLY OBJECT TO

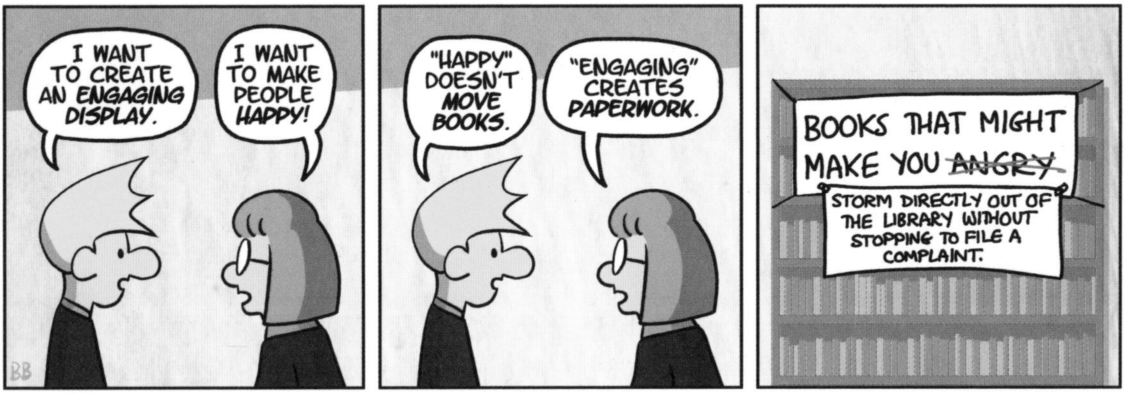
I WANT TO CREATE AN ENGAGING DISPLAY.
I WANT TO MAKE PEOPLE HAPPY!
"HAPPY" DOESN'T MOVE BOOKS.
"ENGAGING" CREATES PAPERWORK.
BOOKS THAT MIGHT MAKE YOU ANGRY
STORM DIRECTLY OUT OF THE LIBRARY WITHOUT STOPPING TO FILE A COMPLAINT.

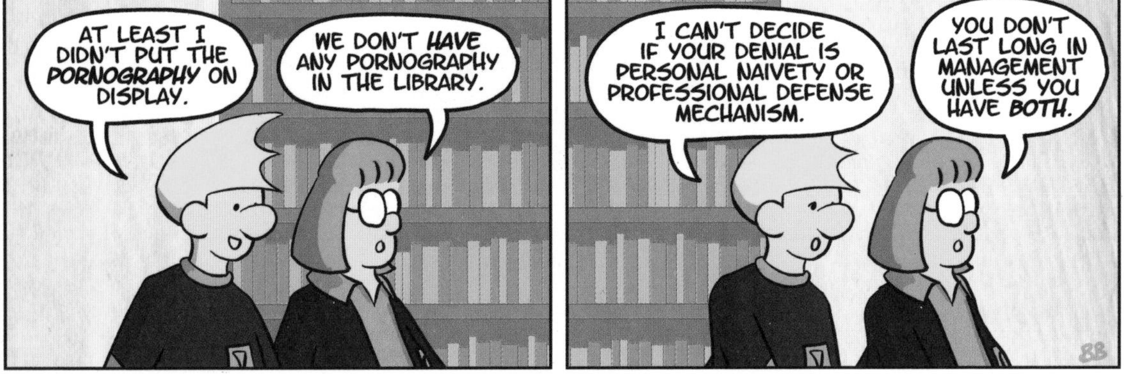
AT LEAST I DIDN'T PUT THE PORNOGRAPHY ON DISPLAY.
WE DON'T HAVE ANY PORNOGRAPHY IN THE LIBRARY.
I CAN'T DECIDE IF YOUR DENIAL IS PERSONAL NAIVETY OR PROFESSIONAL DEFENSE MECHANISM.
YOU DON'T LAST LONG IN MANAGEMENT UNLESS YOU HAVE BOTH.

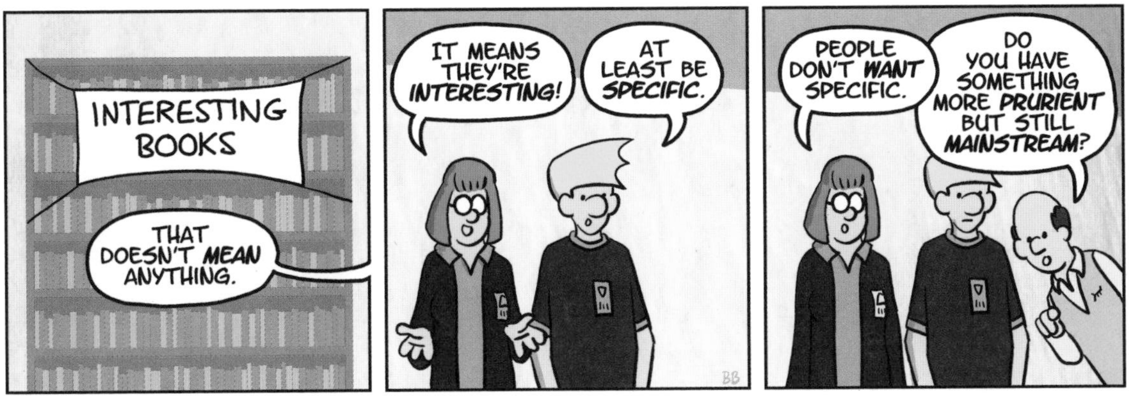
INTERESTING BOOKS
THAT DOESN'T **MEAN** ANYTHING.
IT MEANS THEY'RE ***INTERESTING!***
AT LEAST BE ***SPECIFIC.***
PEOPLE DON'T ***WANT*** SPECIFIC.
DO YOU HAVE SOMETHING MORE ***PRURIENT*** BUT STILL ***MAINSTREAM?***

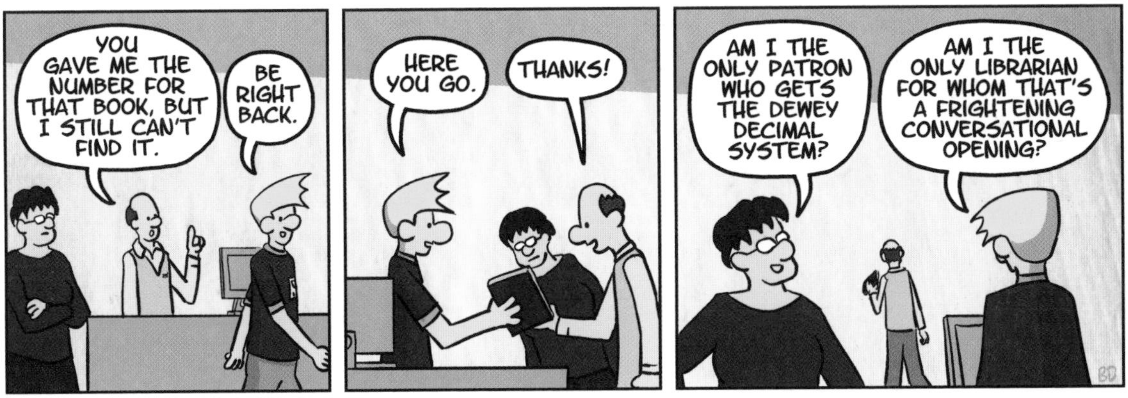
YOU GAVE ME THE NUMBER FOR THAT BOOK, BUT I STILL CAN'T FIND IT.
BE RIGHT BACK.
HERE YOU GO.
THANKS!
AM I THE ONLY PATRON WHO GETS THE DEWEY DECIMAL SYSTEM?
AM I THE ONLY LIBRARIAN FOR WHOM THAT'S A FRIGHTENING CONVERSATIONAL OPENING?

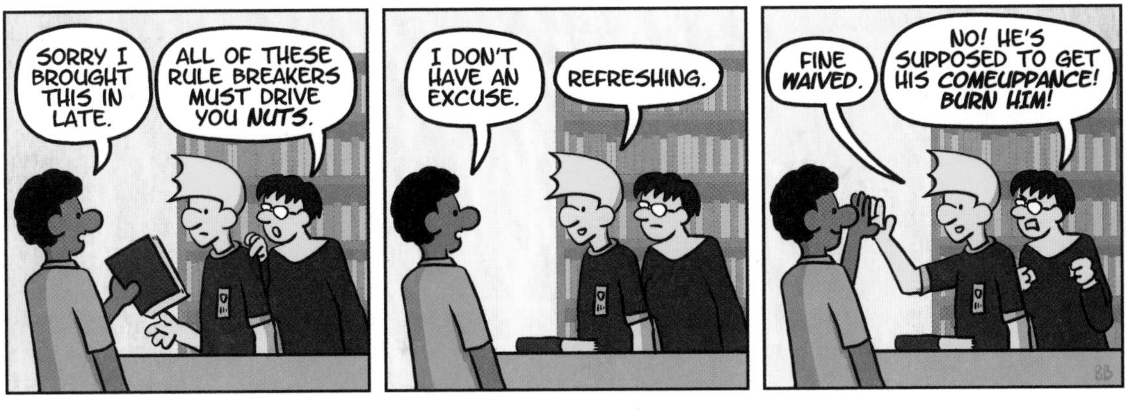
SORRY I BROUGHT THIS IN LATE.
ALL OF THESE RULE BREAKERS MUST DRIVE YOU ***NUTS.***
I DON'T HAVE AN EXCUSE.
REFRESHING.
FINE ***WAIVED.***
NO! HE'S SUPPOSED TO GET HIS ***COMEUPPANCE! BURN HIM!***

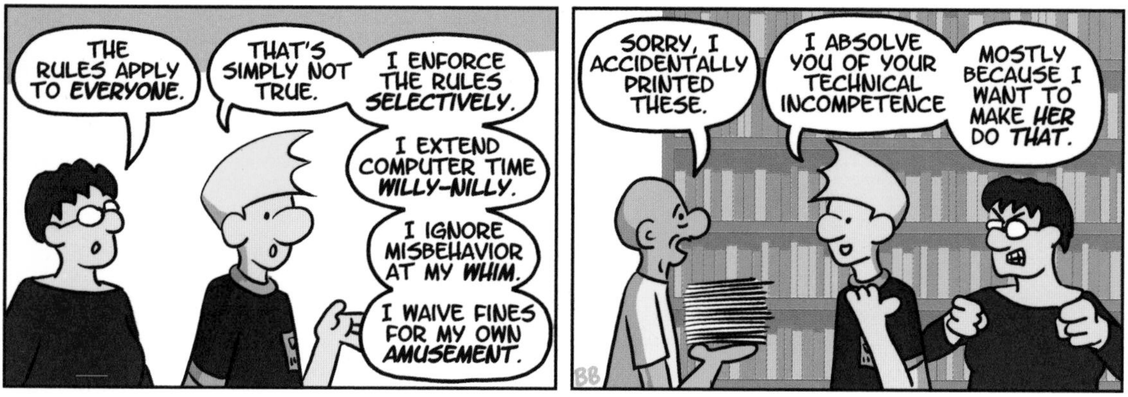
THE RULES APPLY TO EVERYONE.
THAT'S SIMPLY NOT TRUE.
I ENFORCE THE RULES SELECTIVELY.
I EXTEND COMPUTER TIME WILLY-NILLY.
I IGNORE MISBEHAVIOR AT MY WHIM.
I WAIVE FINES FOR MY OWN AMUSEMENT.
SORRY, I ACCIDENTALLY PRINTED THESE.
I ABSOLVE YOU OF YOUR TECHNICAL INCOMPETENCE
MOSTLY BECAUSE I WANT TO MAKE HER DO THAT.
BB

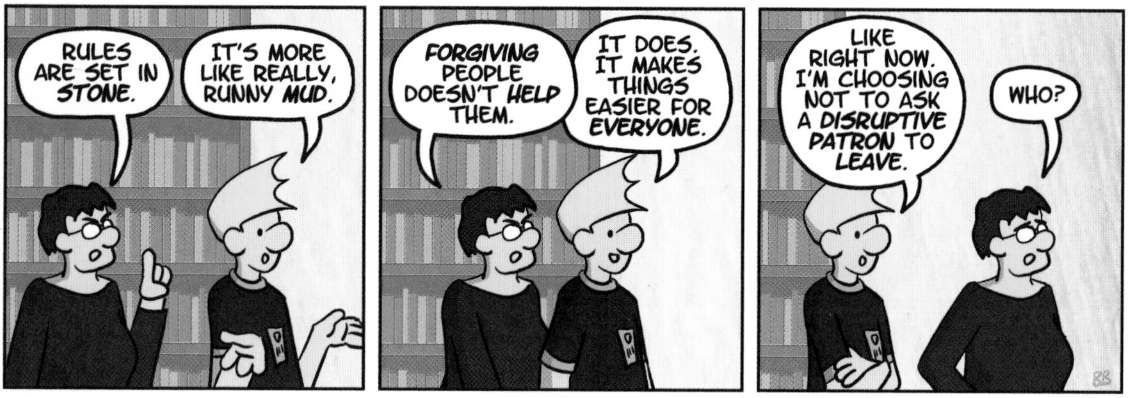
RULES ARE SET IN STONE.
IT'S MORE LIKE REALLY, RUNNY MUD.
FORGIVING PEOPLE DOESN'T HELP THEM.
IT DOES. IT MAKES THINGS EASIER FOR EVERYONE.
LIKE RIGHT NOW. I'M CHOOSING NOT TO ASK A DISRUPTIVE PATRON TO LEAVE.
WHO?
BB

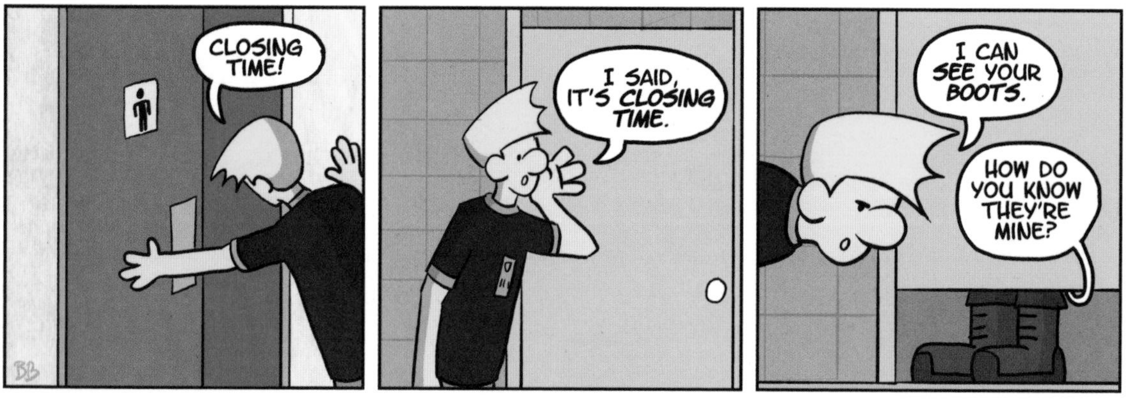
CLOSING TIME!
BB
I SAID, IT'S CLOSING TIME.
I CAN SEE YOUR BOOTS.
HOW DO YOU KNOW THEY'RE MINE?

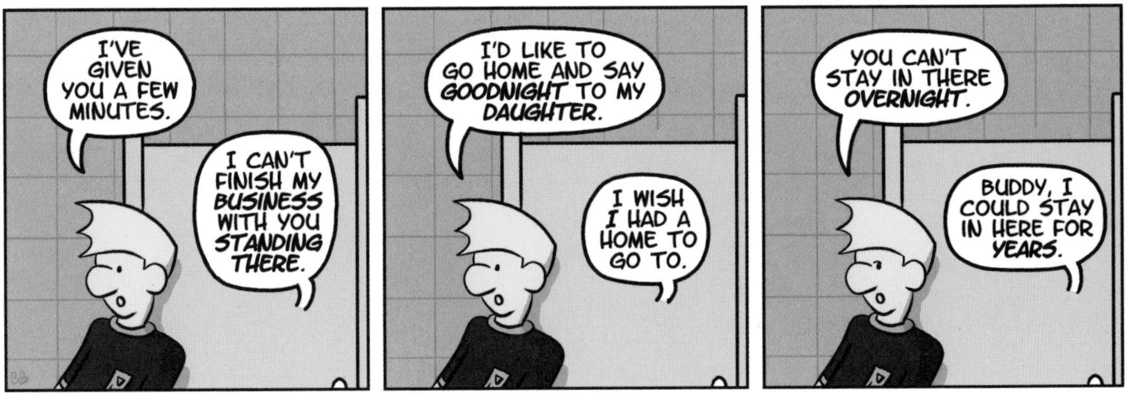
I'VE GIVEN YOU A FEW MINUTES.
I CAN'T FINISH MY BUSINESS WITH YOU STANDING THERE.
I'D LIKE TO GO HOME AND SAY GOODNIGHT TO MY DAUGHTER.
I WISH I HAD A HOME TO GO TO.
YOU CAN'T STAY IN THERE OVERNIGHT.
BUDDY, I COULD STAY IN HERE FOR YEARS.

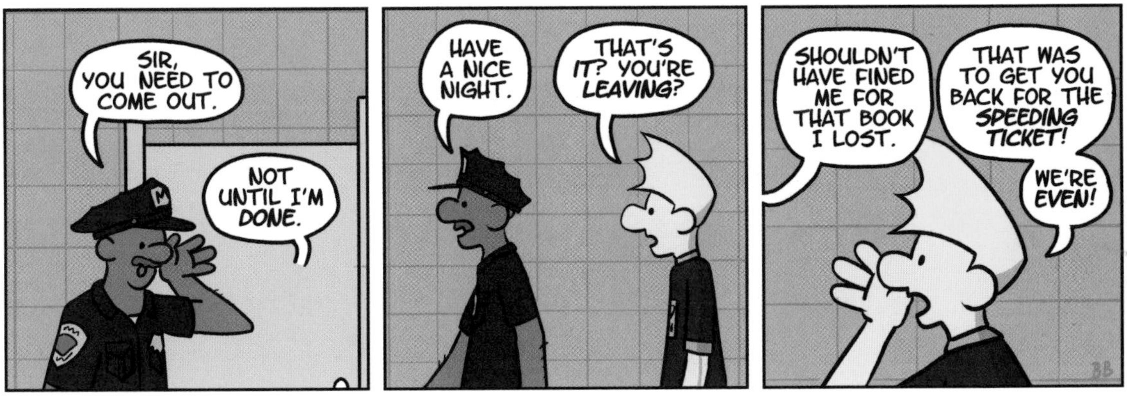
SIR, YOU NEED TO COME OUT.
NOT UNTIL I'M DONE.
HAVE A NICE NIGHT.
THAT'S IT? YOU'RE LEAVING?
SHOULDN'T HAVE FINED ME FOR THAT BOOK I LOST.
THAT WAS TO GET YOU BACK FOR THE SPEEDING TICKET!
WE'RE EVEN!

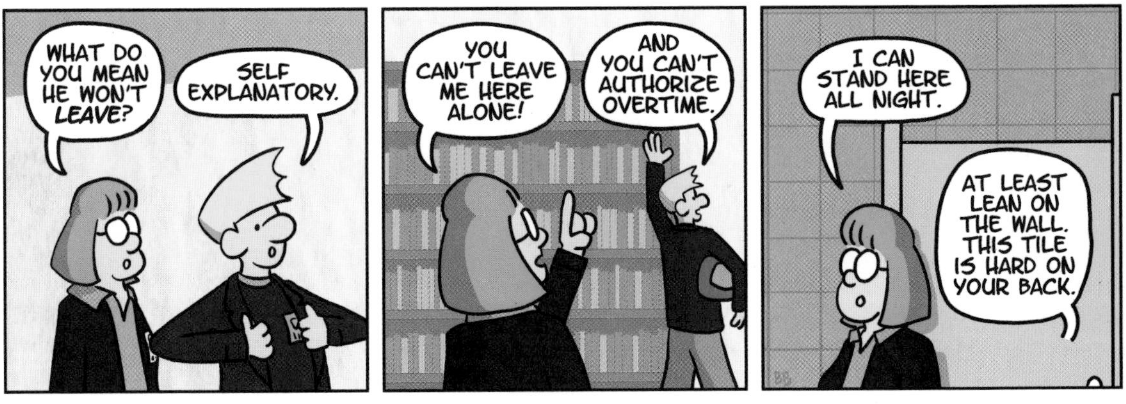
WHAT DO YOU MEAN HE WON'T LEAVE?
SELF EXPLANATORY.
YOU CAN'T LEAVE ME HERE ALONE!
AND YOU CAN'T AUTHORIZE OVERTIME.
I CAN STAND HERE ALL NIGHT.
AT LEAST LEAN ON THE WALL. THIS TILE IS HARD ON YOUR BACK.

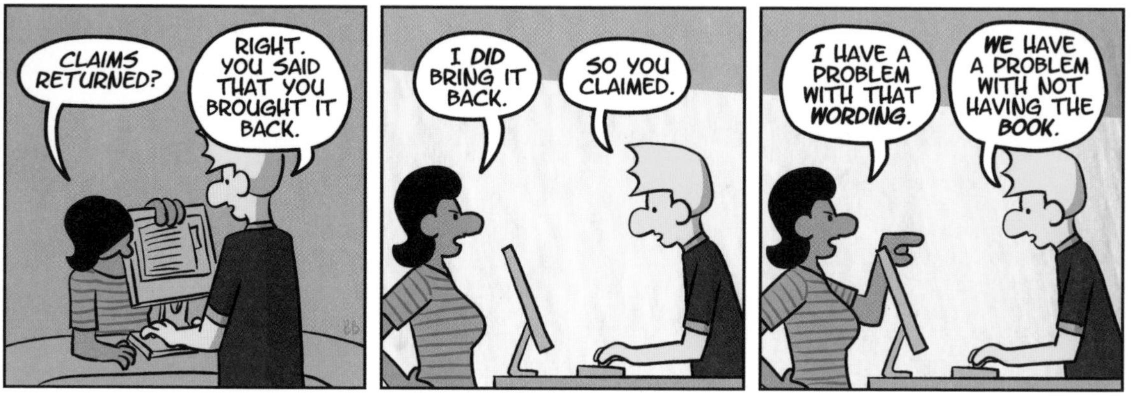
CLAIMS RETURNED?
RIGHT. YOU SAID THAT YOU BROUGHT IT BACK.
I *DID* BRING IT BACK.
SO YOU CLAIMED.
I HAVE A PROBLEM WITH THAT *WORDING*.
WE HAVE A PROBLEM WITH NOT HAVING THE *BOOK*.
BB

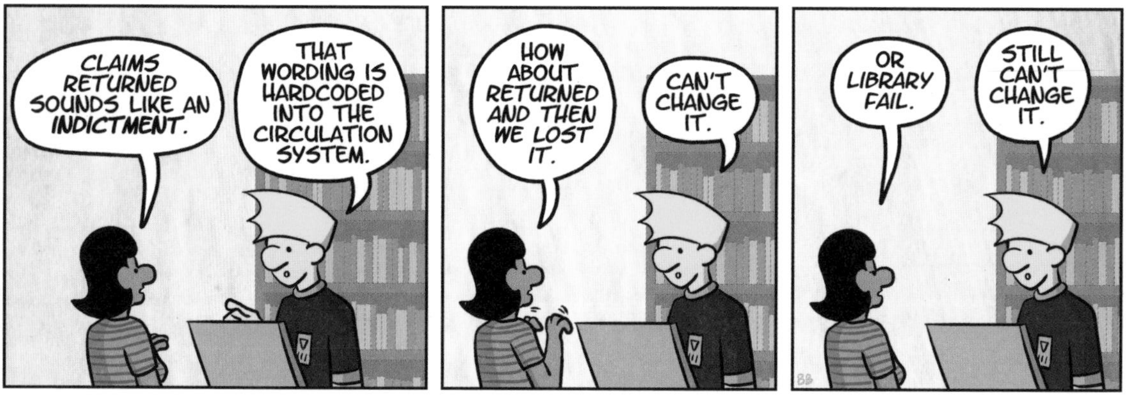
CLAIMS RETURNED SOUNDS LIKE AN *INDICTMENT*.
THAT WORDING IS HARDCODED INTO THE CIRCULATION SYSTEM.
HOW ABOUT RETURNED *AND THEN WE LOST IT*.
CAN'T CHANGE IT.
OR LIBRARY FAIL.
STILL CAN'T CHANGE IT.
BB

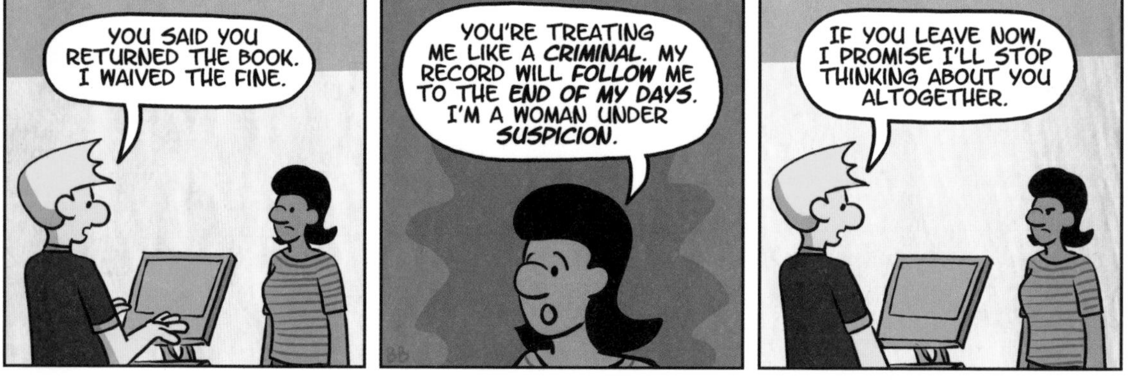
YOU SAID YOU RETURNED THE BOOK. I WAIVED THE FINE.
YOU'RE TREATING ME LIKE A *CRIMINAL*. MY RECORD WILL *FOLLOW* ME TO THE *END OF MY DAYS*. I'M A WOMAN UNDER *SUSPICION*.
BB
IF YOU LEAVE NOW, I PROMISE I'LL STOP THINKING ABOUT YOU ALTOGETHER.

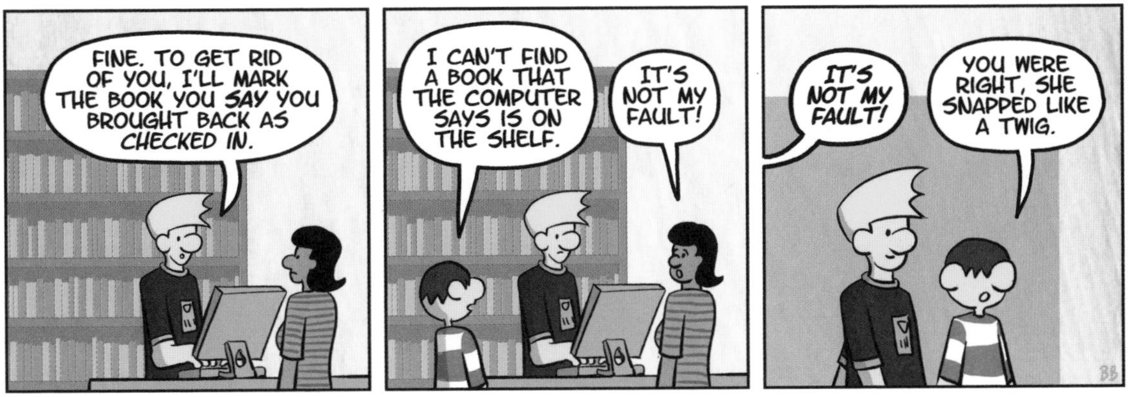
FINE. TO GET RID OF YOU, I'LL MARK THE BOOK YOU *SAY* YOU BROUGHT BACK AS *CHECKED IN*.
I CAN'T FIND A BOOK THAT THE COMPUTER SAYS IS ON THE SHELF.
IT'S NOT MY FAULT!
IT'S NOT MY FAULT!
YOU WERE RIGHT, SHE SNAPPED LIKE A TWIG.
BB

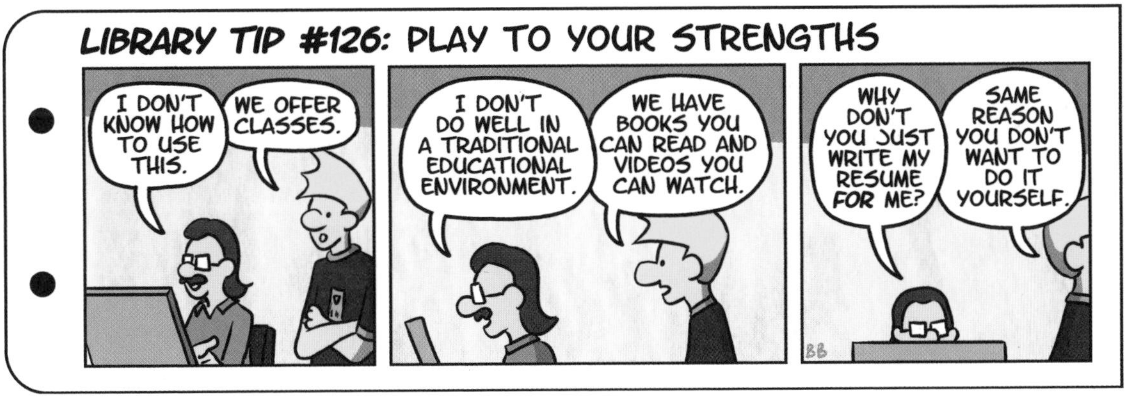
LIBRARY TIP #126: PLAY TO YOUR STRENGTHS
I DON'T KNOW HOW TO USE THIS.
WE OFFER CLASSES.
I DON'T DO WELL IN A TRADITIONAL EDUCATIONAL ENVIRONMENT.
WE HAVE BOOKS YOU CAN READ AND VIDEOS YOU CAN WATCH.
WHY DON'T YOU JUST WRITE MY RESUME *FOR* ME?
SAME REASON YOU DON'T WANT TO DO IT YOURSELF.
BB

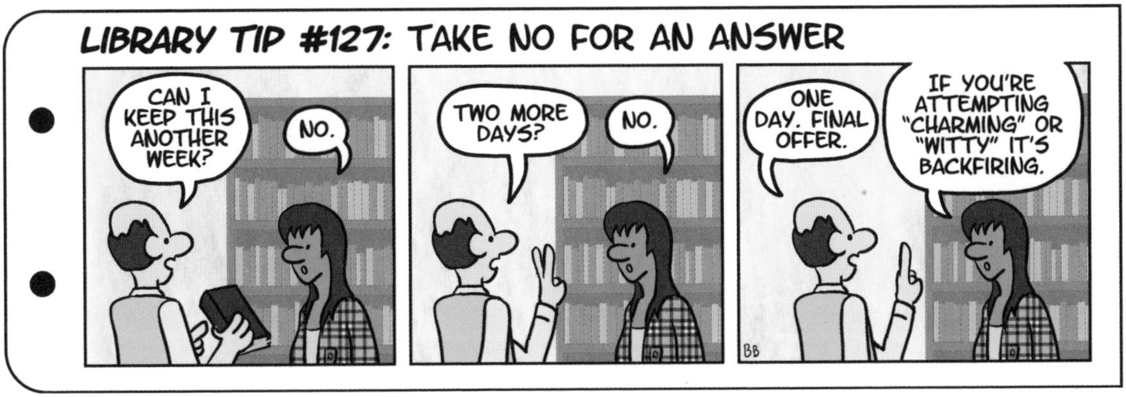
LIBRARY TIP #127: TAKE NO FOR AN ANSWER
CAN I KEEP THIS ANOTHER WEEK?
NO.
TWO MORE DAYS?
NO.
ONE DAY. FINAL OFFER.
IF YOU'RE ATTEMPTING "CHARMING" OR "WITTY" IT'S BACKFIRING.
BB

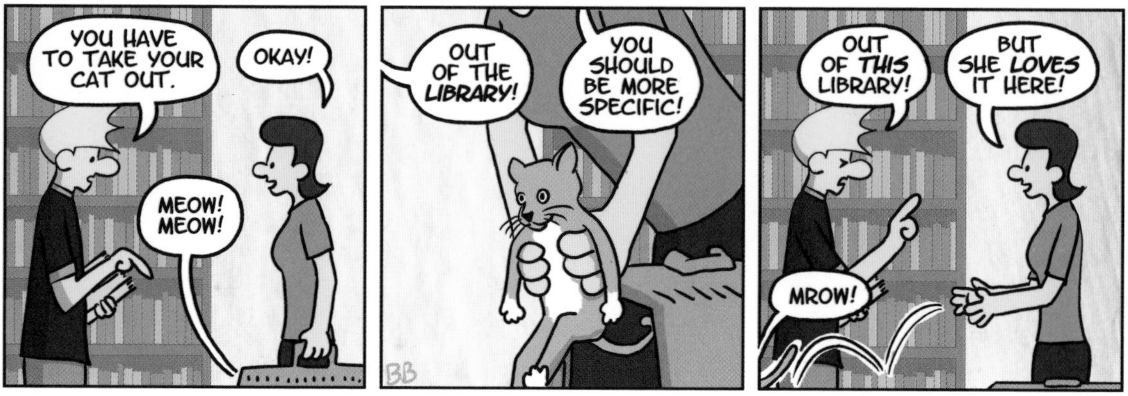
YOU HAVE TO TAKE YOUR CAT OUT.
OKAY!
MEOW! MEOW!
OUT OF THE LIBRARY!
YOU SHOULD BE MORE SPECIFIC!
OUT OF THIS LIBRARY!
BUT SHE LOVES IT HERE!
MROW!
BB

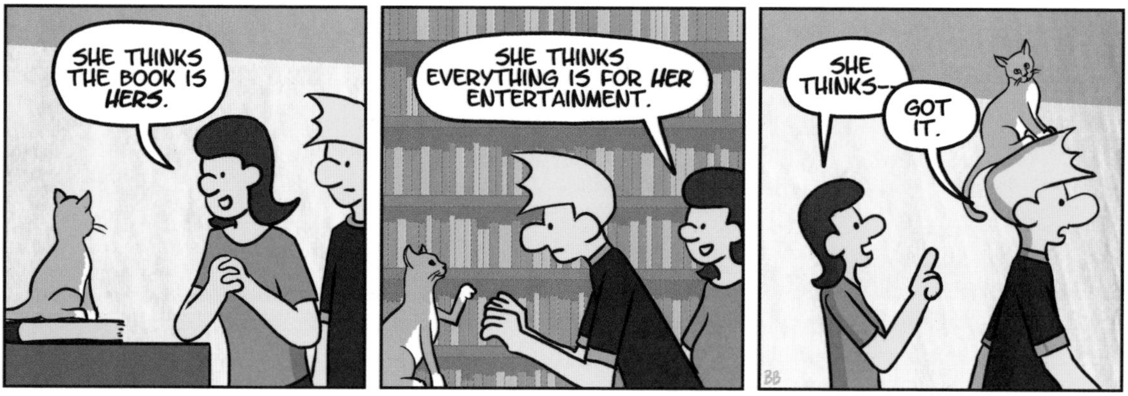
SHE THINKS THE BOOK IS HERS.
SHE THINKS EVERYTHING IS FOR HER ENTERTAINMENT.
SHE THINKS--
GOT IT.
BB

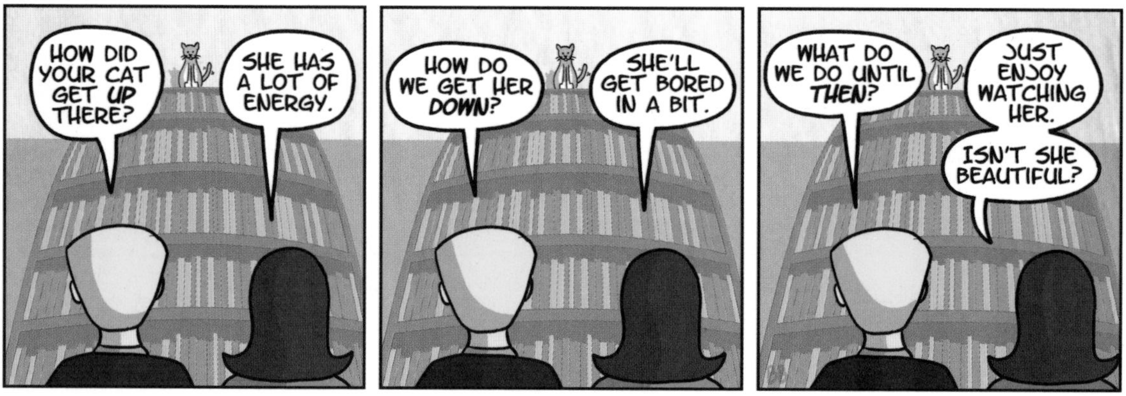
HOW DID YOUR CAT GET UP THERE?
SHE HAS A LOT OF ENERGY.
HOW DO WE GET HER DOWN?
SHE'LL GET BORED IN A BIT.
WHAT DO WE DO UNTIL THEN?
JUST ENJOY WATCHING HER.
ISN'T SHE BEAUTIFUL?

Reads Well With Others

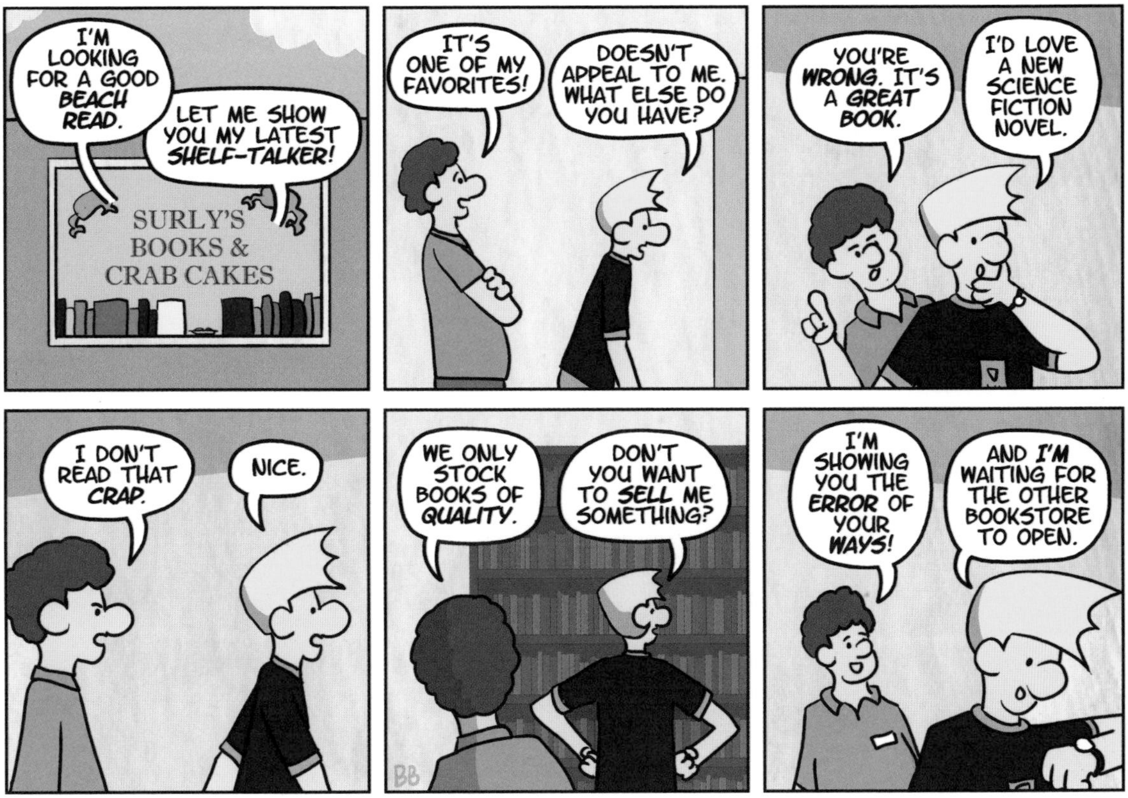
I'M LOOKING FOR A GOOD BEACH READ.
LET ME SHOW YOU MY LATEST SHELF-TALKER!
SURLY'S BOOKS & CRAB CAKES
IT'S ONE OF MY FAVORITES!
DOESN'T APPEAL TO ME. WHAT ELSE DO YOU HAVE?
YOU'RE WRONG. IT'S A GREAT BOOK.
I'D LOVE A NEW SCIENCE FICTION NOVEL.
I DON'T READ THAT CRAP.
NICE.
WE ONLY STOCK BOOKS OF QUALITY.
DON'T YOU WANT TO SELL ME SOMETHING?
BB
I'M SHOWING YOU THE ERROR OF YOUR WAYS!
AND I'M WAITING FOR THE OTHER BOOKSTORE TO OPEN.

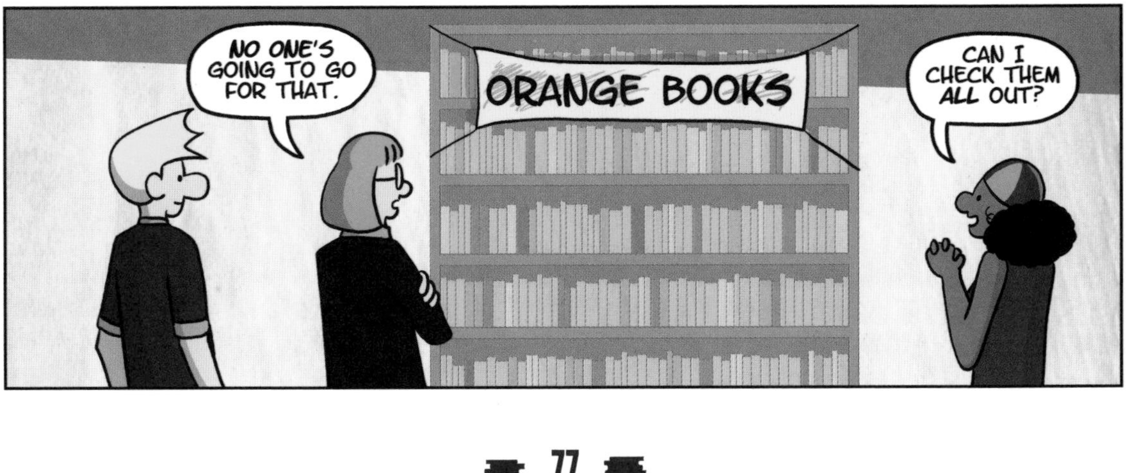
NO ONE'S GOING TO GO FOR THAT.
ORANGE BOOKS
CAN I CHECK THEM ALL OUT?

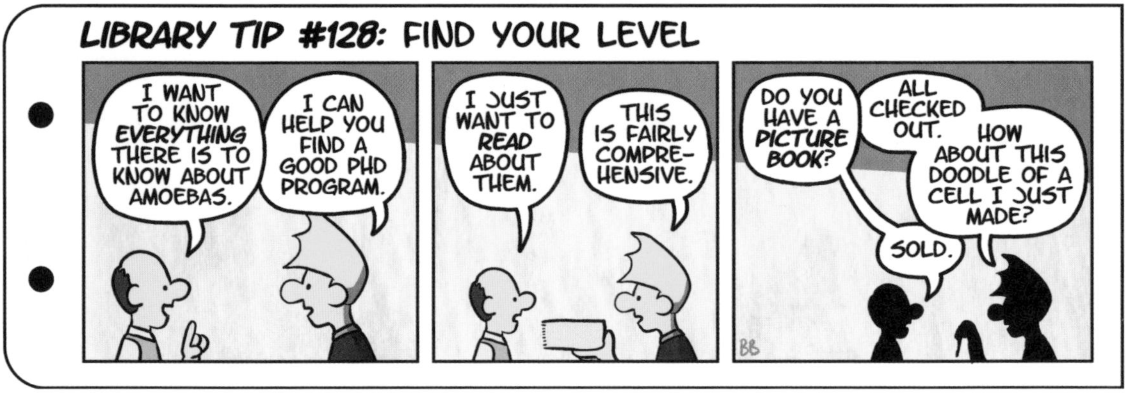
LIBRARY TIP #128: FIND YOUR LEVEL
I WANT TO KNOW EVERYTHING THERE IS TO KNOW ABOUT AMOEBAS.
I CAN HELP YOU FIND A GOOD PHD PROGRAM.
I JUST WANT TO READ ABOUT THEM.
THIS IS FAIRLY COMPRE-HENSIVE.
DO YOU HAVE A PICTURE BOOK?
ALL CHECKED OUT. HOW ABOUT THIS DOODLE OF A CELL I JUST MADE?
SOLD.
BB

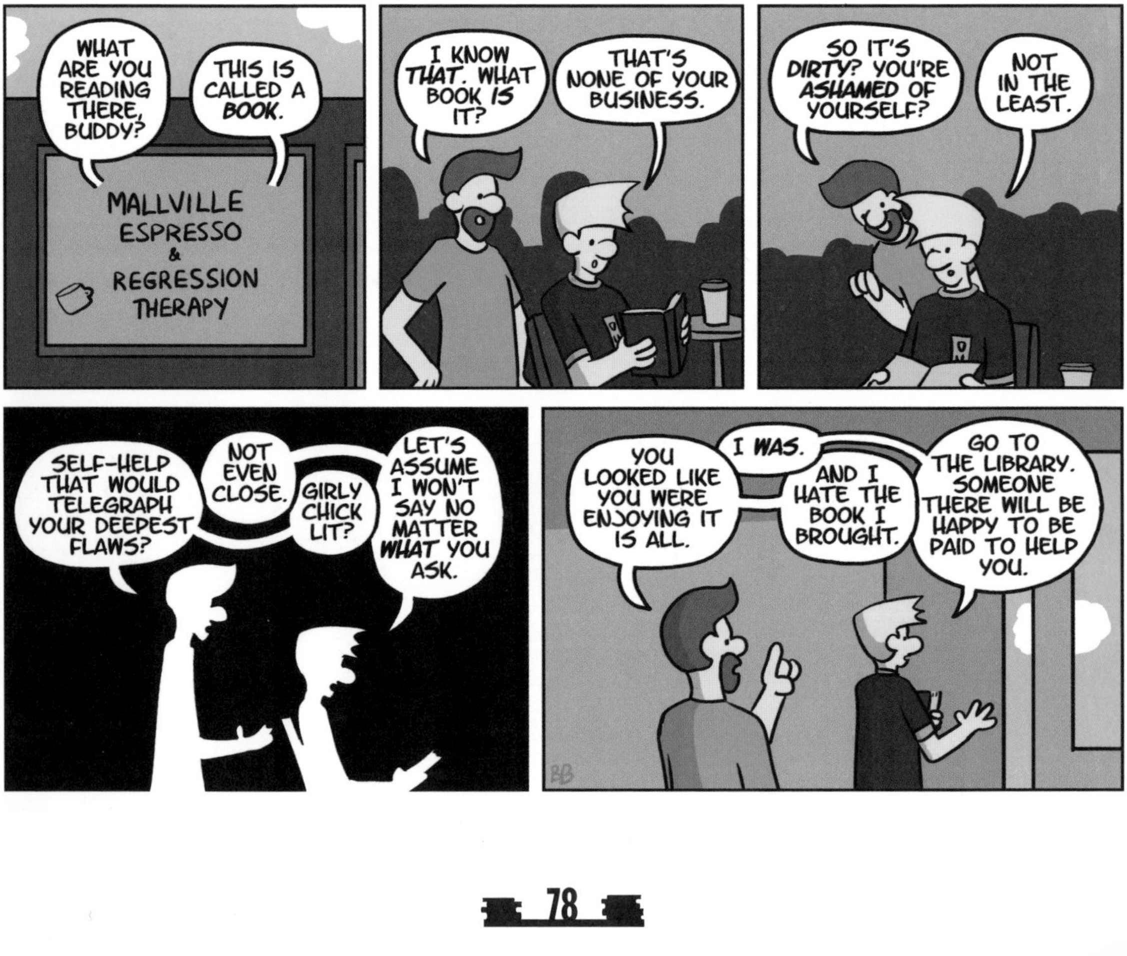
WHAT ARE YOU READING THERE, BUDDY?
THIS IS CALLED A BOOK.
MALLVILLE ESPRESSO & REGRESSION THERAPY
I KNOW THAT. WHAT BOOK IS IT?
THAT'S NONE OF YOUR BUSINESS.
SO IT'S DIRTY? YOU'RE ASHAMED OF YOURSELF?
NOT IN THE LEAST.
SELF-HELP THAT WOULD TELEGRAPH YOUR DEEPEST FLAWS?
NOT EVEN CLOSE.
GIRLY CHICK LIT?
LET'S ASSUME I WON'T SAY NO MATTER WHAT YOU ASK.
YOU LOOKED LIKE YOU WERE ENJOYING IT IS ALL.
I WAS.
AND I HATE THE BOOK I BROUGHT.
GO TO THE LIBRARY. SOMEONE THERE WILL BE HAPPY TO BE PAID TO HELP YOU.
BB

Reads Well With Others

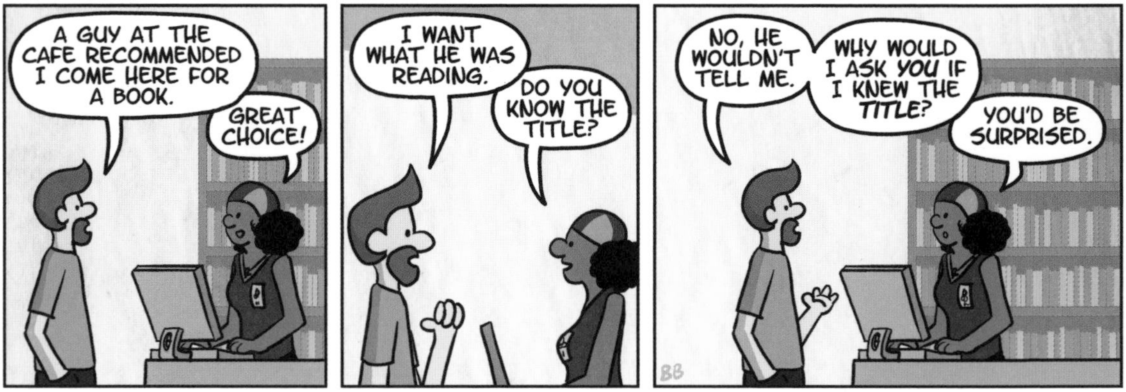
A GUY AT THE CAFE RECOMMENDED I COME HERE FOR A BOOK.
GREAT CHOICE!
I WANT WHAT HE WAS READING.
DO YOU KNOW THE TITLE?
NO, HE WOULDN'T TELL ME.
WHY WOULD I ASK *YOU* IF I KNEW THE *TITLE*?
YOU'D BE SURPRISED.
BB

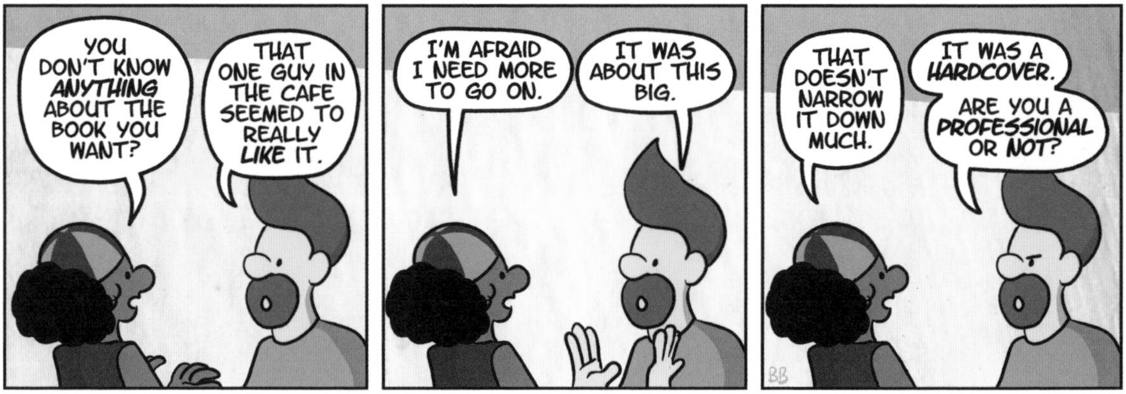
YOU DON'T KNOW *ANYTHING* ABOUT THE BOOK YOU WANT?
THAT ONE GUY IN THE CAFE SEEMED TO REALLY *LIKE* IT.
I'M AFRAID I NEED MORE TO GO ON.
IT WAS ABOUT THIS BIG.
THAT DOESN'T NARROW IT DOWN MUCH.
IT WAS A *HARDCOVER*.
ARE YOU A *PROFESSIONAL* OR *NOT*?
BB

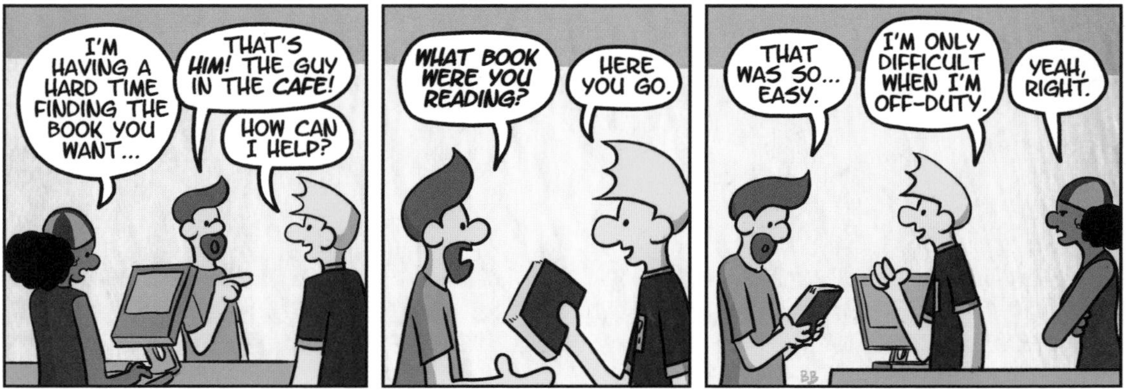
I'M HAVING A HARD TIME FINDING THE BOOK YOU WANT...
THAT'S *HIM*! THE GUY IN THE *CAFE*!
HOW CAN I HELP?
WHAT BOOK WERE YOU READING?
HERE YOU GO.
THAT WAS SO... EASY.
I'M ONLY DIFFICULT WHEN I'M OFF-DUTY.
YEAH, RIGHT.
BB

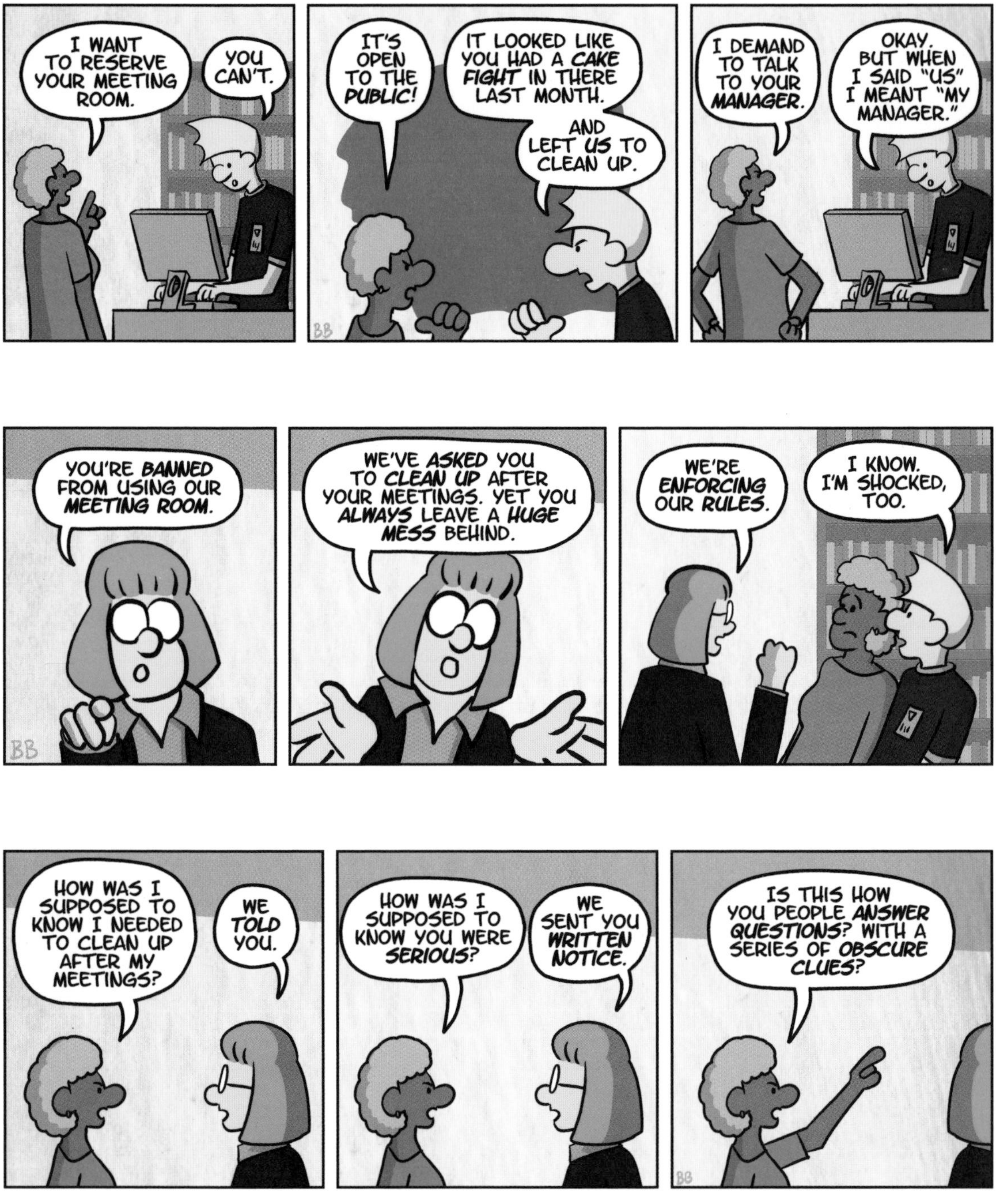
I WANT TO RESERVE YOUR MEETING ROOM.
YOU CAN'T.
IT'S OPEN TO THE PUBLIC!
IT LOOKED LIKE YOU HAD A CAKE FIGHT IN THERE LAST MONTH.
AND LEFT US TO CLEAN UP.
I DEMAND TO TALK TO YOUR MANAGER.
OKAY. BUT WHEN I SAID "US" I MEANT "MY MANAGER."
BB
YOU'RE BANNED FROM USING OUR MEETING ROOM.
WE'VE ASKED YOU TO CLEAN UP AFTER YOUR MEETINGS. YET YOU ALWAYS LEAVE A HUGE MESS BEHIND.
WE'RE ENFORCING OUR RULES.
I KNOW. I'M SHOCKED, TOO.
BB
HOW WAS I SUPPOSED TO KNOW I NEEDED TO CLEAN UP AFTER MY MEETINGS?
WE TOLD YOU.
HOW WAS I SUPPOSED TO KNOW YOU WERE SERIOUS?
WE SENT YOU WRITTEN NOTICE.
IS THIS HOW YOU PEOPLE ANSWER QUESTIONS? WITH A SERIES OF OBSCURE CLUES?
BB

Reads Well With Others

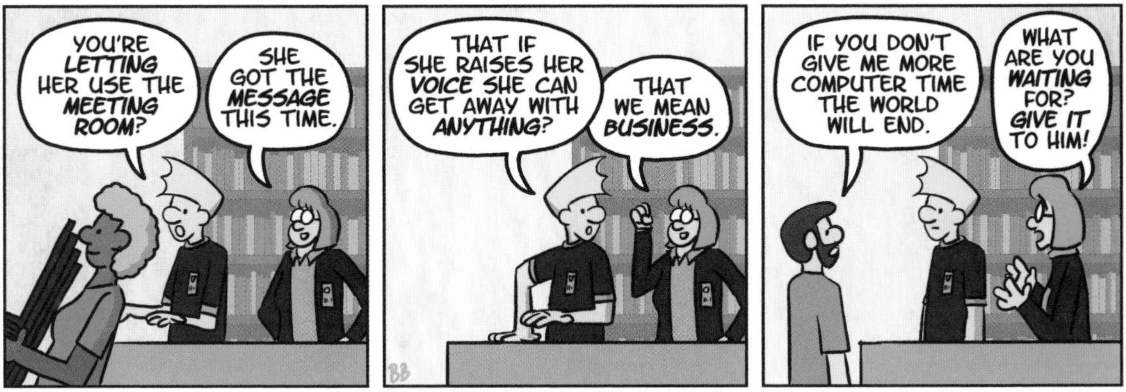

YOU'RE LETTING HER USE THE MEETING ROOM?
SHE GOT THE MESSAGE THIS TIME.
THAT IF SHE RAISES HER VOICE SHE CAN GET AWAY WITH ANYTHING?
THAT WE MEAN BUSINESS.
BB
IF YOU DON'T GIVE ME MORE COMPUTER TIME THE WORLD WILL END.
WHAT ARE YOU WAITING FOR? GIVE IT TO HIM!

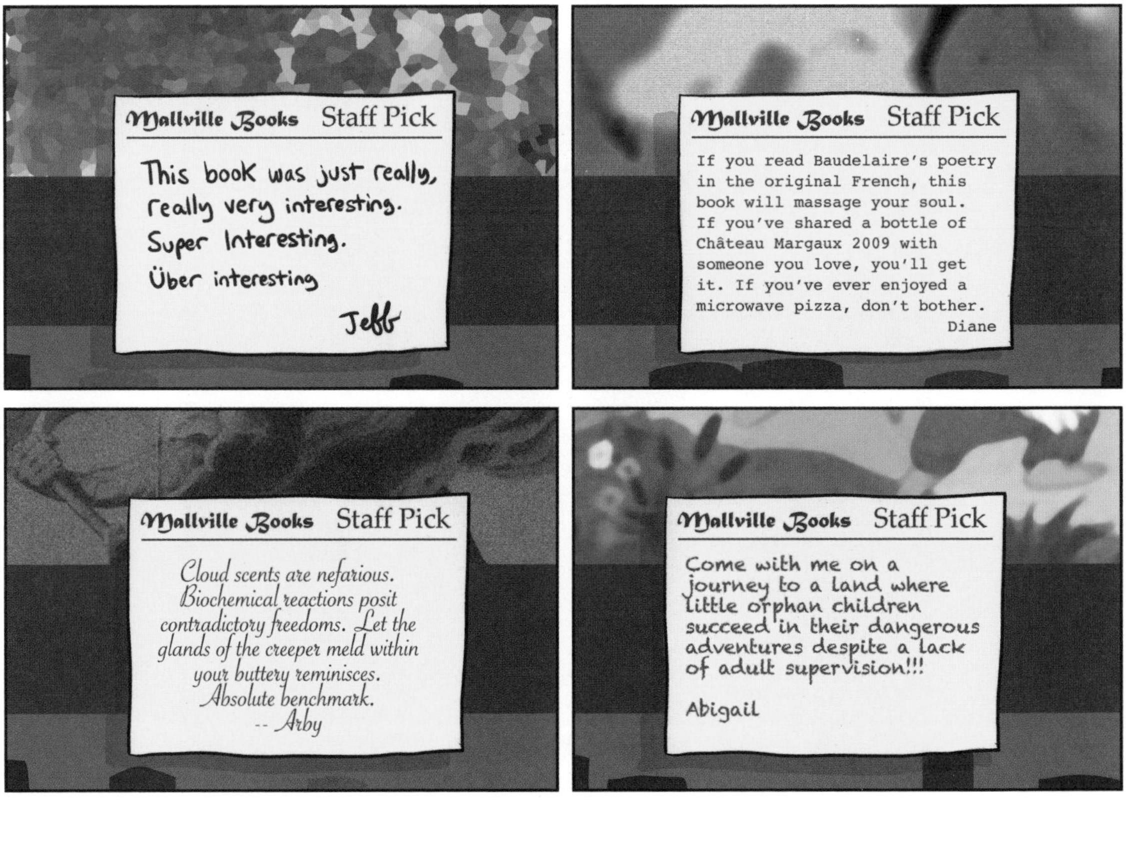

Mallville Books Staff Pick
This book was just really, really very interesting. Super Interesting. Über interesting
Jeff
Mallville Books Staff Pick
If you read Baudelaire's poetry in the original French, this book will massage your soul. If you've shared a bottle of Château Margaux 2009 with someone you love, you'll get it. If you've ever enjoyed a microwave pizza, don't bother.
Diane
Mallville Books Staff Pick
Cloud scents are nefarious. Biochemical reactions posit contradictory freedoms. Let the glands of the creeper meld within your buttery reminisces. Absolute benchmark.
-- Arby
Mallville Books Staff Pick
Come with me on a journey to a land where little orphan children succeed in their dangerous adventures despite a lack of adult supervision!!!
Abigail

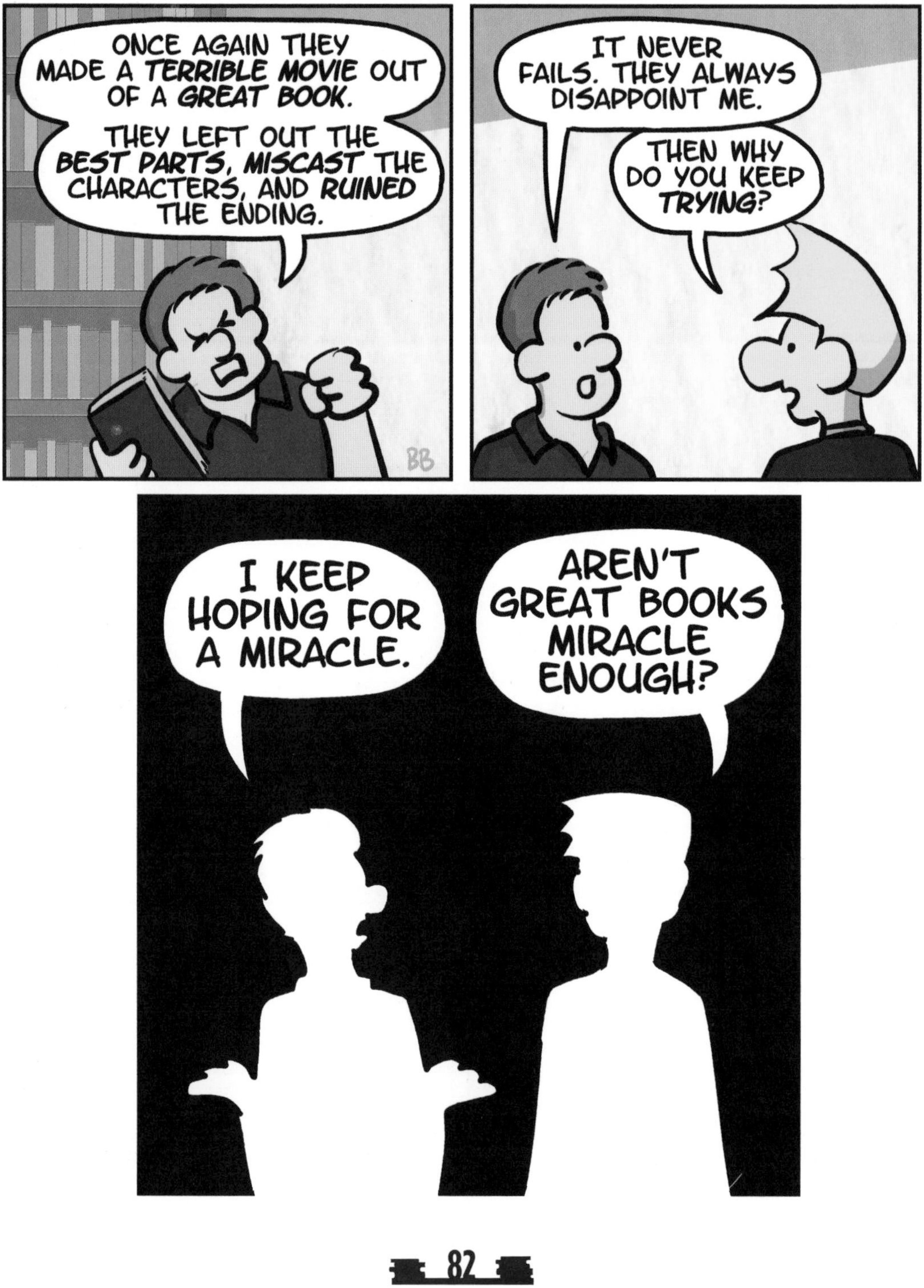
ONCE AGAIN THEY MADE A TERRIBLE MOVIE OUT OF A GREAT BOOK.
THEY LEFT OUT THE BEST PARTS, MISCAST THE CHARACTERS, AND RUINED THE ENDING.
BB
IT NEVER FAILS. THEY ALWAYS DISAPPOINT ME.
THEN WHY DO YOU KEEP TRYING?
I KEEP HOPING FOR A MIRACLE.
AREN'T GREAT BOOKS MIRACLE ENOUGH?

Reads Well With Others

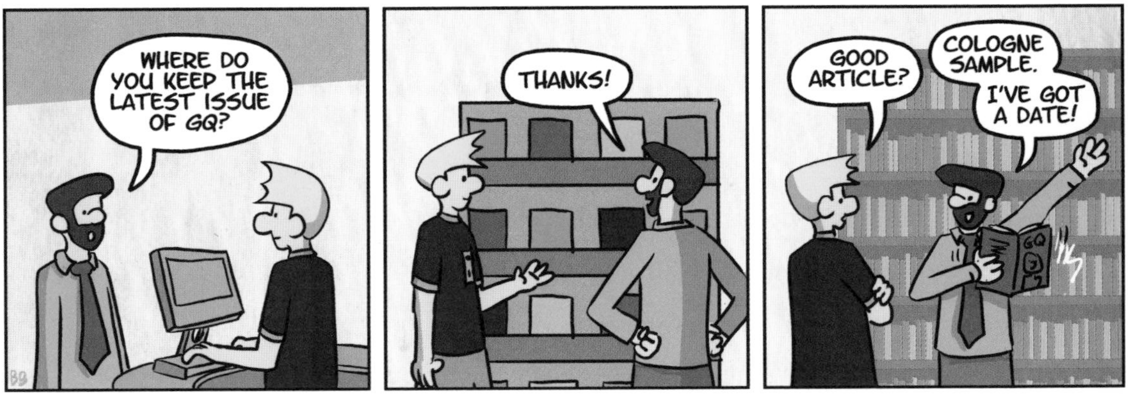
WHERE DO YOU KEEP THE LATEST ISSUE OF GQ?
THANKS!
GOOD ARTICLE?
COLOGNE SAMPLE.
I'VE GOT A DATE!
GQ

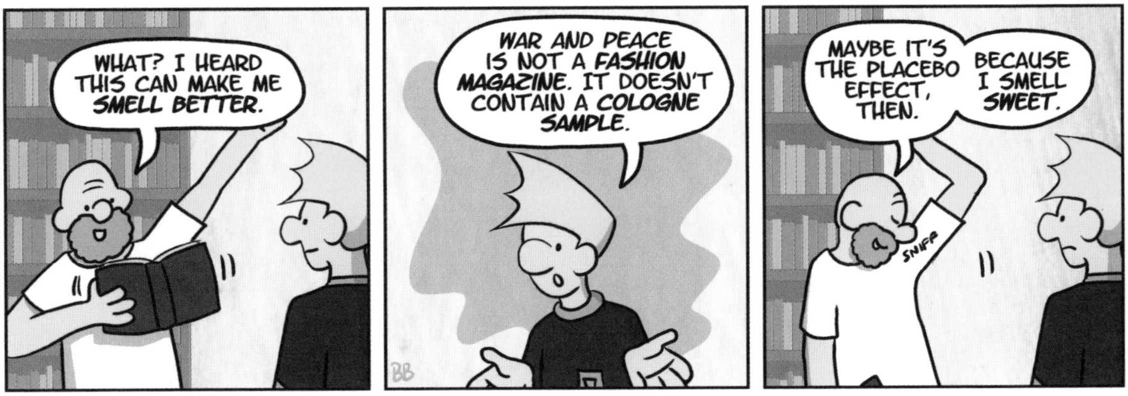
WHAT? I HEARD THIS CAN MAKE ME SMELL BETTER.
WAR AND PEACE IS NOT A FASHION MAGAZINE. IT DOESN'T CONTAIN A COLOGNE SAMPLE.
MAYBE IT'S THE PLACEBO EFFECT, THEN.
BECAUSE I SMELL SWEET.
SNIFF

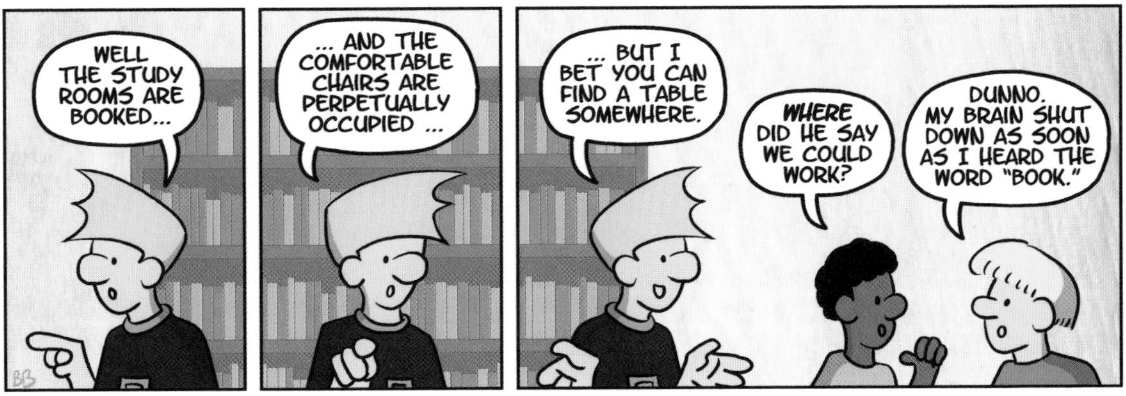
WELL THE STUDY ROOMS ARE BOOKED...
... AND THE COMFORTABLE CHAIRS ARE PERPETUALLY OCCUPIED ...
... BUT I BET YOU CAN FIND A TABLE SOMEWHERE.
WHERE DID HE SAY WE COULD WORK?
DUNNO. MY BRAIN SHUT DOWN AS SOON AS I HEARD THE WORD "BOOK."

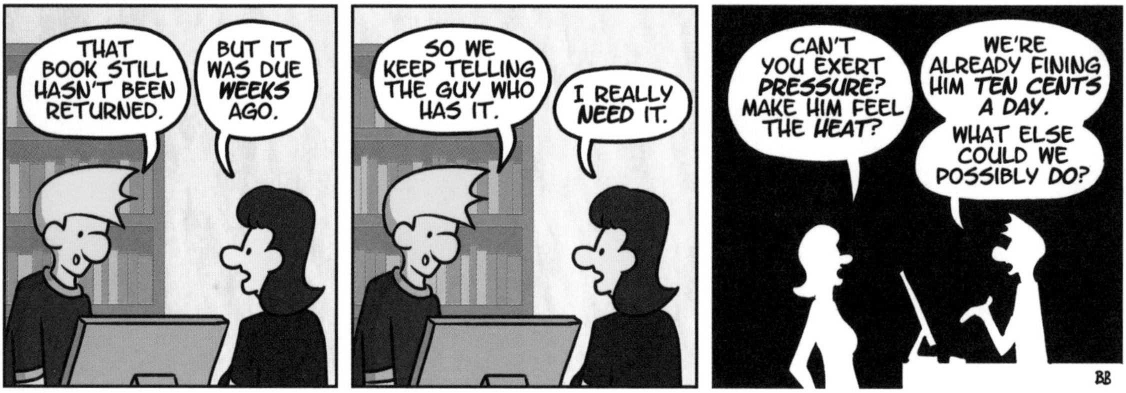
THAT BOOK STILL HASN'T BEEN RETURNED.
BUT IT WAS DUE **WEEKS** AGO.
SO WE KEEP TELLING THE GUY WHO HAS IT.
I REALLY **NEED** IT.
CAN'T YOU EXERT **PRESSURE?** MAKE HIM FEEL THE **HEAT?**
WE'RE ALREADY FINING HIM **TEN CENTS A DAY.**
WHAT ELSE COULD WE POSSIBLY **DO?**
BB

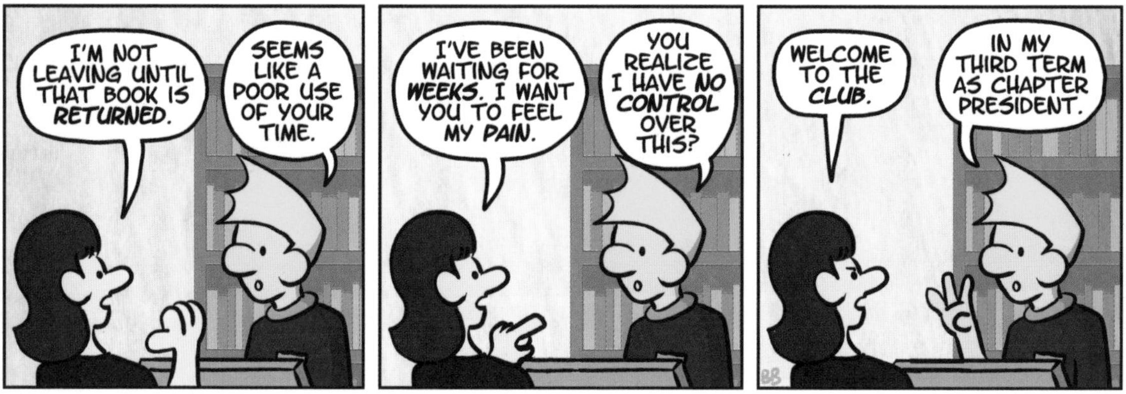
I'M NOT LEAVING UNTIL THAT BOOK IS **RETURNED.**
SEEMS LIKE A POOR USE OF YOUR TIME.
I'VE BEEN WAITING FOR **WEEKS.** I WANT YOU TO FEEL MY **PAIN.**
YOU REALIZE I HAVE **NO CONTROL** OVER THIS?
WELCOME TO THE **CLUB.**
IN MY THIRD TERM AS CHAPTER PRESIDENT.
BB

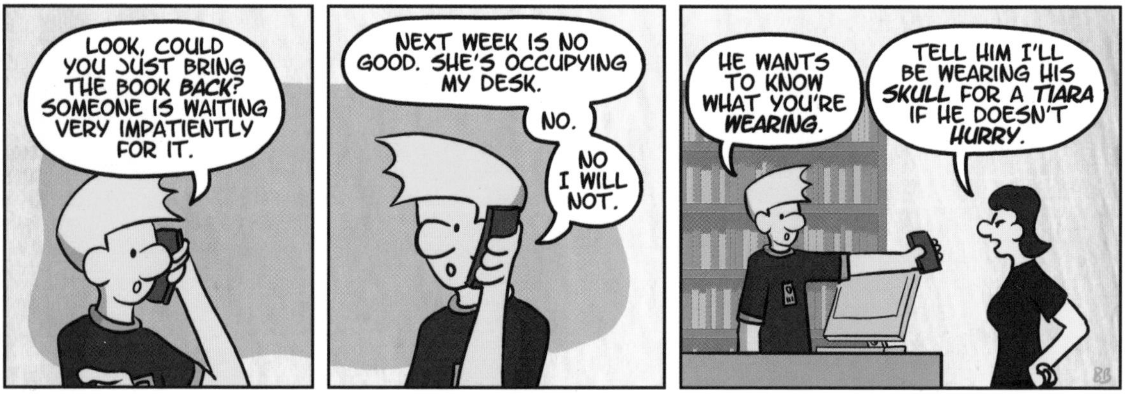
LOOK, COULD YOU JUST BRING THE BOOK **BACK?** SOMEONE IS WAITING VERY IMPATIENTLY FOR IT.
NEXT WEEK IS NO GOOD. SHE'S OCCUPYING MY DESK.
NO.
NO I WILL NOT.
HE WANTS TO KNOW WHAT YOU'RE **WEARING.**
TELL HIM I'LL BE WEARING HIS **SKULL** FOR A **TIARA** IF HE DOESN'T **HURRY.**
BB

Reads Well With Others

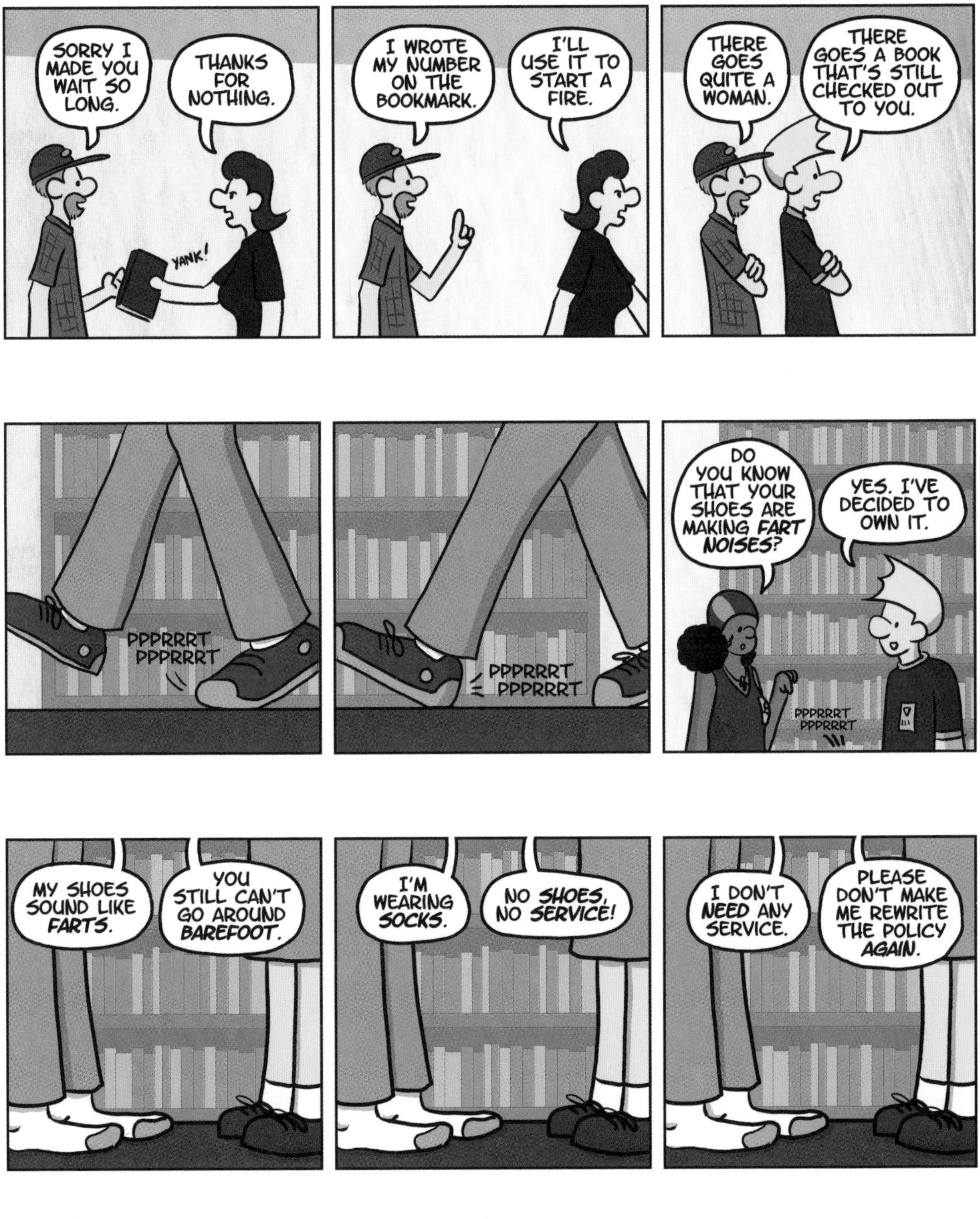

SORRY I MADE YOU WAIT SO LONG.
THANKS FOR NOTHING.
YANK!
I WROTE MY NUMBER ON THE BOOKMARK.
I'LL USE IT TO START A FIRE.
THERE GOES QUITE A WOMAN.
THERE GOES A BOOK THAT'S STILL CHECKED OUT TO YOU.
PPPRRRT PPPRRRT
PPPRRRT PPPRRRT
DO YOU KNOW THAT YOUR SHOES ARE MAKING FART NOISES?
YES. I'VE DECIDED TO OWN IT.
PPPRRRT PPPRRRT
MY SHOES SOUND LIKE FARTS.
YOU STILL CAN'T GO AROUND BAREFOOT.
I'M WEARING SOCKS.
NO SHOES, NO SERVICE!
I DON'T NEED ANY SERVICE.
PLEASE DON'T MAKE ME REWRITE THE POLICY AGAIN.

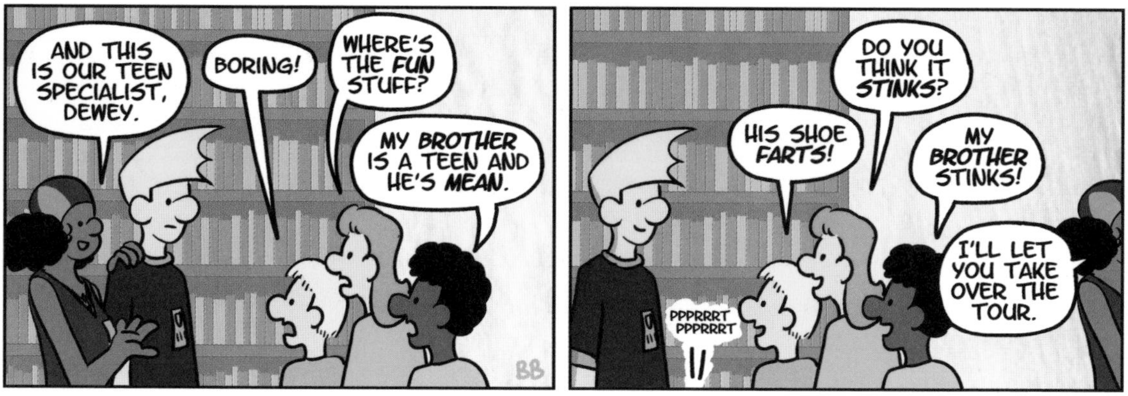
AND THIS IS OUR TEEN SPECIALIST, DEWEY.
BORING!
WHERE'S THE FUN STUFF?
MY BROTHER IS A TEEN AND HE'S MEAN.
BB
DO YOU THINK IT STINKS?
HIS SHOE FARTS!
MY BROTHER STINKS!
I'LL LET YOU TAKE OVER THE TOUR.
PPPRRRT PPPRRRT

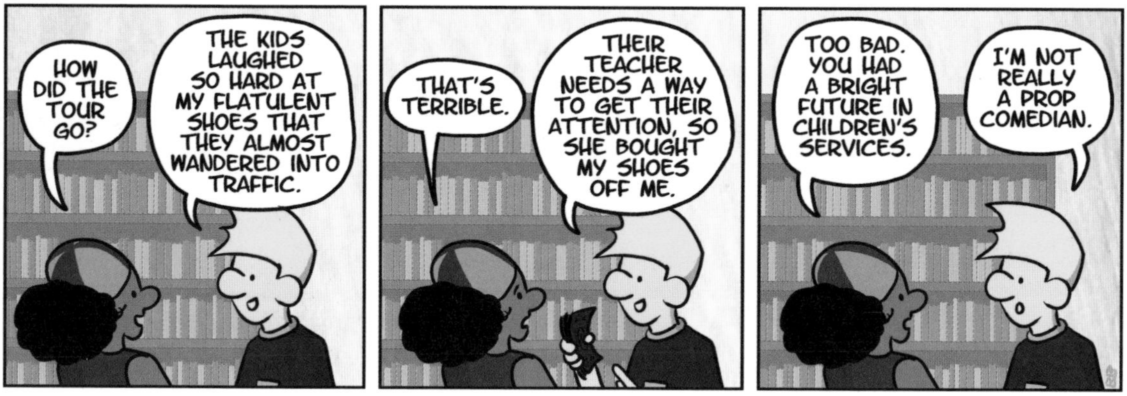
HOW DID THE TOUR GO?
THE KIDS LAUGHED SO HARD AT MY FLATULENT SHOES THAT THEY ALMOST WANDERED INTO TRAFFIC.
THAT'S TERRIBLE.
THEIR TEACHER NEEDS A WAY TO GET THEIR ATTENTION, SO SHE BOUGHT MY SHOES OFF ME.
TOO BAD. YOU HAD A BRIGHT FUTURE IN CHILDREN'S SERVICES.
I'M NOT REALLY A PROP COMEDIAN.

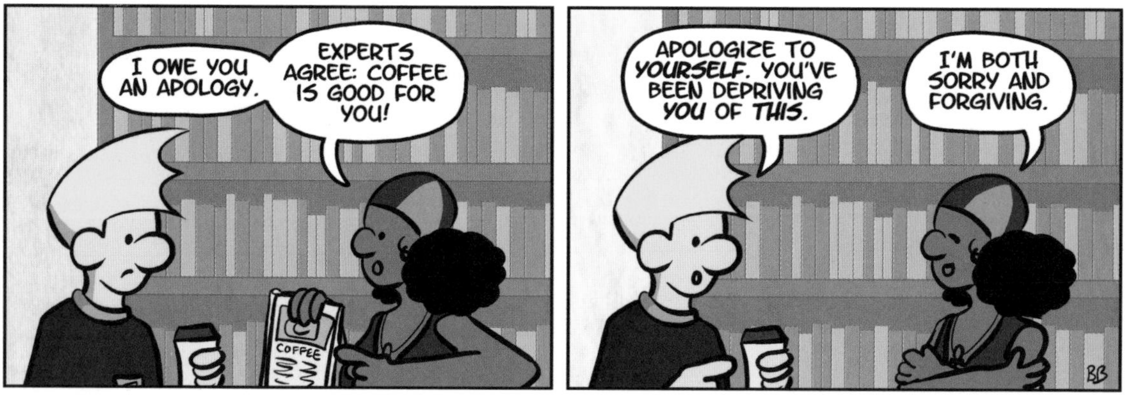
I OWE YOU AN APOLOGY.
EXPERTS AGREE: COFFEE IS GOOD FOR YOU!
COFFEE
APOLOGIZE TO YOURSELF. YOU'VE BEEN DEPRIVING YOU OF THIS.
I'M BOTH SORRY AND FORGIVING.
BB

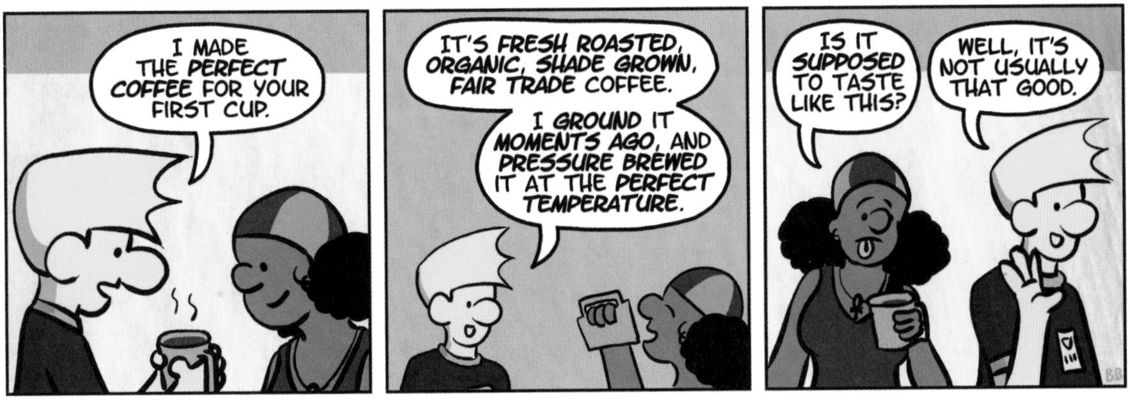
I MADE THE PERFECT COFFEE FOR YOUR FIRST CUP.
IT'S FRESH ROASTED, ORGANIC, SHADE GROWN, FAIR TRADE COFFEE.
I GROUND IT MOMENTS AGO, AND PRESSURE BREWED IT AT THE PERFECT TEMPERATURE.
IS IT SUPPOSED TO TASTE LIKE THIS?
WELL, IT'S NOT USUALLY THAT GOOD.
BB

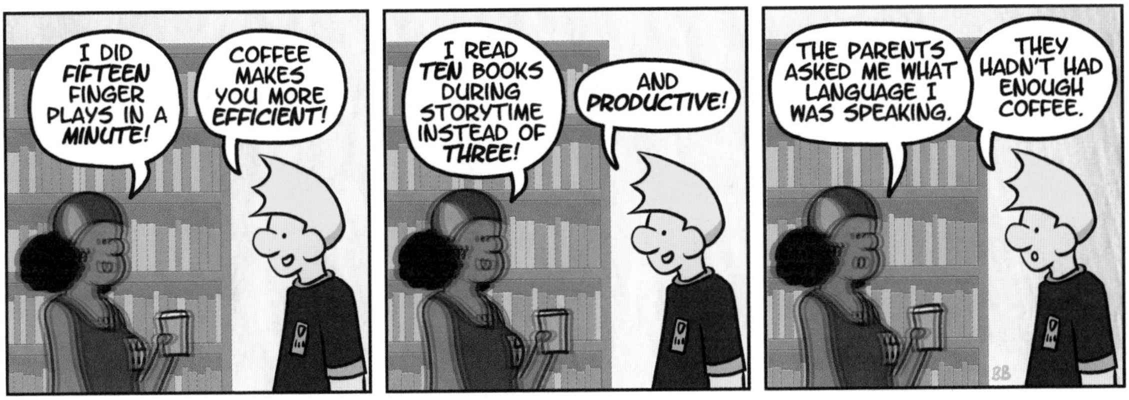
I DID FIFTEEN FINGER PLAYS IN A MINUTE!
COFFEE MAKES YOU MORE EFFICIENT!
I READ TEN BOOKS DURING STORYTIME INSTEAD OF THREE!
AND PRODUCTIVE!
THE PARENTS ASKED ME WHAT LANGUAGE I WAS SPEAKING.
THEY HADN'T HAD ENOUGH COFFEE.
BB

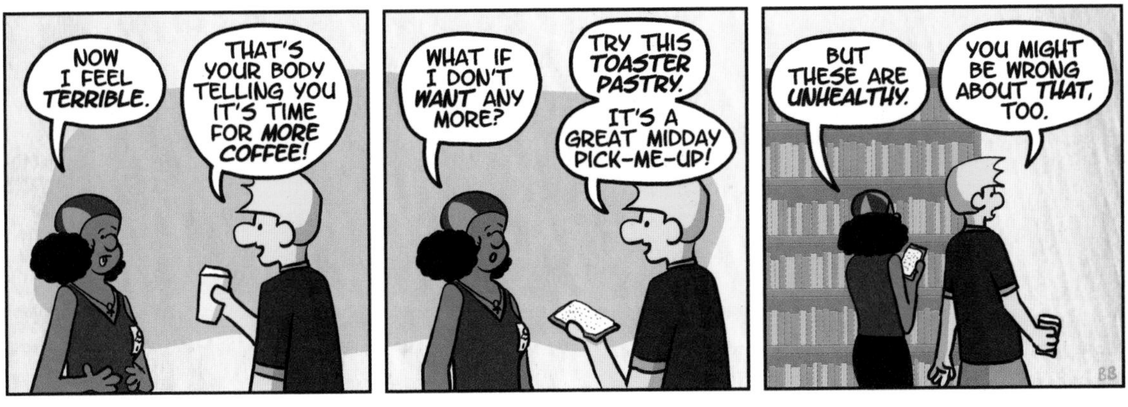
NOW I FEEL TERRIBLE.
THAT'S YOUR BODY TELLING YOU IT'S TIME FOR MORE COFFEE!
WHAT IF I DON'T WANT ANY MORE?
TRY THIS TOASTER PASTRY.
IT'S A GREAT MIDDAY PICK-ME-UP!
BUT THESE ARE UNHEALTHY.
YOU MIGHT BE WRONG ABOUT THAT, TOO.
BB

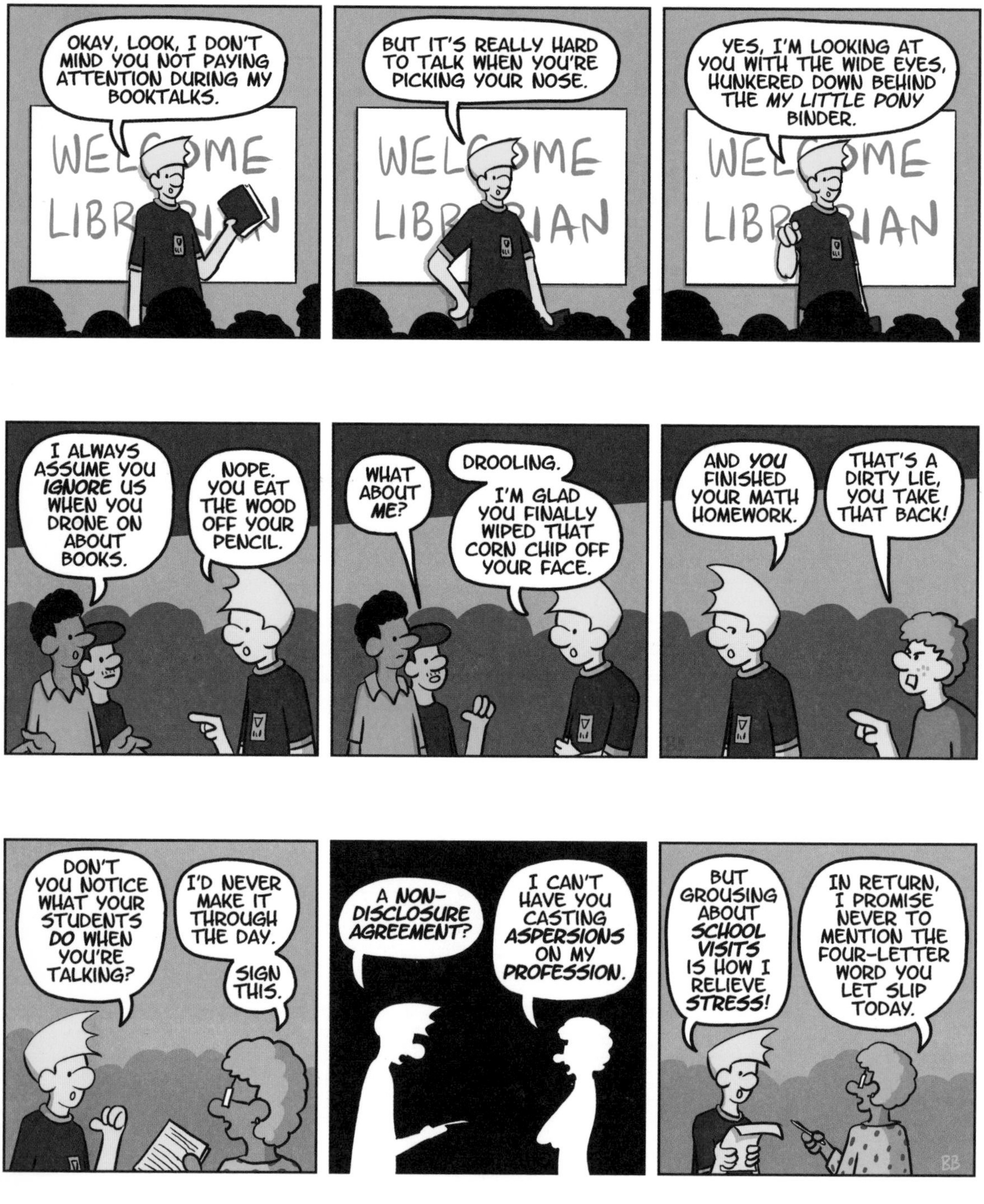
OKAY, LOOK, I DON'T MIND YOU NOT PAYING ATTENTION DURING MY BOOKTALKS.
WELCOME LIBRARIAN
BUT IT'S REALLY HARD TO TALK WHEN YOU'RE PICKING YOUR NOSE.
YES, I'M LOOKING AT YOU WITH THE WIDE EYES, HUNKERED DOWN BEHIND THE *MY LITTLE PONY* BINDER.
I ALWAYS ASSUME YOU **IGNORE** US WHEN YOU DRONE ON ABOUT BOOKS.
NOPE. YOU EAT THE WOOD OFF YOUR PENCIL.
WHAT ABOUT ***ME***?
DROOLING.
I'M GLAD YOU FINALLY WIPED THAT CORN CHIP OFF YOUR FACE.
AND ***YOU*** FINISHED YOUR MATH HOMEWORK.
THAT'S A DIRTY LIE, YOU TAKE THAT BACK!
DON'T YOU NOTICE WHAT YOUR STUDENTS ***DO*** WHEN YOU'RE TALKING?
I'D NEVER MAKE IT THROUGH THE DAY.
SIGN THIS.
A ***NON-DISCLOSURE AGREEMENT***?
I CAN'T HAVE YOU CASTING ***ASPERSIONS*** ON MY ***PROFESSION***.
BUT GROUSING ABOUT ***SCHOOL VISITS*** IS HOW I RELIEVE ***STRESS***!
IN RETURN, I PROMISE NEVER TO MENTION THE FOUR-LETTER WORD YOU LET SLIP TODAY.
BB

Reads Well With Others

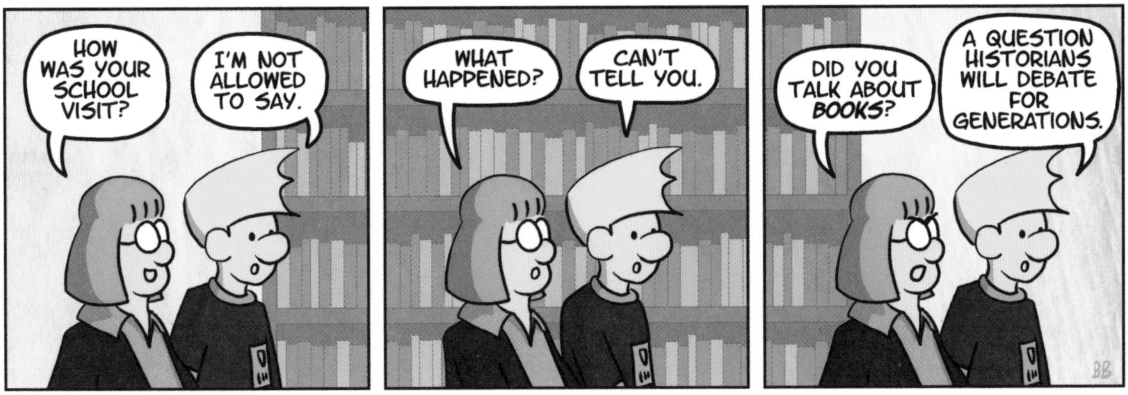

HOW WAS YOUR SCHOOL VISIT?
I'M NOT ALLOWED TO SAY.
WHAT HAPPENED?
CAN'T TELL YOU.
DID YOU TALK ABOUT *BOOKS*?
A QUESTION HISTORIANS WILL DEBATE FOR GENERATIONS.
BB

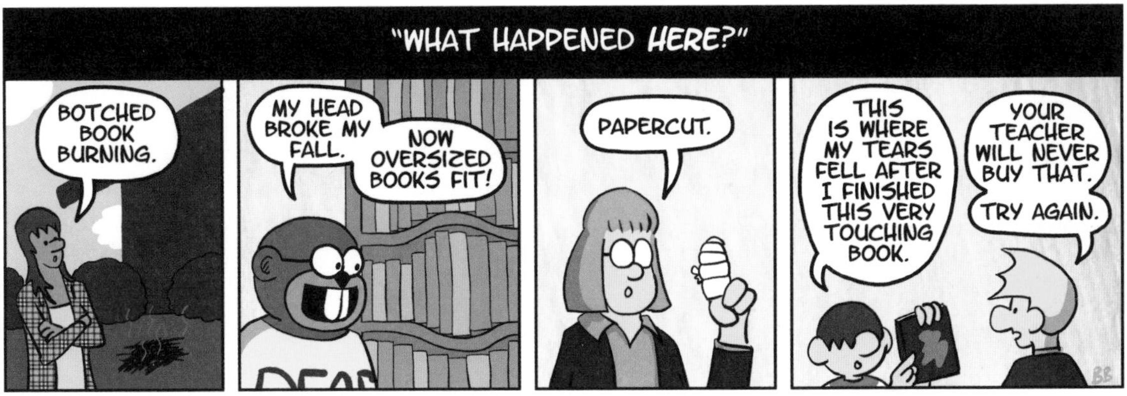

"WHAT HAPPENED *HERE*?"
BOTCHED BOOK BURNING.
MY HEAD BROKE MY FALL.
NOW OVERSIZED BOOKS FIT!
PAPERCUT.
THIS IS WHERE MY TEARS FELL AFTER I FINISHED THIS VERY TOUCHING BOOK.
YOUR TEACHER WILL NEVER BUY THAT.
TRY AGAIN.
BB

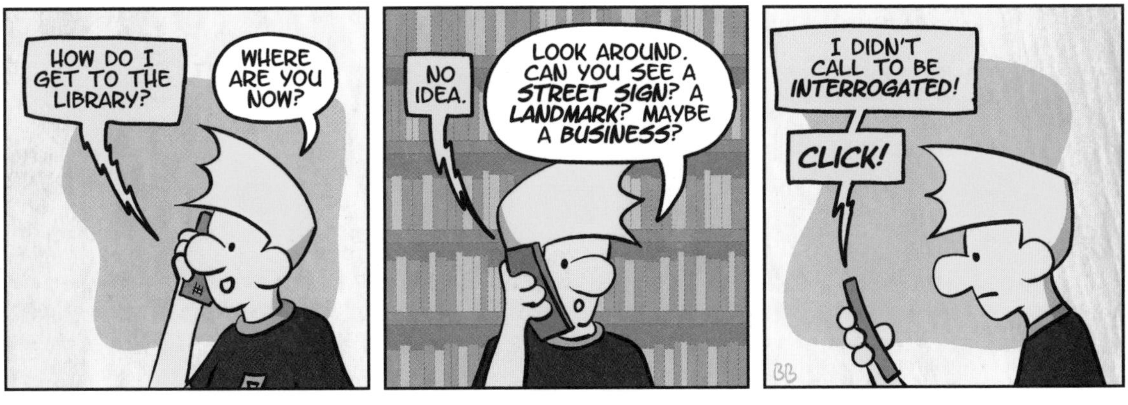

HOW DO I GET TO THE LIBRARY?
WHERE ARE YOU NOW?
NO IDEA.
LOOK AROUND. CAN YOU SEE A *STREET SIGN*? A *LANDMARK*? MAYBE A *BUSINESS*?
I DIDN'T CALL TO BE *INTERROGATED*!
CLICK!
BB

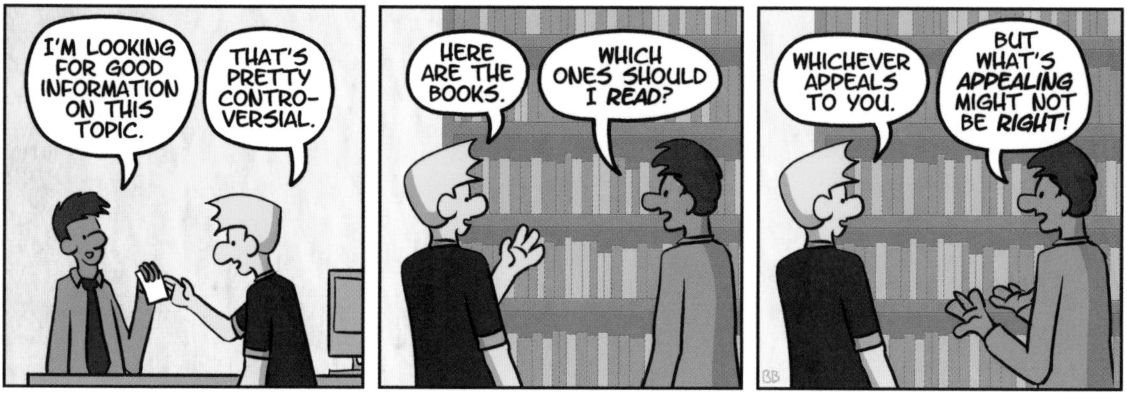
I'M LOOKING FOR GOOD INFORMATION ON THIS TOPIC.
THAT'S PRETTY CONTRO-VERSIAL.
HERE ARE THE BOOKS.
WHICH ONES SHOULD I *READ*?
WHICHEVER APPEALS TO YOU.
BUT WHAT'S *APPEALING* MIGHT NOT BE *RIGHT*!

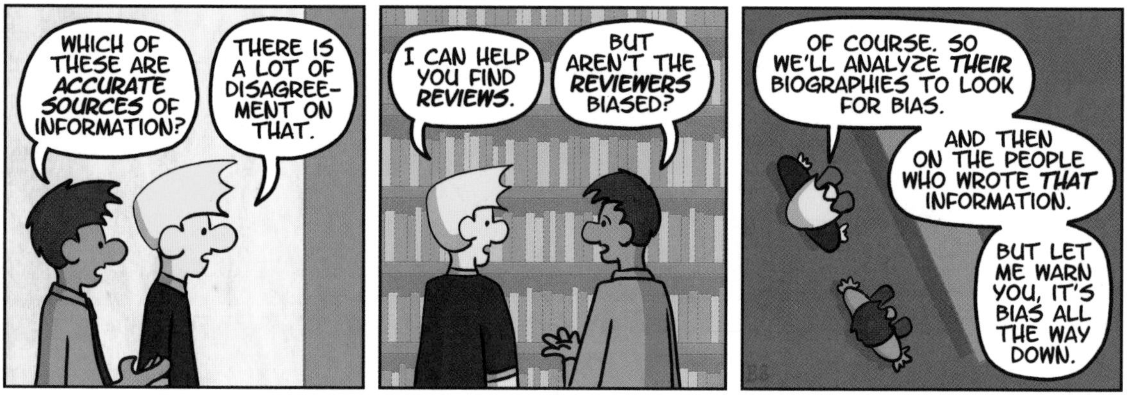
WHICH OF THESE ARE *ACCURATE SOURCES* OF INFORMATION?
THERE IS A LOT OF DISAGREE-MENT ON THAT.
I CAN HELP YOU FIND *REVIEWS*.
BUT AREN'T THE *REVIEWERS* BIASED?
OF COURSE. SO WE'LL ANALYZE *THEIR* BIOGRAPHIES TO LOOK FOR BIAS.
AND THEN ON THE PEOPLE WHO WROTE *THAT* INFORMATION.
BUT LET ME WARN YOU, IT'S BIAS ALL THE WAY DOWN.

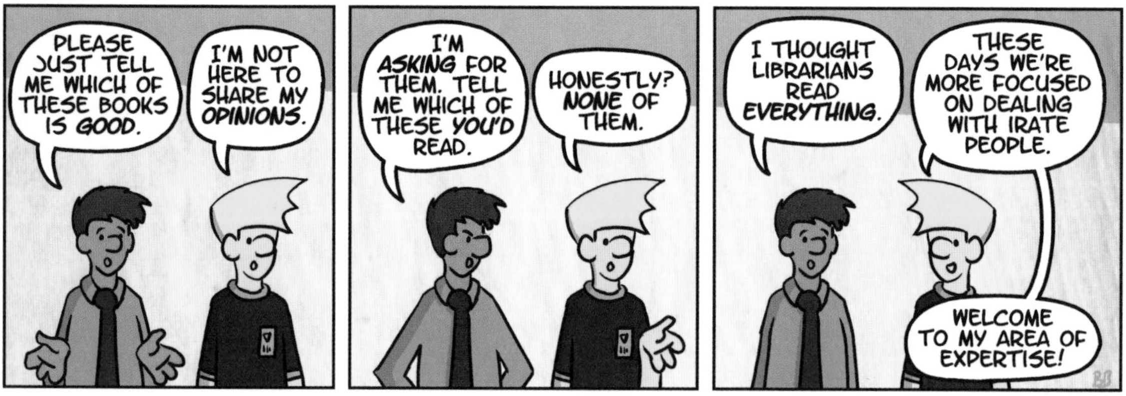
PLEASE JUST TELL ME WHICH OF THESE BOOKS IS *GOOD*.
I'M NOT HERE TO SHARE MY *OPINIONS*.
I'M *ASKING* FOR THEM. TELL ME WHICH OF THESE *YOU'D* READ.
HONESTLY? *NONE* OF THEM.
I THOUGHT LIBRARIANS READ *EVERYTHING*.
THESE DAYS WE'RE MORE FOCUSED ON DEALING WITH IRATE PEOPLE.
WELCOME TO MY AREA OF EXPERTISE!

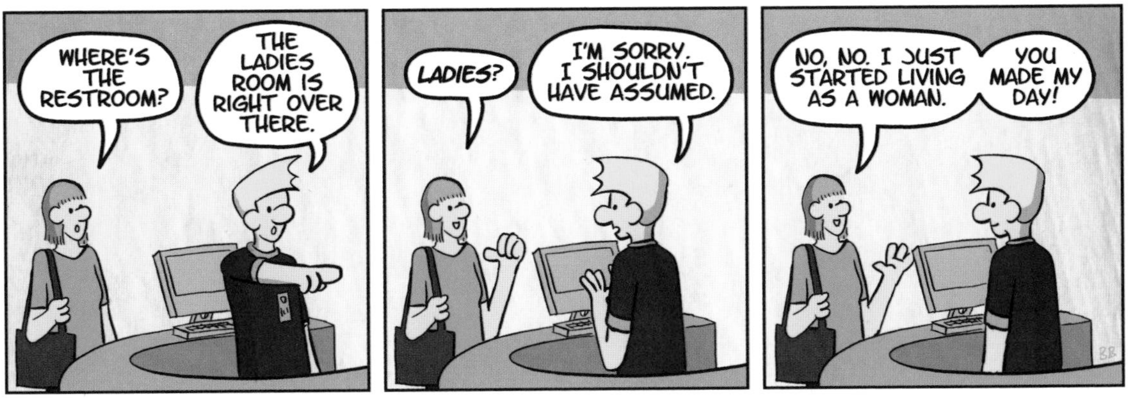
WHERE'S THE RESTROOM?
THE LADIES ROOM IS RIGHT OVER THERE.
LADIES?
I'M SORRY. I SHOULDN'T HAVE ASSUMED.
NO, NO. I JUST STARTED LIVING AS A WOMAN.
YOU MADE MY DAY!
BB

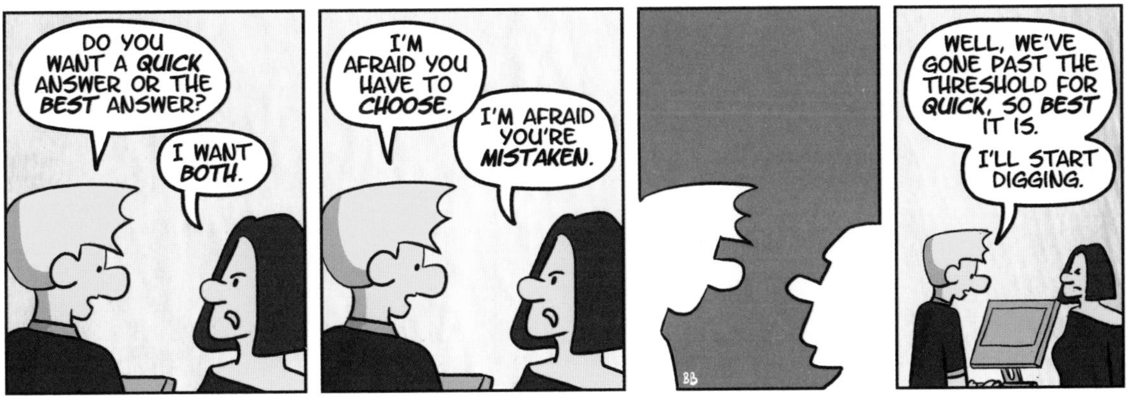
DO YOU WANT A QUICK ANSWER OR THE BEST ANSWER?
I WANT BOTH.
I'M AFRAID YOU HAVE TO CHOOSE.
I'M AFRAID YOU'RE MISTAKEN.
BB
WELL, WE'VE GONE PAST THE THRESHOLD FOR QUICK, SO BEST IT IS.
I'LL START DIGGING.

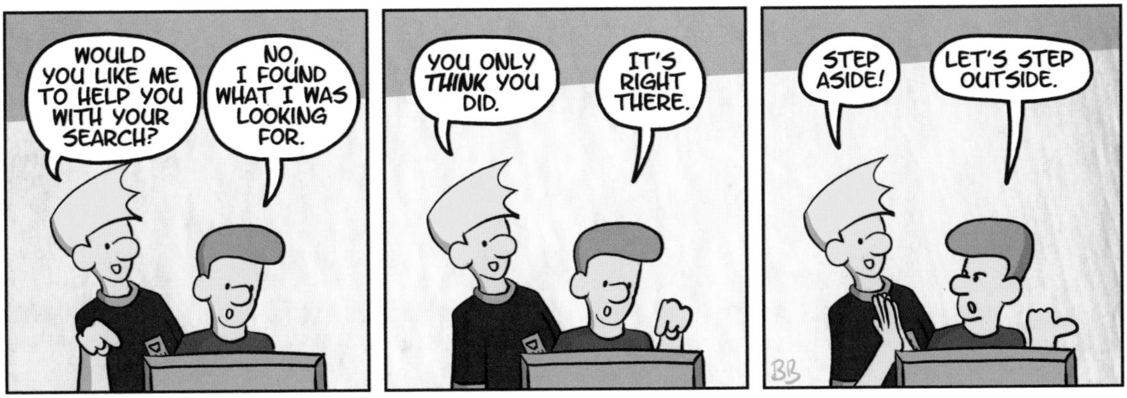
WOULD YOU LIKE ME TO HELP YOU WITH YOUR SEARCH?
NO, I FOUND WHAT I WAS LOOKING FOR.
YOU ONLY THINK YOU DID.
IT'S RIGHT THERE.
STEP ASIDE!
LET'S STEP OUTSIDE.
BB

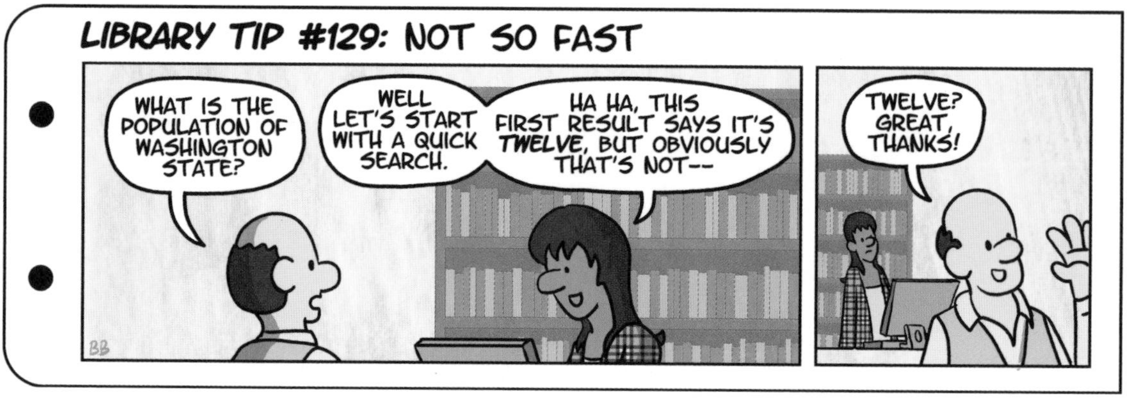
LIBRARY TIP #129: NOT SO FAST
WHAT IS THE POPULATION OF WASHINGTON STATE?
WELL LET'S START WITH A QUICK SEARCH.
HA HA, THIS FIRST RESULT SAYS IT'S *TWELVE*, BUT OBVIOUSLY THAT'S NOT--
TWELVE? GREAT, THANKS!

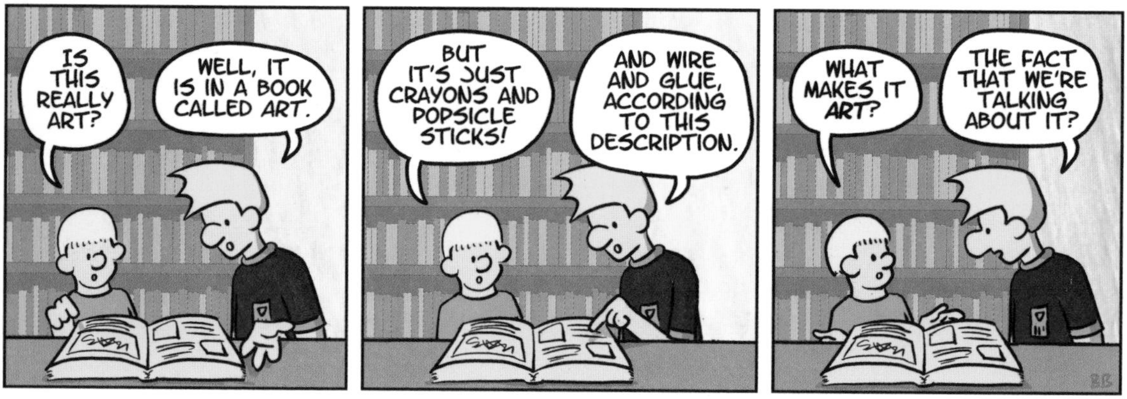
IS THIS REALLY ART?
WELL, IT IS IN A BOOK CALLED *ART*.
BUT IT'S JUST CRAYONS AND POPSICLE STICKS!
AND WIRE AND GLUE, ACCORDING TO THIS DESCRIPTION.
WHAT MAKES IT ***ART***?
THE FACT THAT WE'RE TALKING ABOUT IT?

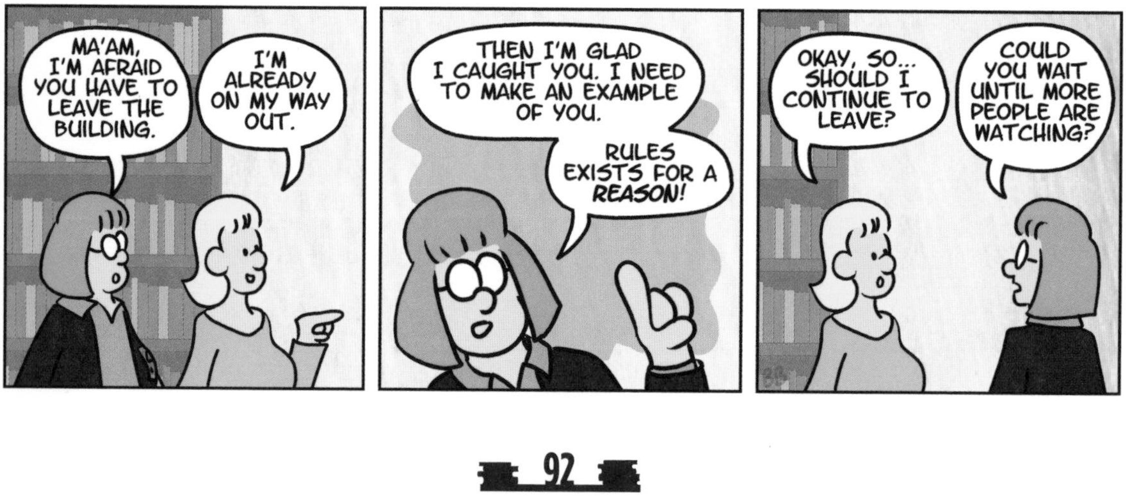
MA'AM, I'M AFRAID YOU HAVE TO LEAVE THE BUILDING.
I'M ALREADY ON MY WAY OUT.
THEN I'M GLAD I CAUGHT YOU. I NEED TO MAKE AN EXAMPLE OF YOU.
RULES EXISTS FOR A ***REASON***!
OKAY, SO... SHOULD I CONTINUE TO LEAVE?
COULD YOU WAIT UNTIL MORE PEOPLE ARE WATCHING?

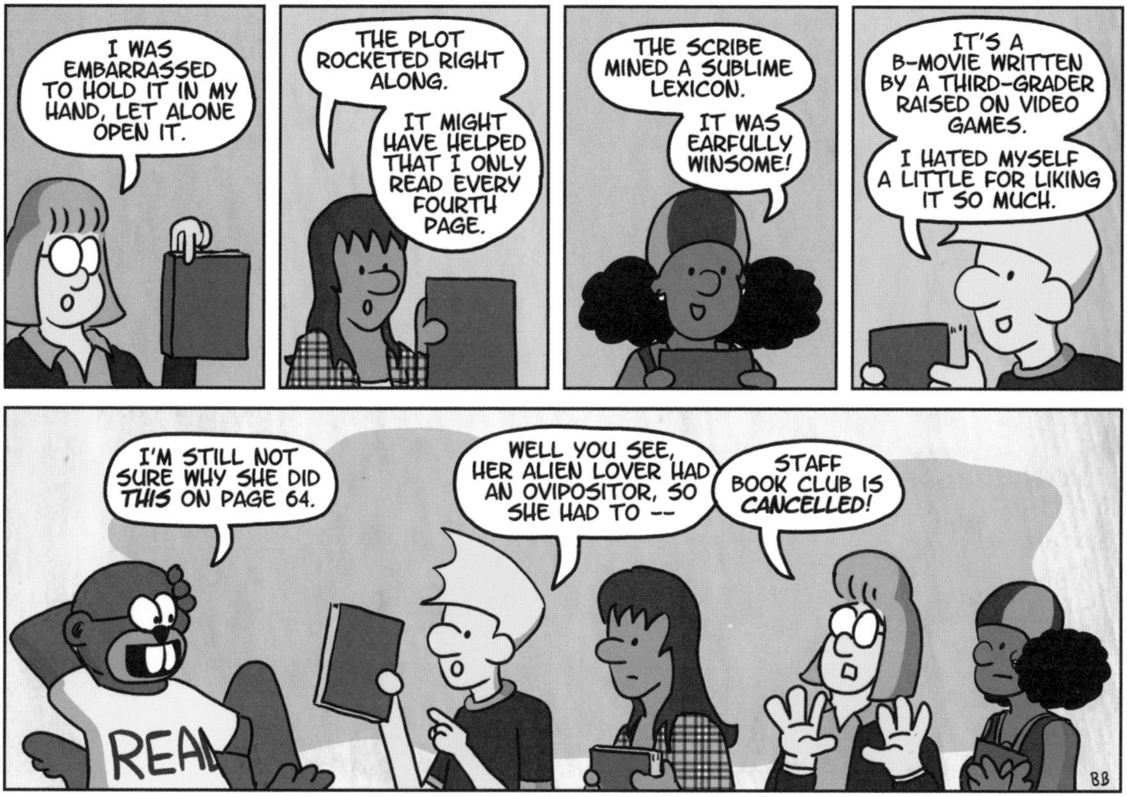
I WAS EMBARRASSED TO HOLD IT IN MY HAND, LET ALONE OPEN IT.
THE PLOT ROCKETED RIGHT ALONG.
IT MIGHT HAVE HELPED THAT I ONLY READ EVERY FOURTH PAGE.
THE SCRIBE MINED A SUBLIME LEXICON.
IT WAS EARFULLY WINSOME!
IT'S A B-MOVIE WRITTEN BY A THIRD-GRADER RAISED ON VIDEO GAMES.
I HATED MYSELF A LITTLE FOR LIKING IT SO MUCH.
I'M STILL NOT SURE WHY SHE DID THIS ON PAGE 64.
WELL YOU SEE, HER ALIEN LOVER HAD AN OVIPOSITOR, SO SHE HAD TO --
STAFF BOOK CLUB IS CANCELLED!
REAL
BB

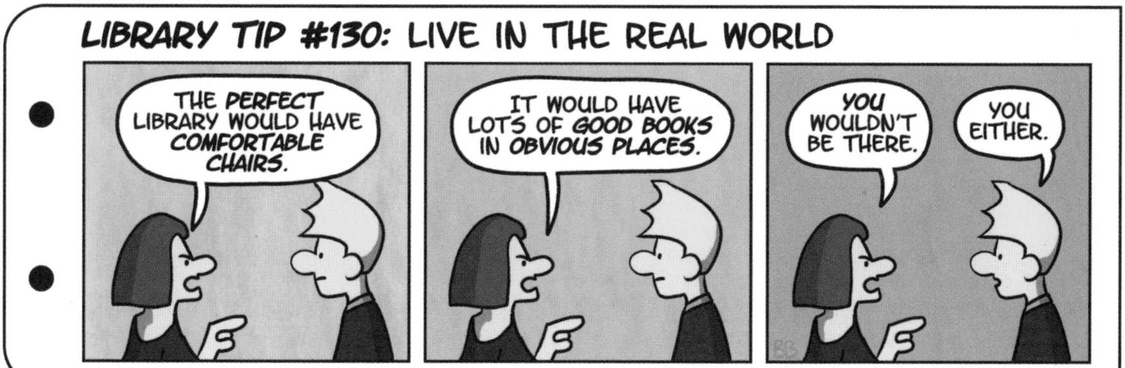
LIBRARY TIP #130: LIVE IN THE REAL WORLD
THE PERFECT LIBRARY WOULD HAVE COMFORTABLE CHAIRS.
IT WOULD HAVE LOTS OF GOOD BOOKS IN OBVIOUS PLACES.
YOU WOULDN'T BE THERE.
YOU EITHER.
BB

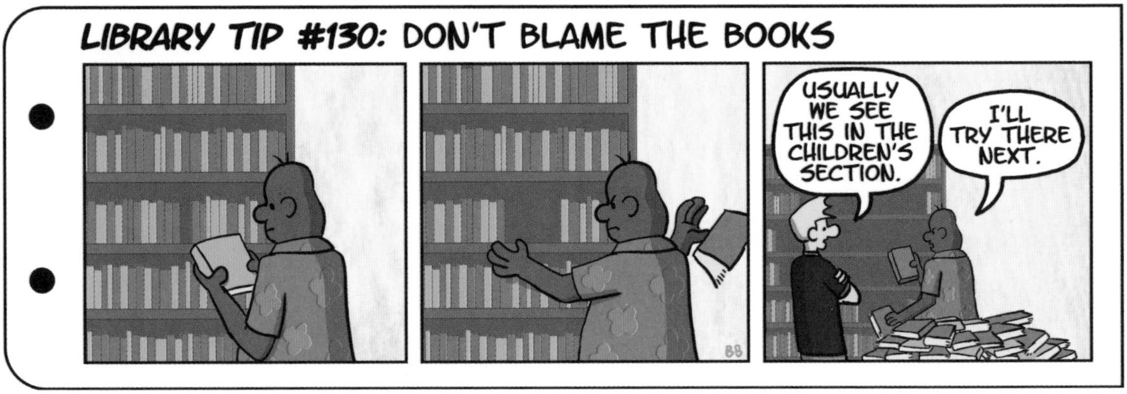
LIBRARY TIP #130: DON'T BLAME THE BOOKS
USUALLY WE SEE THIS IN THE CHILDREN'S SECTION.
I'LL TRY THERE NEXT.

This is Desmond, from Bill's other comic strip *Not Invented Here*, guest starring as part of an epic crossover between the two strips, which began at **http://j.mp/epiccrossover**

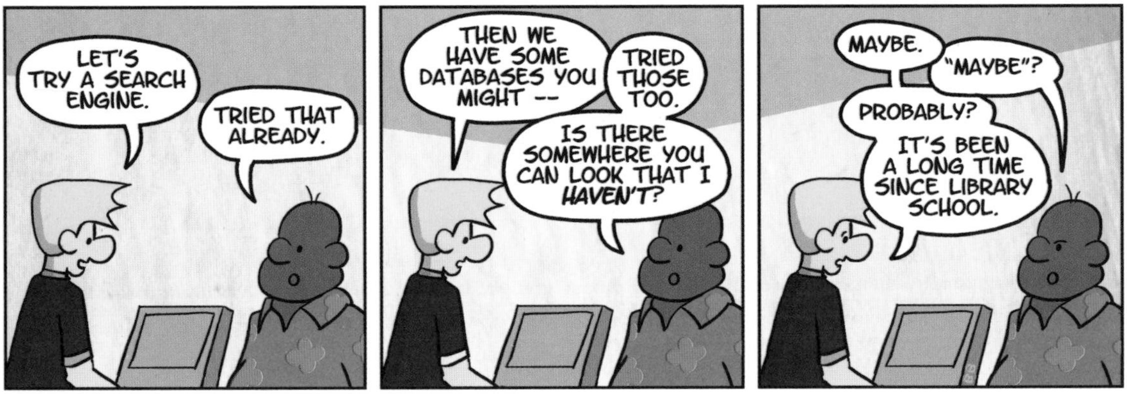
LET'S TRY A SEARCH ENGINE.
TRIED THAT ALREADY.
THEN WE HAVE SOME DATABASES YOU MIGHT --
TRIED THOSE TOO.
IS THERE SOMEWHERE YOU CAN LOOK THAT I *HAVEN'T*?
MAYBE.
"MAYBE"?
PROBABLY?
IT'S BEEN A LONG TIME SINCE LIBRARY SCHOOL.

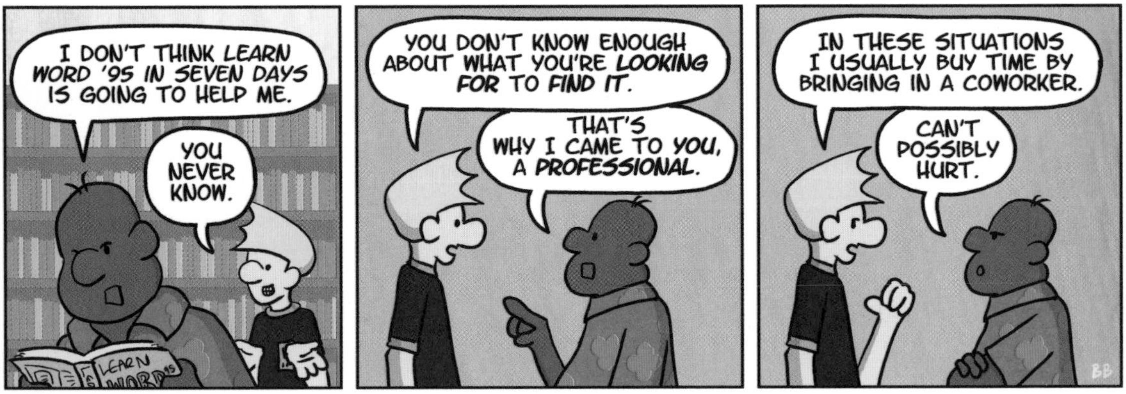
I DON'T THINK *LEARN WORD '95 IN SEVEN DAYS* IS GOING TO HELP ME.
YOU NEVER KNOW.
YOU DON'T KNOW ENOUGH ABOUT WHAT YOU'RE *LOOKING FOR* TO *FIND IT*.
THAT'S WHY I CAME TO *YOU*, A *PROFESSIONAL*.
IN THESE SITUATIONS I USUALLY BUY TIME BY BRINGING IN A COWORKER.
CAN'T POSSIBLY HURT.

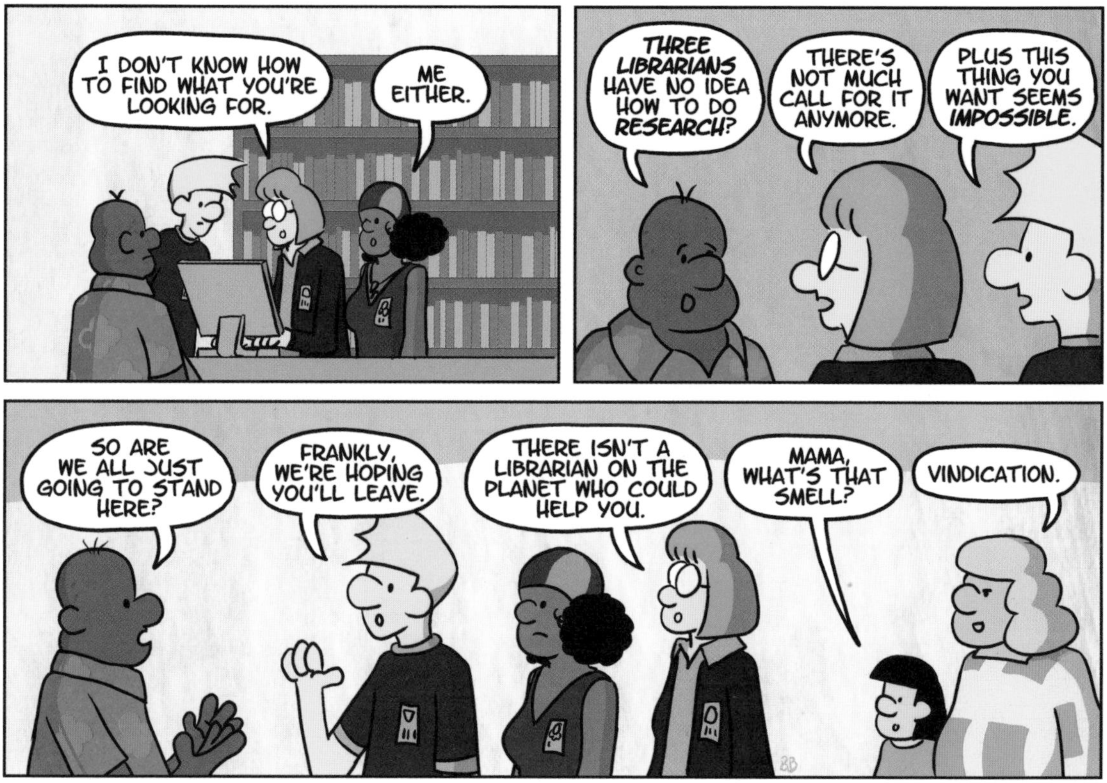
I DON'T KNOW HOW TO FIND WHAT YOU'RE LOOKING FOR.
ME EITHER.
THREE LIBRARIANS HAVE NO IDEA HOW TO DO RESEARCH?
THERE'S NOT MUCH CALL FOR IT ANYMORE.
PLUS THIS THING YOU WANT SEEMS IMPOSSIBLE.
SO ARE WE ALL JUST GOING TO STAND HERE?
FRANKLY, WE'RE HOPING YOU'LL LEAVE.
THERE ISN'T A LIBRARIAN ON THE PLANET WHO COULD HELP YOU.
MAMA, WHAT'S THAT SMELL?
VINDICATION.
BB

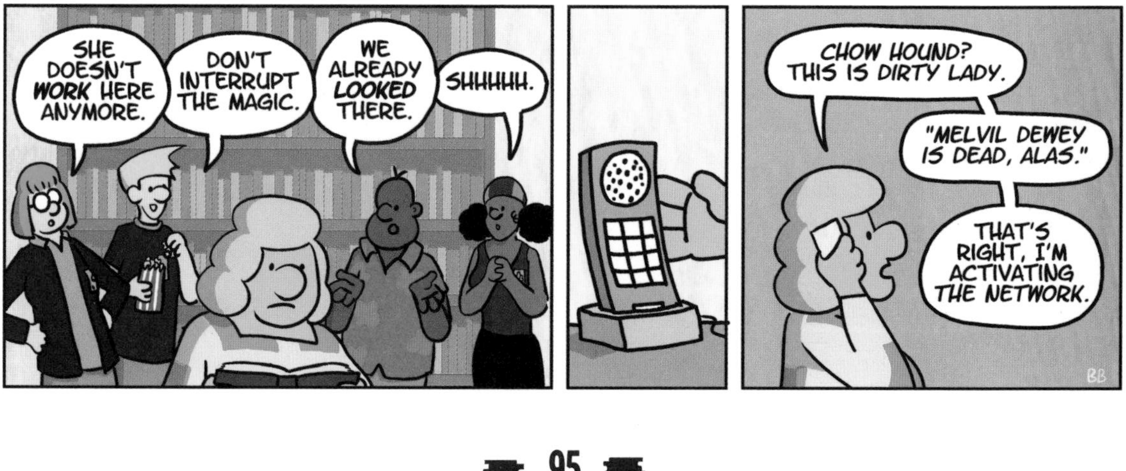
SHE DOESN'T WORK HERE ANYMORE.
DON'T INTERRUPT THE MAGIC.
WE ALREADY LOOKED THERE.
SHHHHH.
CHOW HOUND? THIS IS DIRTY LADY.
"MELVIL DEWEY IS DEAD, ALAS."
THAT'S RIGHT, I'M ACTIVATING THE NETWORK.
BB

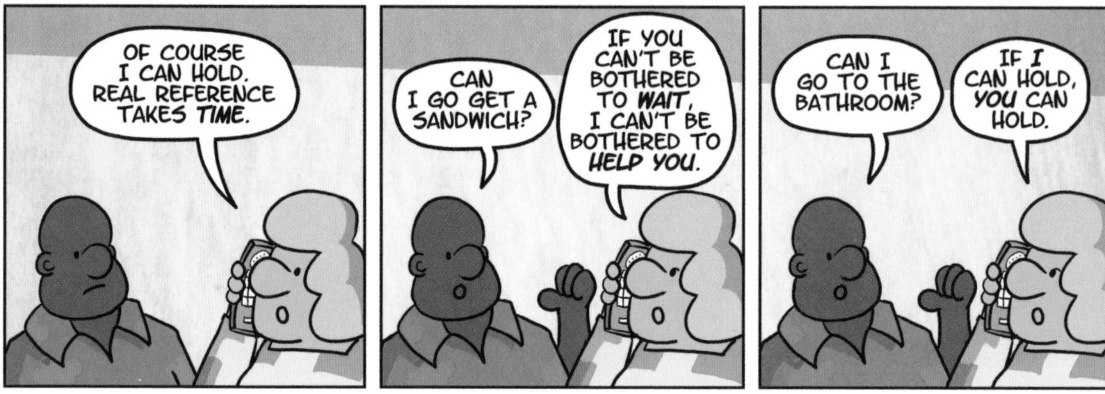
OF COURSE I CAN HOLD. REAL REFERENCE TAKES *TIME*.
CAN I GO GET A SANDWICH?
IF YOU CAN'T BE BOTHERED TO *WAIT*, I CAN'T BE BOTHERED TO *HELP YOU*.
CAN I GO TO THE BATHROOM?
IF *I* CAN HOLD, *YOU* CAN HOLD.

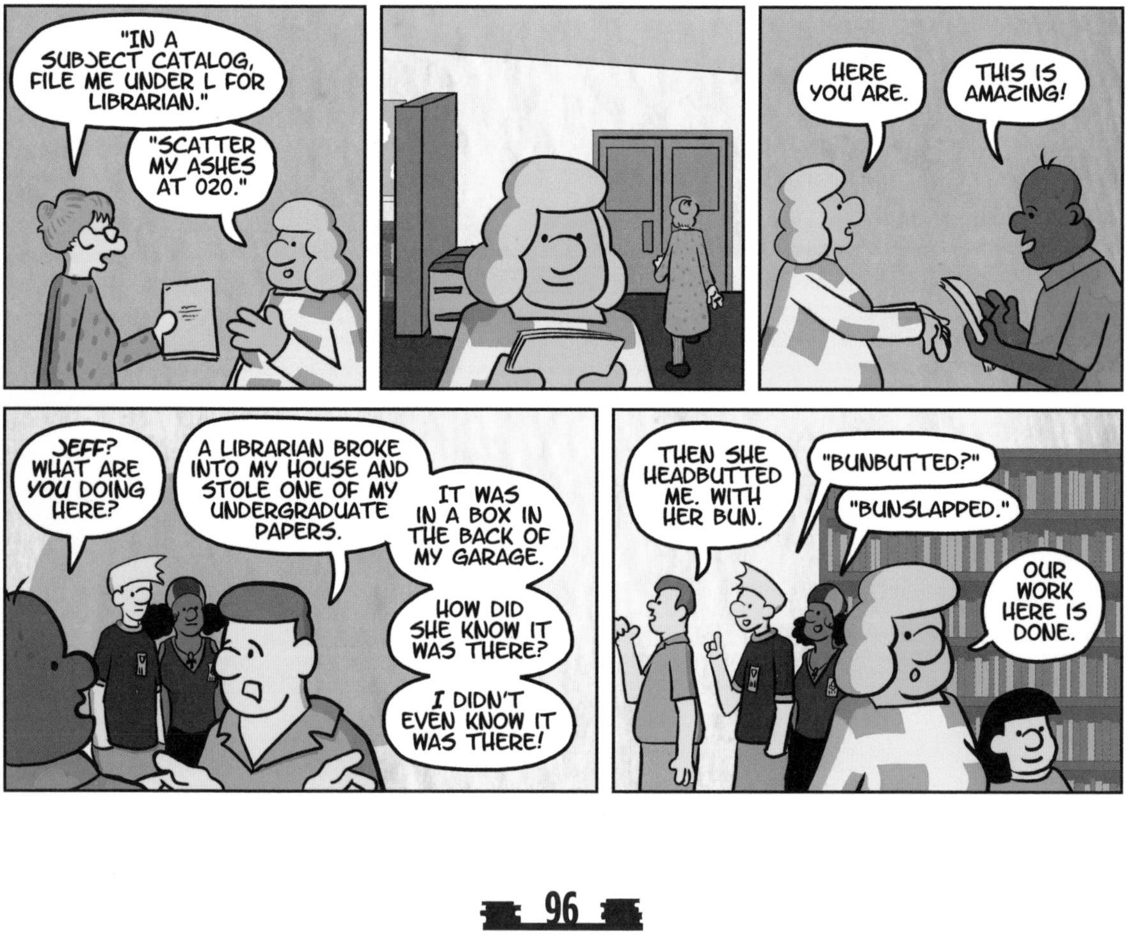
"IN A SUBJECT CATALOG, FILE ME UNDER L FOR LIBRARIAN."
"SCATTER MY ASHES AT 020."
HERE YOU ARE.
THIS IS AMAZING!
JEFF? WHAT ARE *YOU* DOING HERE?
A LIBRARIAN BROKE INTO MY HOUSE AND STOLE ONE OF MY UNDERGRADUATE PAPERS.
IT WAS IN A BOX IN THE BACK OF MY GARAGE.
HOW DID SHE KNOW IT WAS THERE?
I DIDN'T EVEN KNOW IT WAS THERE!
THEN SHE HEADBUTTED ME. WITH HER BUN.
"BUNBUTTED?"
"BUNSLAPPED."
OUR WORK HERE IS DONE.

Reads Well With Others

LIBRARY TIP #131: SILENCE IS GOLDEN

WE CAN'T ALLOW THIS TO GO ON.

AS LONG AS THEY'RE COMPLETELY QUIET, THEY'RE IN COMPLIANCE WITH POLICY.

I JUST RECOMMENDED A BOOK TO THAT GUY. HE'S *TOTALLY PSYCHED* TO READ IT.

YOU MUST HAVE *LOVED* IT!

NO, I *HATED* IT! BUT *HE'S* GOING TO LOVE IT.

YOU PRACTICED *EMPATHY!*

I DID! I PUT MYSELF IN HIS SHOES...

I'M SO *PROUD* OF YOU!

... HIS DUMB, UGLY SHOES.

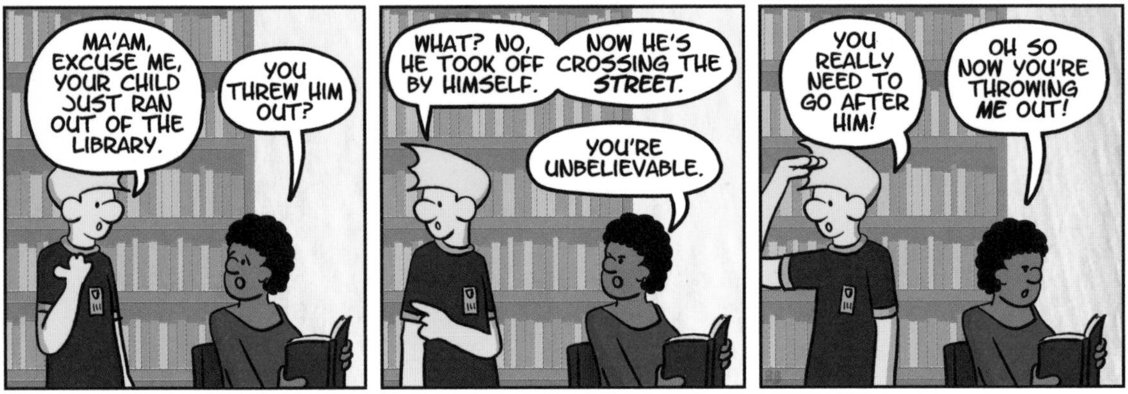
MA'AM, EXCUSE ME, YOUR CHILD JUST RAN OUT OF THE LIBRARY.
YOU THREW HIM OUT?
WHAT? NO, HE TOOK OFF BY HIMSELF.
NOW HE'S CROSSING THE **STREET**.
YOU'RE UNBELIEVABLE.
YOU REALLY NEED TO GO AFTER HIM!
OH SO NOW YOU'RE THROWING **ME** OUT!

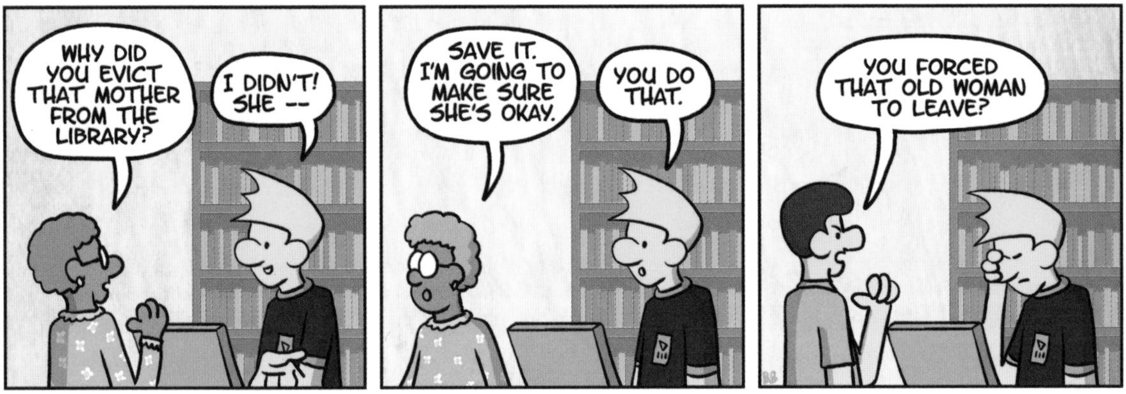
WHY DID YOU EVICT THAT MOTHER FROM THE LIBRARY?
I DIDN'T! SHE --
SAVE IT. I'M GOING TO MAKE SURE SHE'S OKAY.
YOU DO THAT.
YOU FORCED THAT OLD WOMAN TO LEAVE?

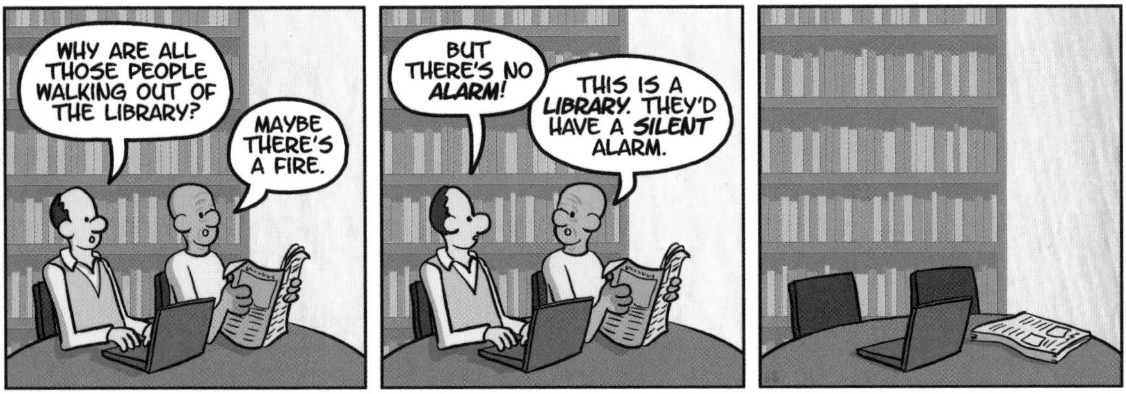
WHY ARE ALL THOSE PEOPLE WALKING OUT OF THE LIBRARY?
MAYBE THERE'S A FIRE.
BUT THERE'S NO **ALARM**!
THIS IS A **LIBRARY**. THEY'D HAVE A **SILENT** ALARM.

Reads Well With Others

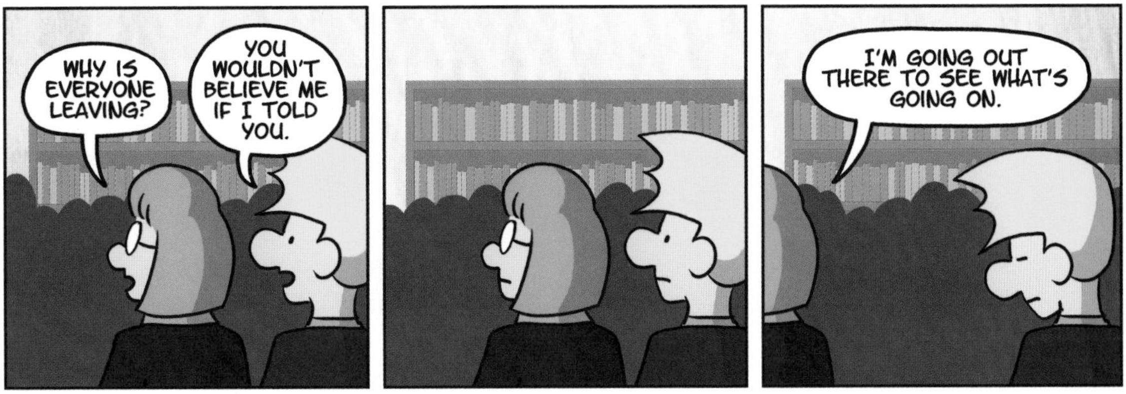
WHY IS EVERYONE LEAVING?
YOU WOULDN'T BELIEVE ME IF I TOLD YOU.
I'M GOING OUT THERE TO SEE WHAT'S GOING ON.

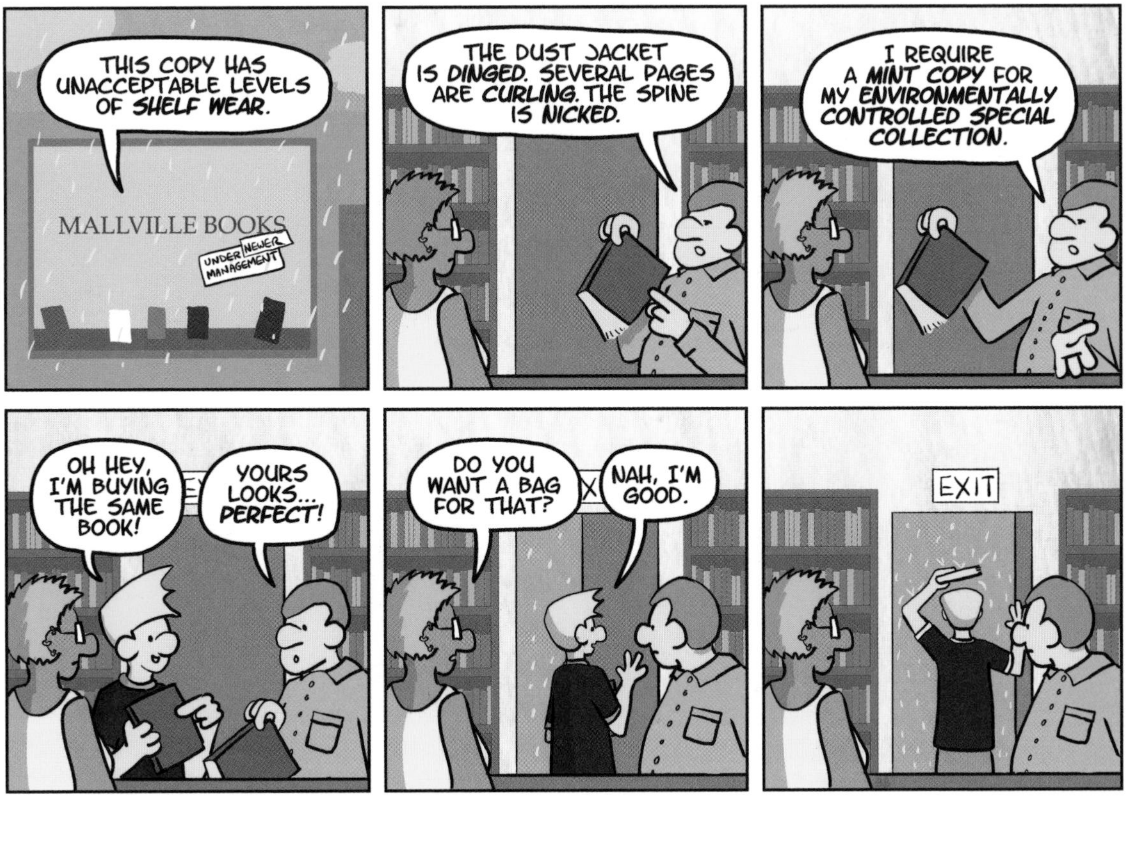
THIS COPY HAS UNACCEPTABLE LEVELS OF SHELF WEAR.
MALLVILLE BOOKS
UNDER NEWER MANAGEMENT
THE DUST JACKET IS DINGED. SEVERAL PAGES ARE CURLING. THE SPINE IS NICKED.
I REQUIRE A MINT COPY FOR MY ENVIRONMENTALLY CONTROLLED SPECIAL COLLECTION.
OH HEY, I'M BUYING THE SAME BOOK!
YOURS LOOKS... PERFECT!
DO YOU WANT A BAG FOR THAT?
NAH, I'M GOOD.
EXIT

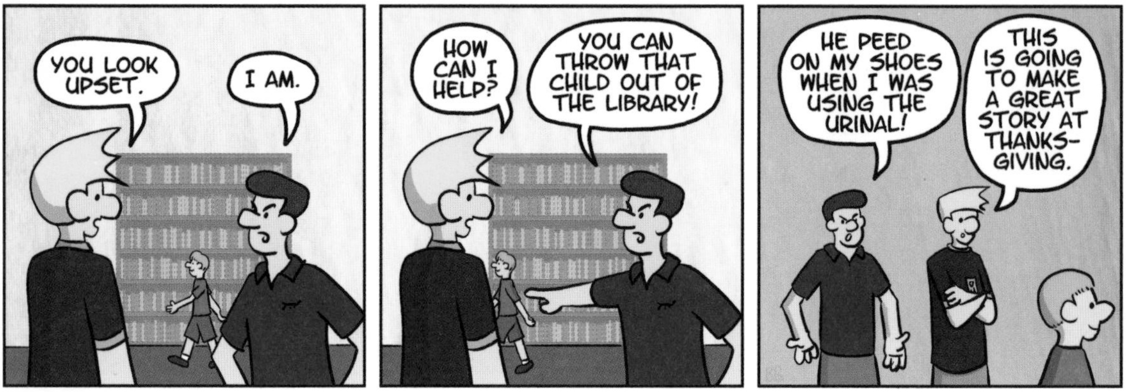
YOU LOOK UPSET.
I AM.
HOW CAN I HELP?
YOU CAN THROW THAT CHILD OUT OF THE LIBRARY!
HE PEED ON MY SHOES WHEN I WAS USING THE URINAL!
THIS IS GOING TO MAKE A GREAT STORY AT THANKS-GIVING.

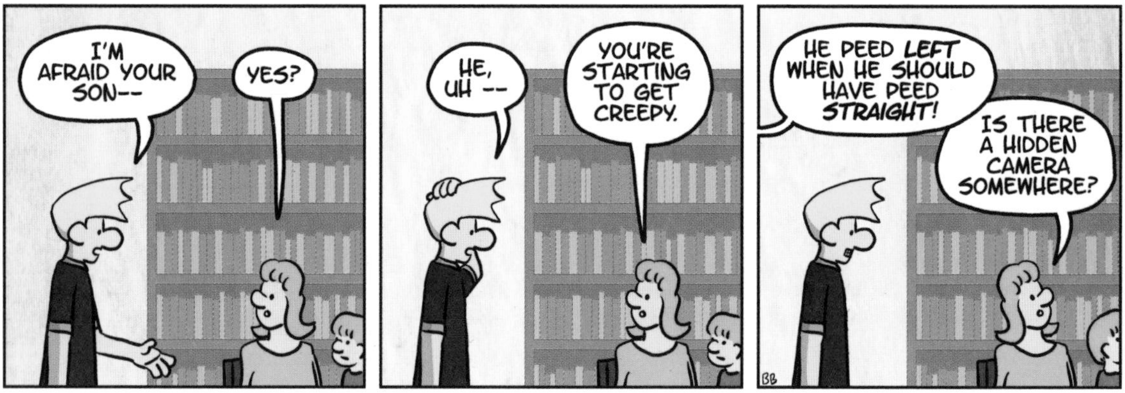
I'M AFRAID YOUR SON--
YES?
HE, UH --
YOU'RE STARTING TO GET CREEPY.
HE PEED **LEFT** WHEN HE SHOULD HAVE PEED ***STRAIGHT***!
IS THERE A HIDDEN CAMERA SOMEWHERE?
BB

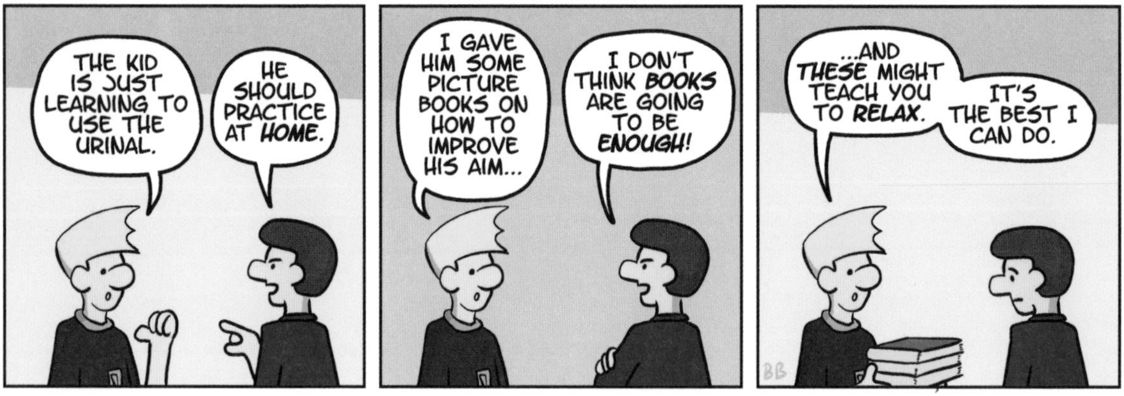
THE KID IS JUST LEARNING TO USE THE URINAL.
HE SHOULD PRACTICE AT ***HOME***.
I GAVE HIM SOME PICTURE BOOKS ON HOW TO IMPROVE HIS AIM...
I DON'T THINK ***BOOKS*** ARE GOING TO BE ***ENOUGH***!
...AND ***THESE*** MIGHT TEACH YOU TO ***RELAX***.
IT'S THE BEST I CAN DO.
BB

Reads Well With Others

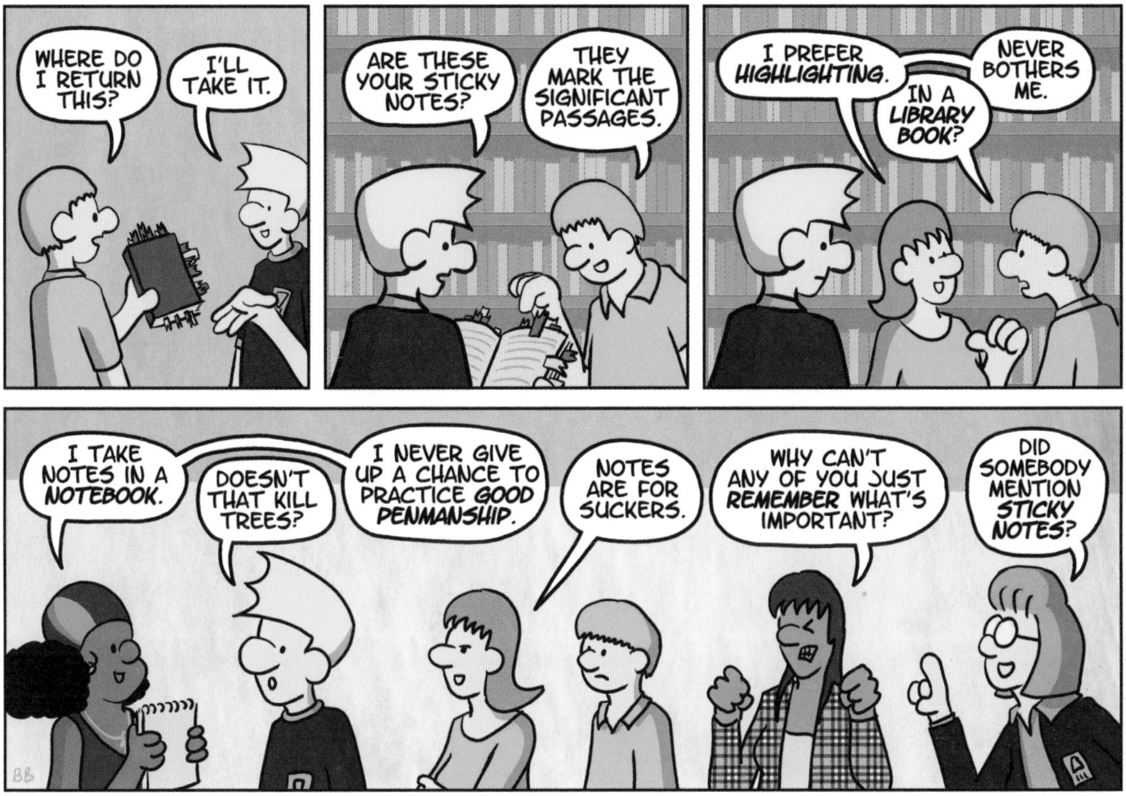
WHERE DO I RETURN THIS?
I'LL TAKE IT.
ARE THESE YOUR STICKY NOTES?
THEY MARK THE SIGNIFICANT PASSAGES.
I PREFER HIGHLIGHTING.
IN A LIBRARY BOOK?
NEVER BOTHERS ME.
I TAKE NOTES IN A NOTEBOOK.
DOESN'T THAT KILL TREES?
I NEVER GIVE UP A CHANCE TO PRACTICE GOOD PENMANSHIP.
NOTES ARE FOR SUCKERS.
WHY CAN'T ANY OF YOU JUST REMEMBER WHAT'S IMPORTANT?
DID SOMEBODY MENTION STICKY NOTES?
BB

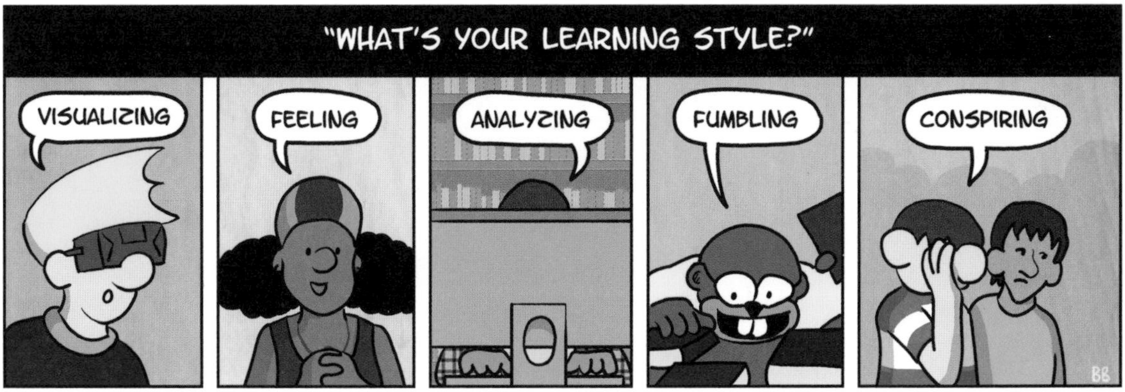
"WHAT'S YOUR LEARNING STYLE?"
VISUALIZING
FEELING
ANALYZING
FUMBLING
CONSPIRING
BB

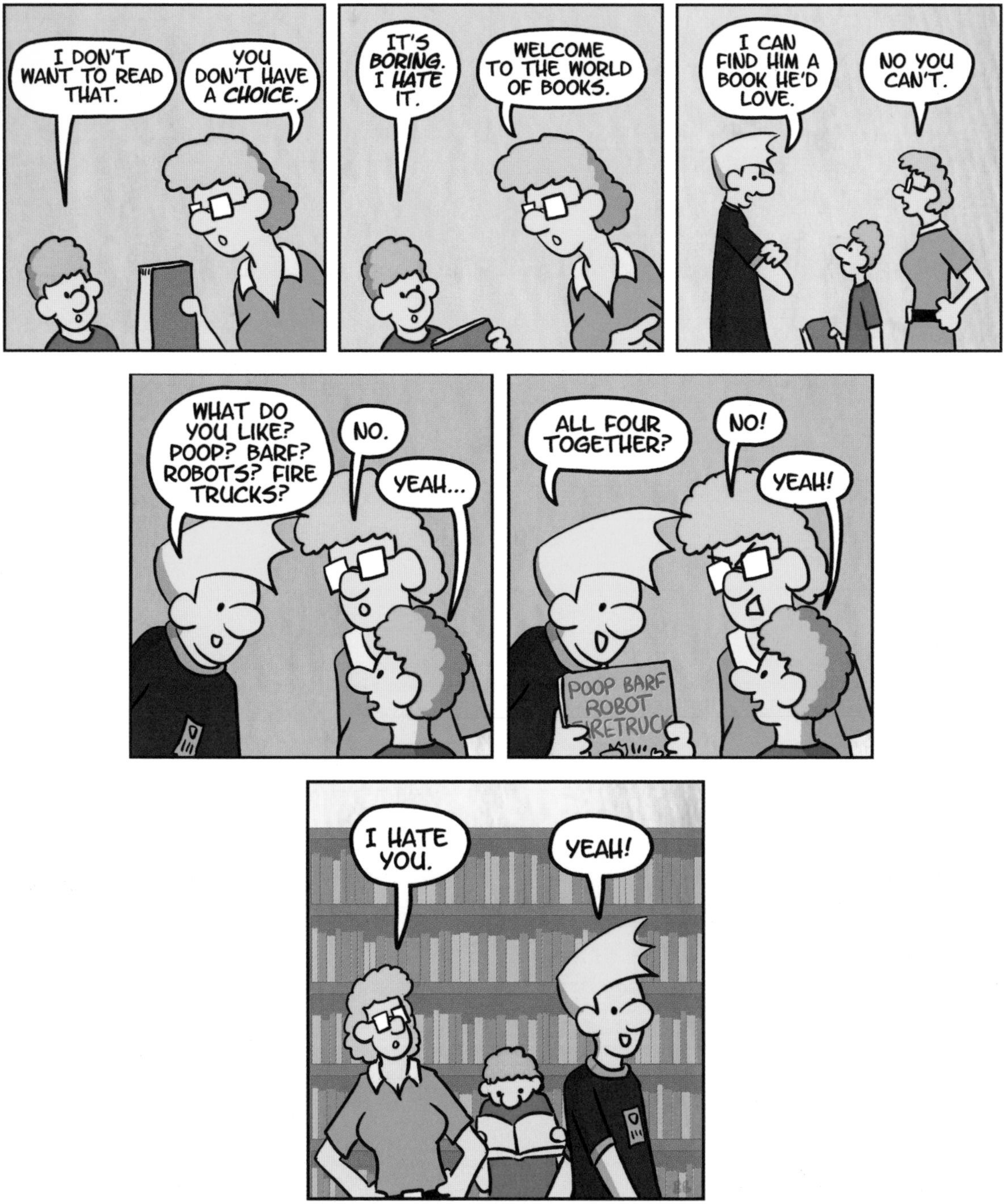

I DON'T WANT TO READ THAT.
YOU DON'T HAVE A *CHOICE*.
IT'S *BORING*. I *HATE* IT.
WELCOME TO THE WORLD OF BOOKS.
I CAN FIND HIM A BOOK HE'D LOVE.
NO YOU CAN'T.
WHAT DO YOU LIKE? POOP? BARF? ROBOTS? FIRE TRUCKS?
NO.
YEAH...
ALL FOUR TOGETHER?
NO!
YEAH!
POOP BARF ROBOT
I HATE YOU.
YEAH!

Reads Well With Others

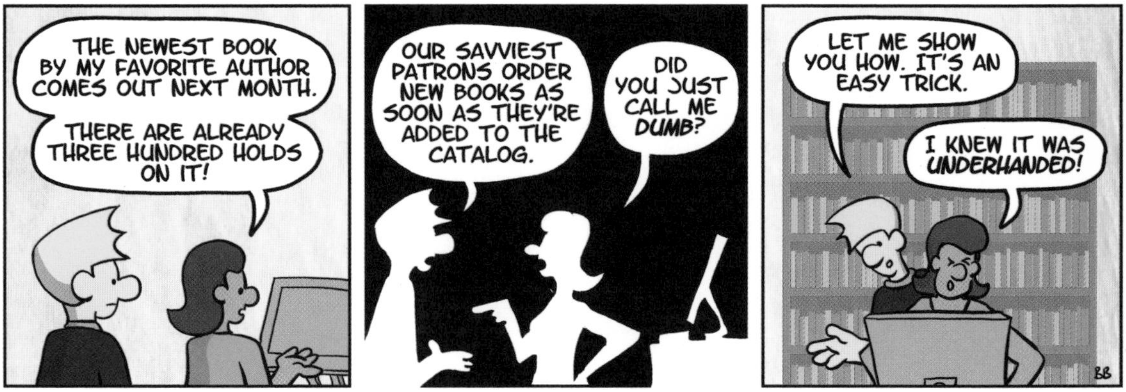
THE NEWEST BOOK BY MY FAVORITE AUTHOR COMES OUT NEXT MONTH.
THERE ARE ALREADY THREE HUNDRED HOLDS ON IT!
OUR SAVVIEST PATRONS ORDER NEW BOOKS AS SOON AS THEY'RE ADDED TO THE CATALOG.
DID YOU JUST CALL ME *DUMB*?
LET ME SHOW YOU HOW. IT'S AN EASY TRICK.
I KNEW IT WAS *UNDERHANDED!*
BB

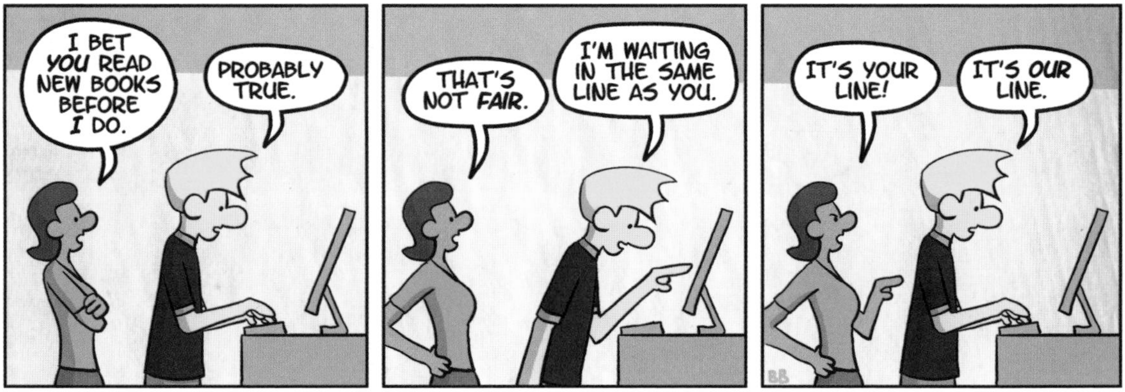
I BET *YOU* READ NEW BOOKS BEFORE *I* DO.
PROBABLY TRUE.
THAT'S NOT *FAIR.*
I'M WAITING IN THE SAME LINE AS YOU.
IT'S YOUR LINE!
IT'S *OUR* LINE.
BB

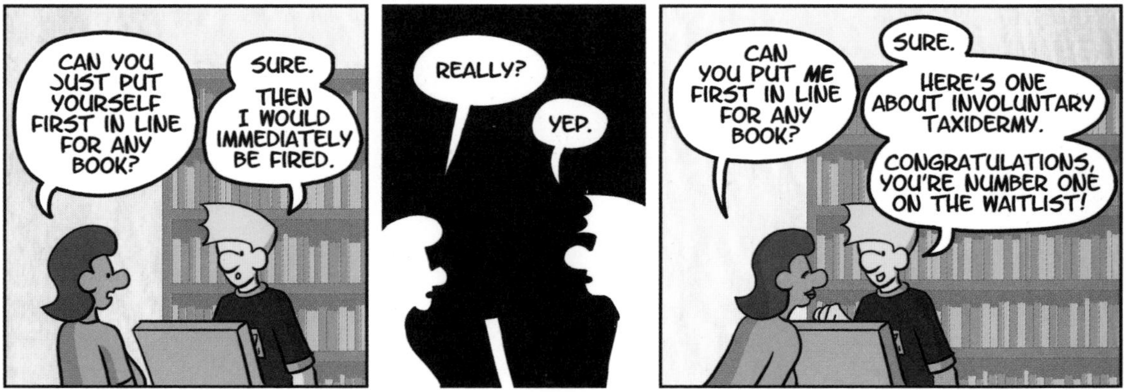
CAN YOU JUST PUT YOURSELF FIRST IN LINE FOR ANY BOOK?
SURE.
THEN I WOULD IMMEDIATELY BE FIRED.
REALLY?
YEP.
CAN YOU PUT *ME* FIRST IN LINE FOR ANY BOOK?
SURE.
HERE'S ONE ABOUT INVOLUNTARY TAXIDERMY.
CONGRATULATIONS, YOU'RE NUMBER ONE ON THE WAITLIST!

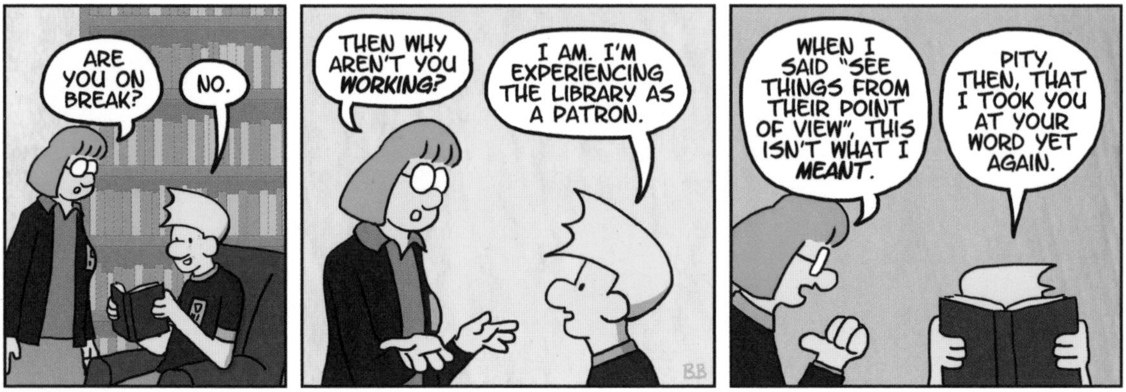
ARE YOU ON BREAK?
NO.
THEN WHY AREN'T YOU *WORKING?*
I AM. I'M EXPERIENCING THE LIBRARY AS A PATRON.
BB
WHEN I SAID "SEE THINGS FROM THEIR POINT OF VIEW", THIS ISN'T WHAT I *MEANT*.
PITY, THEN, THAT I TOOK YOU AT YOUR WORD YET AGAIN.

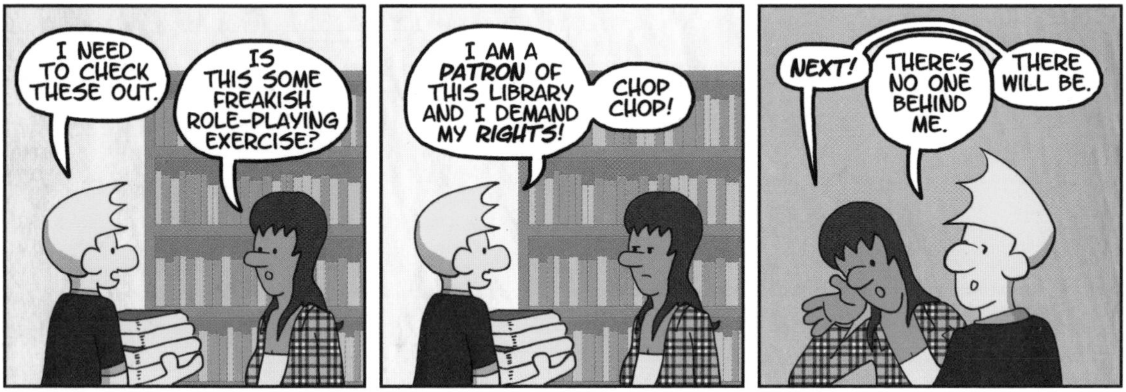
I NEED TO CHECK THESE OUT.
IS THIS SOME FREAKISH ROLE-PLAYING EXERCISE?
I AM A *PATRON* OF THIS LIBRARY AND I DEMAND MY *RIGHTS*!
CHOP CHOP!
NEXT!
THERE'S NO ONE BEHIND ME.
THERE WILL BE.

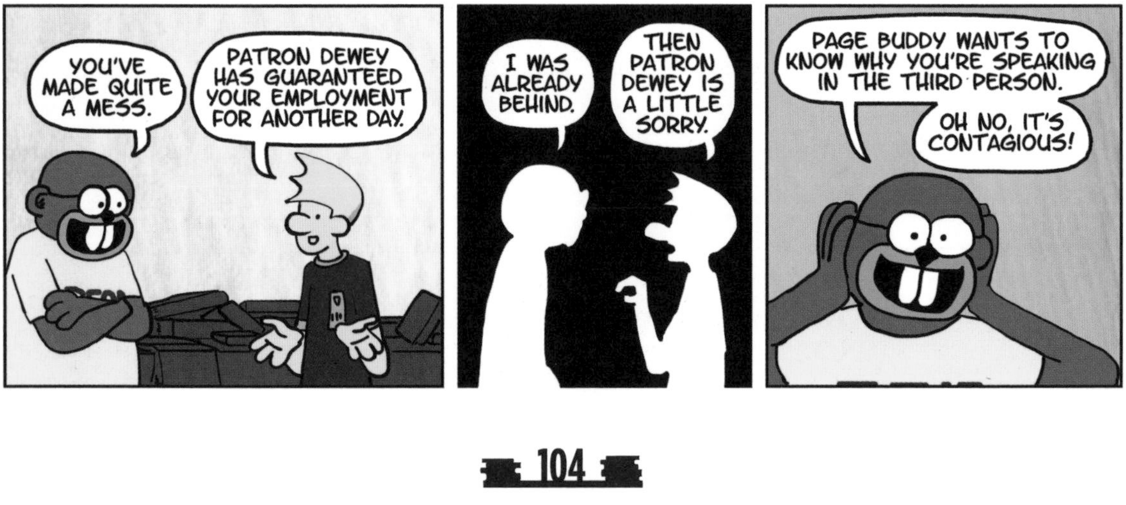
YOU'VE MADE QUITE A MESS.
PATRON DEWEY HAS GUARANTEED YOUR EMPLOYMENT FOR ANOTHER DAY.
I WAS ALREADY BEHIND.
THEN PATRON DEWEY IS A LITTLE SORRY.
PAGE BUDDY WANTS TO KNOW WHY YOU'RE SPEAKING IN THE THIRD PERSON.
OH NO, IT'S CONTAGIOUS!

Reads Well With Others

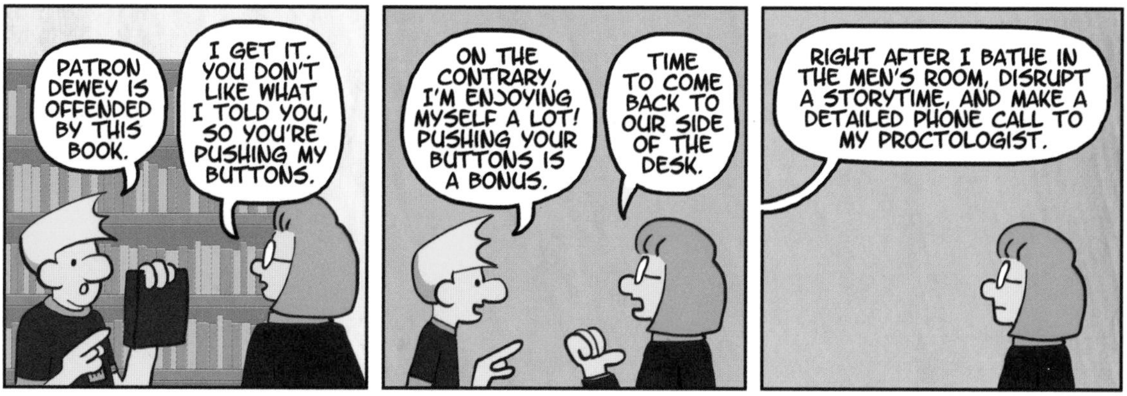
PATRON DEWEY IS OFFENDED BY THIS BOOK.
I GET IT. YOU DON'T LIKE WHAT I TOLD YOU, SO YOU'RE PUSHING MY BUTTONS.
ON THE CONTRARY, I'M ENJOYING MYSELF A LOT! PUSHING YOUR BUTTONS IS A BONUS.
TIME TO COME BACK TO OUR SIDE OF THE DESK.
RIGHT AFTER I BATHE IN THE MEN'S ROOM, DISRUPT A STORYTIME, AND MAKE A DETAILED PHONE CALL TO MY PROCTOLOGIST.

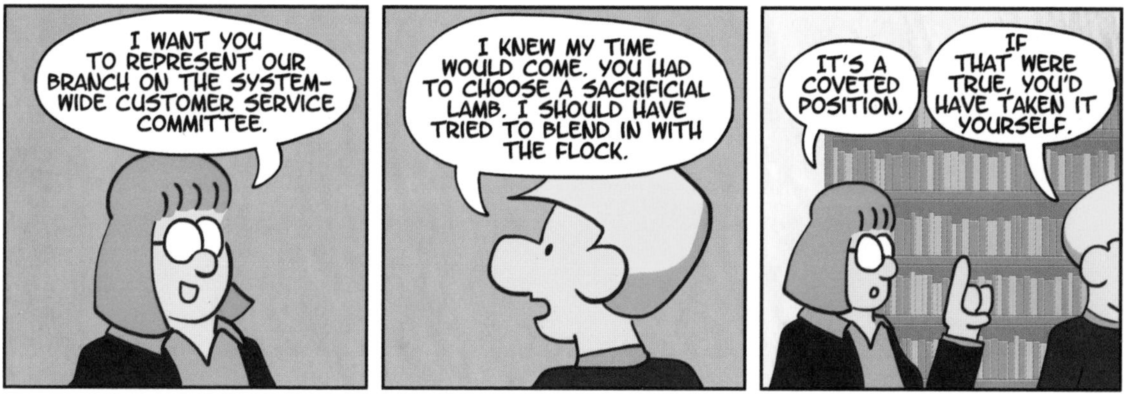
I WANT YOU TO REPRESENT OUR BRANCH ON THE SYSTEM-WIDE CUSTOMER SERVICE COMMITTEE.
I KNEW MY TIME WOULD COME. YOU HAD TO CHOOSE A SACRIFICIAL LAMB. I SHOULD HAVE TRIED TO BLEND IN WITH THE FLOCK.
IT'S A COVETED POSITION.
IF THAT WERE TRUE, YOU'D HAVE TAKEN IT YOURSELF.

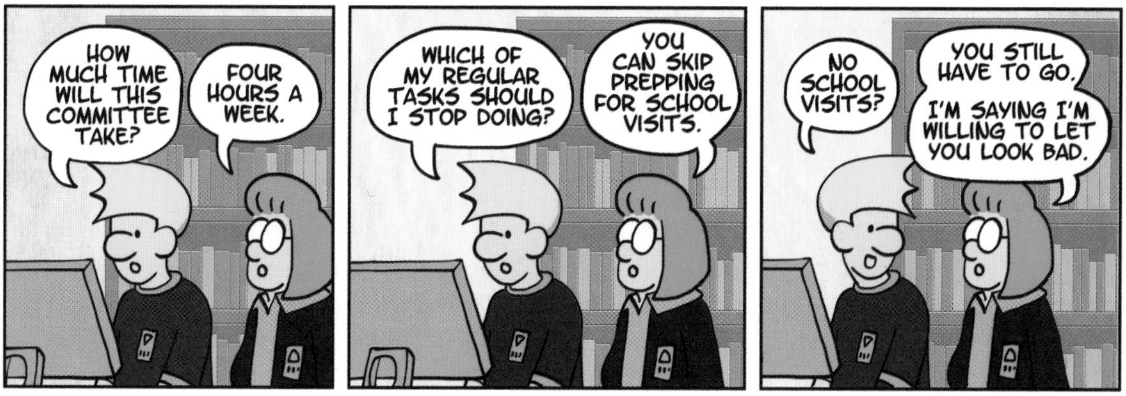
HOW MUCH TIME WILL THIS COMMITTEE TAKE?
FOUR HOURS A WEEK.
WHICH OF MY REGULAR TASKS SHOULD I STOP DOING?
YOU CAN SKIP PREPPING FOR SCHOOL VISITS.
NO SCHOOL VISITS?
YOU STILL HAVE TO GO.
I'M SAYING I'M WILLING TO LET YOU LOOK BAD.

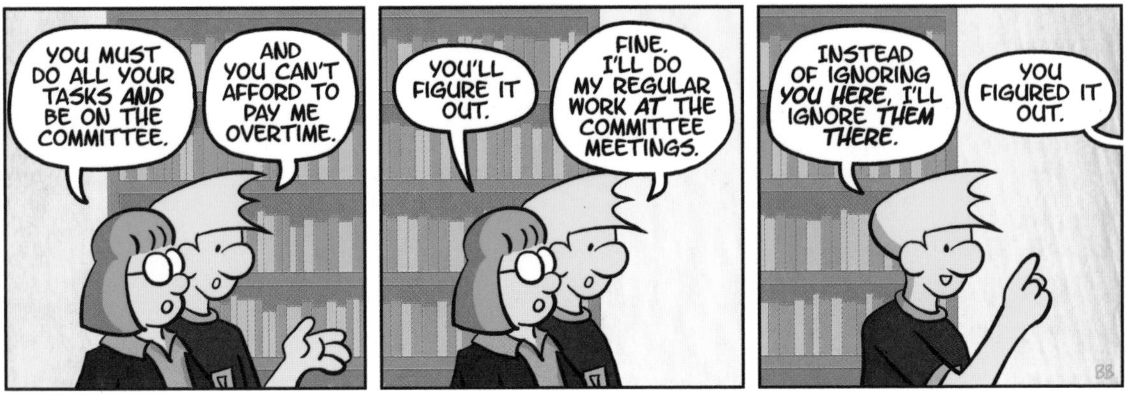
YOU MUST DO ALL YOUR TASKS AND BE ON THE COMMITTEE.
AND YOU CAN'T AFFORD TO PAY ME OVERTIME.
YOU'LL FIGURE IT OUT.
FINE. I'LL DO MY REGULAR WORK AT THE COMMITTEE MEETINGS.
INSTEAD OF IGNORING YOU HERE, I'LL IGNORE THEM THERE.
YOU FIGURED IT OUT.

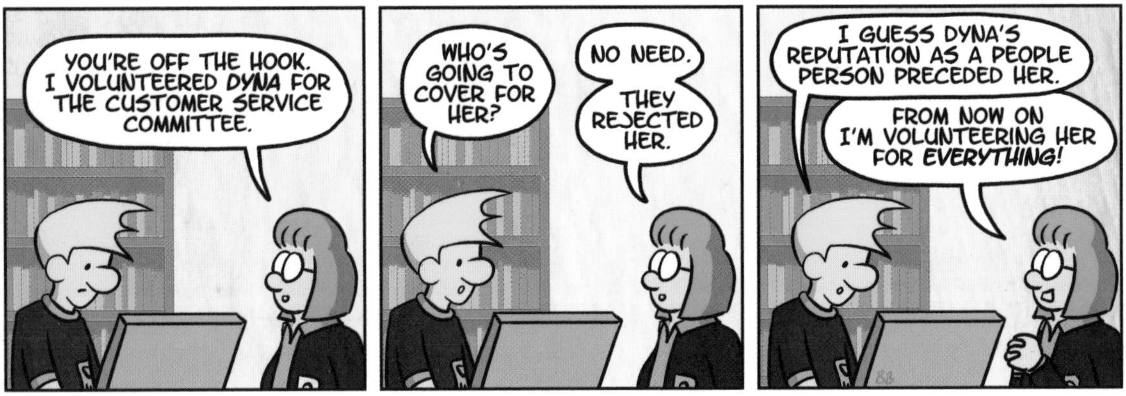
YOU'RE OFF THE HOOK. I VOLUNTEERED DYNA FOR THE CUSTOMER SERVICE COMMITTEE.
WHO'S GOING TO COVER FOR HER?
NO NEED.
THEY REJECTED HER.
I GUESS DYNA'S REPUTATION AS A PEOPLE PERSON PRECEDED HER.
FROM NOW ON I'M VOLUNTEERING HER FOR EVERYTHING!

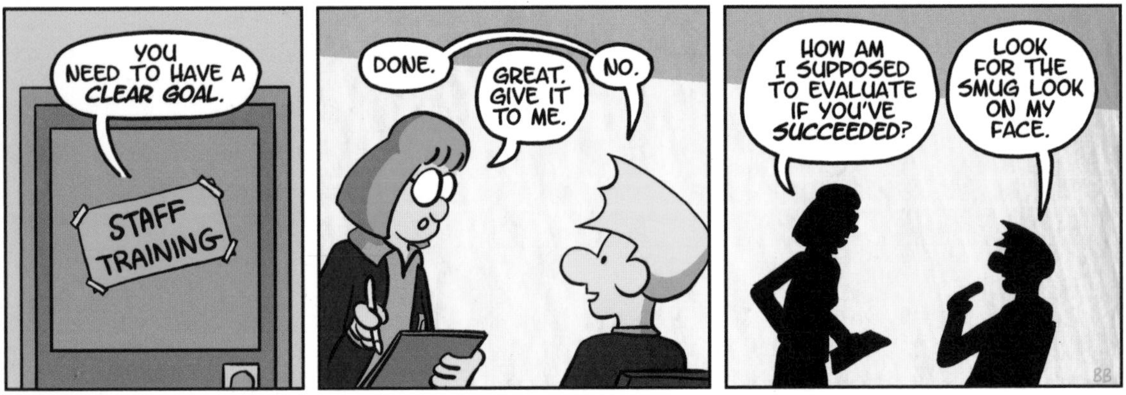
YOU NEED TO HAVE A CLEAR GOAL.
STAFF TRAINING
DONE.
GREAT. GIVE IT TO ME.
NO.
HOW AM I SUPPOSED TO EVALUATE IF YOU'VE SUCCEEDED?
LOOK FOR THE SMUG LOOK ON MY FACE.

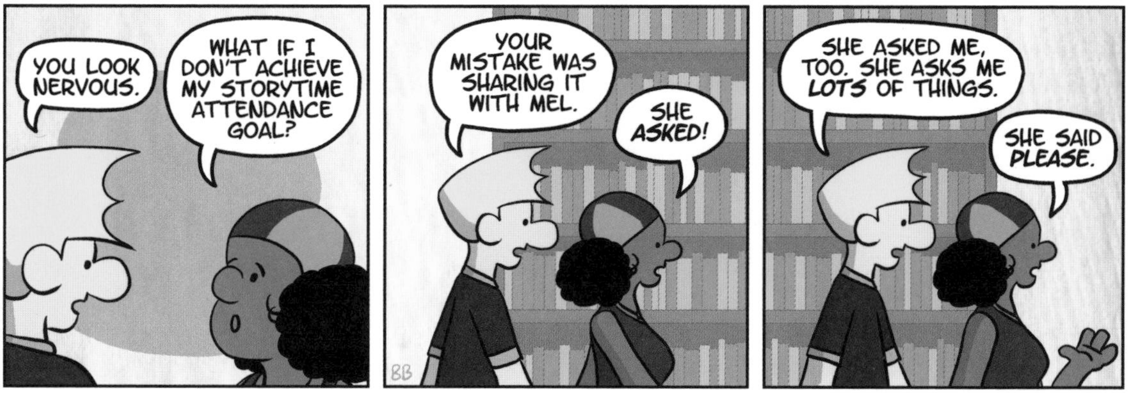
YOU LOOK NERVOUS.
WHAT IF I DON'T ACHIEVE MY STORYTIME ATTENDANCE GOAL?
YOUR MISTAKE WAS SHARING IT WITH MEL.
SHE ASKED!
SHE ASKED ME, TOO. SHE ASKS ME LOTS OF THINGS.
SHE SAID PLEASE.

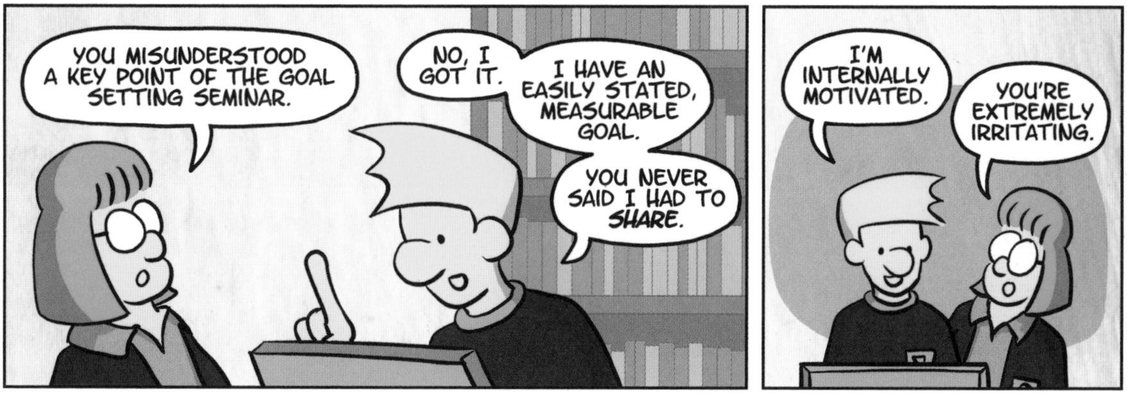
YOU MISUNDERSTOOD A KEY POINT OF THE GOAL SETTING SEMINAR.
NO, I GOT IT.
I HAVE AN EASILY STATED, MEASURABLE GOAL.
YOU NEVER SAID I HAD TO SHARE.
I'M INTERNALLY MOTIVATED.
YOU'RE EXTREMELY IRRITATING.

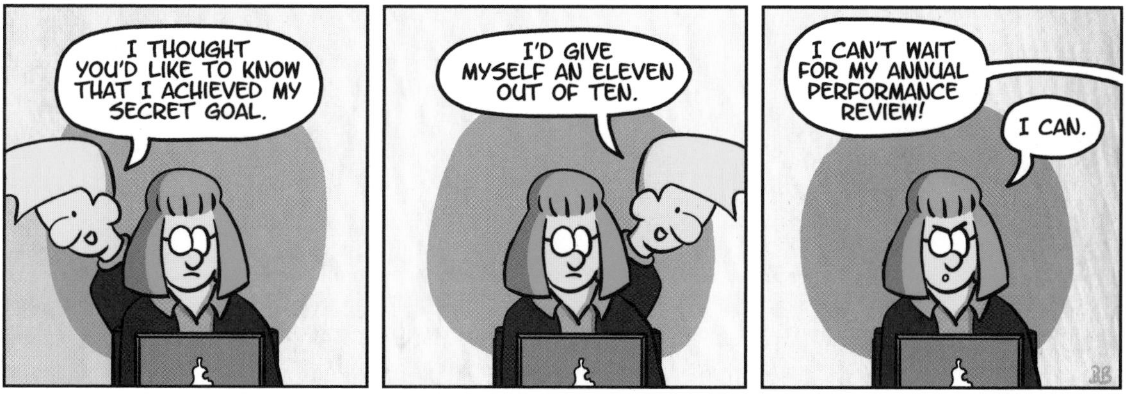
I THOUGHT YOU'D LIKE TO KNOW THAT I ACHIEVED MY SECRET GOAL.
I'D GIVE MYSELF AN ELEVEN OUT OF TEN.
I CAN'T WAIT FOR MY ANNUAL PERFORMANCE REVIEW!
I CAN.

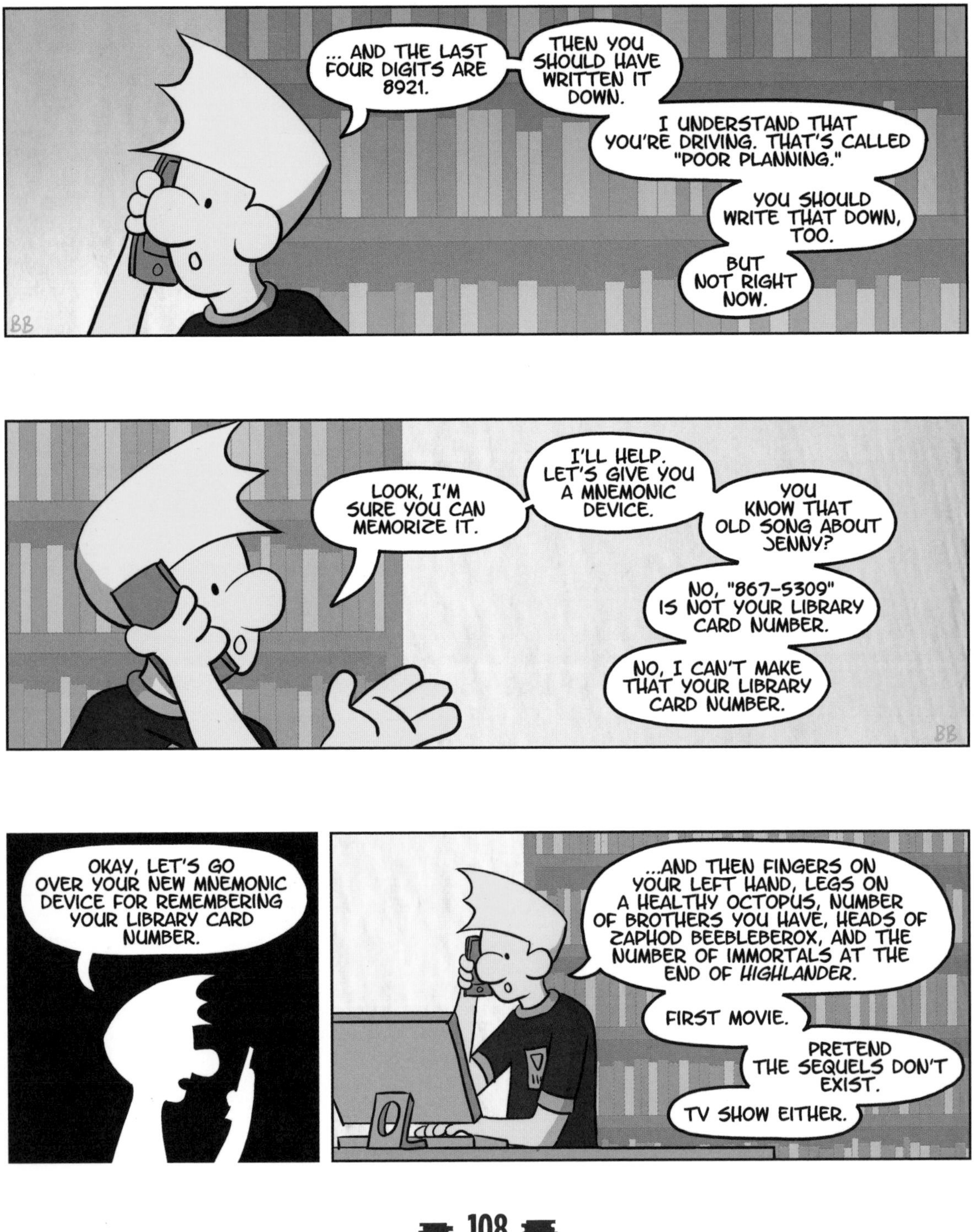
... AND THE LAST FOUR DIGITS ARE 8921.
THEN YOU SHOULD HAVE WRITTEN IT DOWN.
I UNDERSTAND THAT YOU'RE DRIVING. THAT'S CALLED "POOR PLANNING."
YOU SHOULD WRITE THAT DOWN, TOO.
BUT NOT RIGHT NOW.
BB
LOOK, I'M SURE YOU CAN MEMORIZE IT.
I'LL HELP. LET'S GIVE YOU A MNEMONIC DEVICE.
YOU KNOW THAT OLD SONG ABOUT JENNY?
NO, "867-5309" IS NOT YOUR LIBRARY CARD NUMBER.
NO, I CAN'T MAKE THAT YOUR LIBRARY CARD NUMBER.
BB
OKAY, LET'S GO OVER YOUR NEW MNEMONIC DEVICE FOR REMEMBERING YOUR LIBRARY CARD NUMBER.
...AND THEN FINGERS ON YOUR LEFT HAND, LEGS ON A HEALTHY OCTOPUS, NUMBER OF BROTHERS YOU HAVE, HEADS OF ZAPHOD BEEBLEBEROX, AND THE NUMBER OF IMMORTALS AT THE END OF *HIGHLANDER*.
FIRST MOVIE.
PRETEND THE SEQUELS DON'T EXIST.
TV SHOW EITHER.

Reads Well With Others

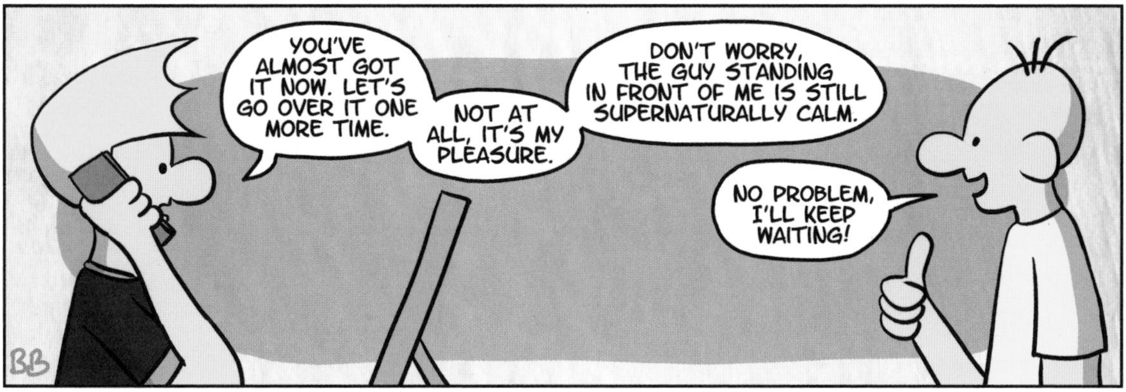
YOU'VE ALMOST GOT IT NOW. LET'S GO OVER IT ONE MORE TIME.
NOT AT ALL, IT'S MY PLEASURE.
DON'T WORRY, THE GUY STANDING IN FRONT OF ME IS STILL SUPERNATURALLY CALM.
NO PROBLEM, I'LL KEEP WAITING!
BB

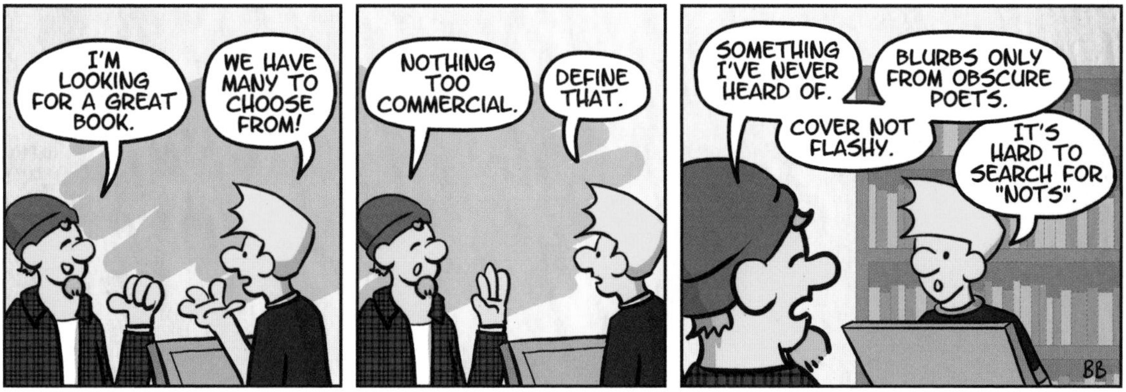
I'M LOOKING FOR A GREAT BOOK.
WE HAVE MANY TO CHOOSE FROM!
NOTHING TOO COMMERCIAL.
DEFINE THAT.
SOMETHING I'VE NEVER HEARD OF.
BLURBS ONLY FROM OBSCURE POETS.
COVER NOT FLASHY.
IT'S HARD TO SEARCH FOR "NOTS".
BB

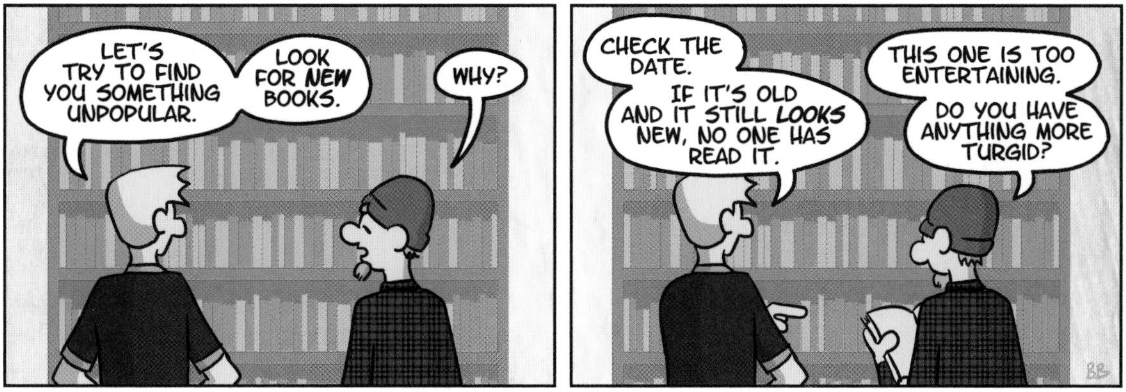
LET'S TRY TO FIND YOU SOMETHING UNPOPULAR.
LOOK FOR NEW BOOKS.
WHY?
CHECK THE DATE.
IF IT'S OLD AND IT STILL LOOKS NEW, NO ONE HAS READ IT.
THIS ONE IS TOO ENTERTAINING.
DO YOU HAVE ANYTHING MORE TURGID?
BB

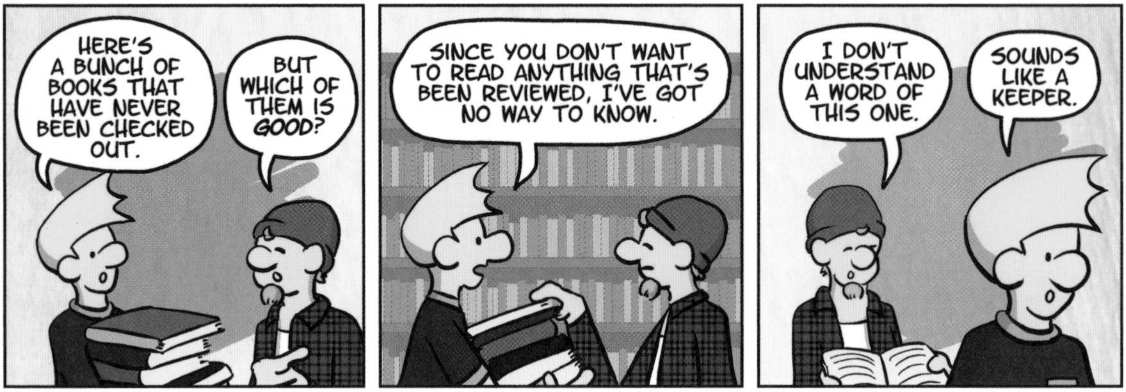
HERE'S A BUNCH OF BOOKS THAT HAVE NEVER BEEN CHECKED OUT.
BUT WHICH OF THEM IS *GOOD?*
SINCE YOU DON'T WANT TO READ ANYTHING THAT'S BEEN REVIEWED, I'VE GOT NO WAY TO KNOW.
I DON'T UNDERSTAND A WORD OF THIS ONE.
SOUNDS LIKE A KEEPER.

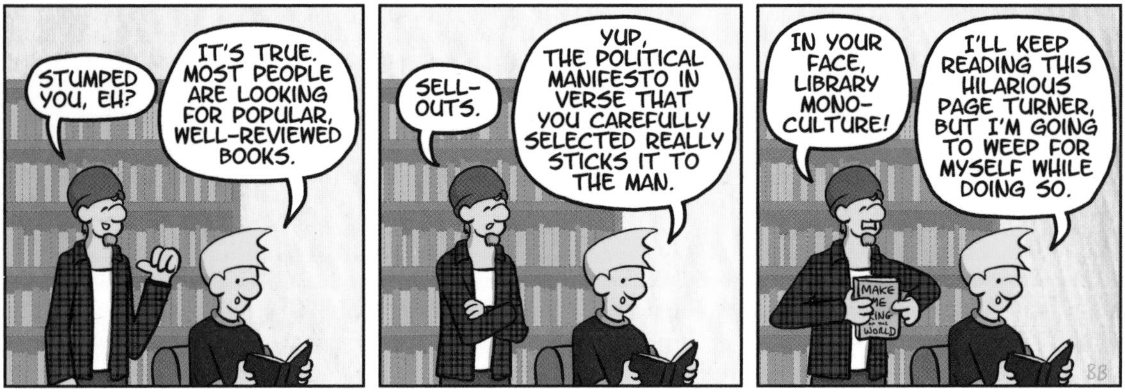
STUMPED YOU, EH?
IT'S TRUE. MOST PEOPLE ARE LOOKING FOR POPULAR, WELL-REVIEWED BOOKS.
SELL-OUTS.
YUP, THE POLITICAL MANIFESTO IN VERSE THAT YOU CAREFULLY SELECTED REALLY STICKS IT TO THE MAN.
IN YOUR FACE, LIBRARY MONO-CULTURE!
I'LL KEEP READING THIS HILARIOUS PAGE TURNER, BUT I'M GOING TO WEEP FOR MYSELF WHILE DOING SO.
BB

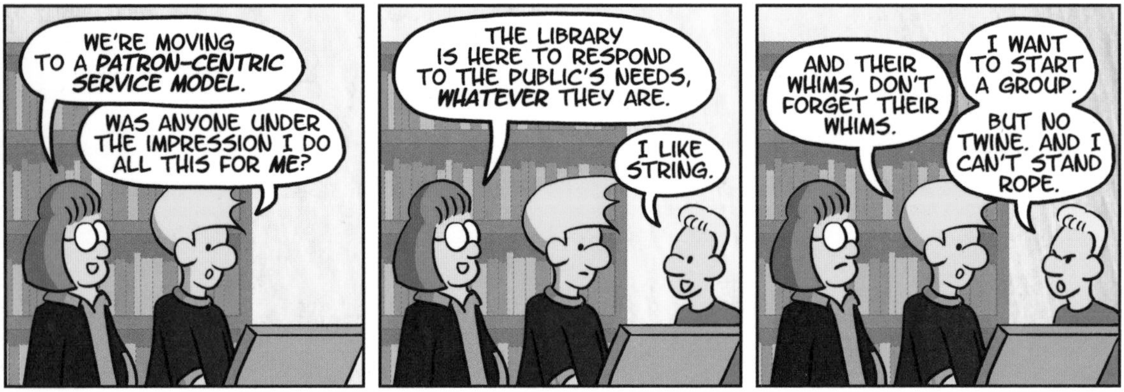
WE'RE MOVING TO A ***PATRON-CENTRIC SERVICE MODEL***.
WAS ANYONE UNDER THE IMPRESSION I DO ALL THIS FOR *ME?*
THE LIBRARY IS HERE TO RESPOND TO THE PUBLIC'S NEEDS, ***WHATEVER*** THEY ARE.
I LIKE STRING.
AND THEIR WHIMS, DON'T FORGET THEIR WHIMS.
I WANT TO START A GROUP.
BUT NO TWINE. AND I CAN'T STAND ROPE.

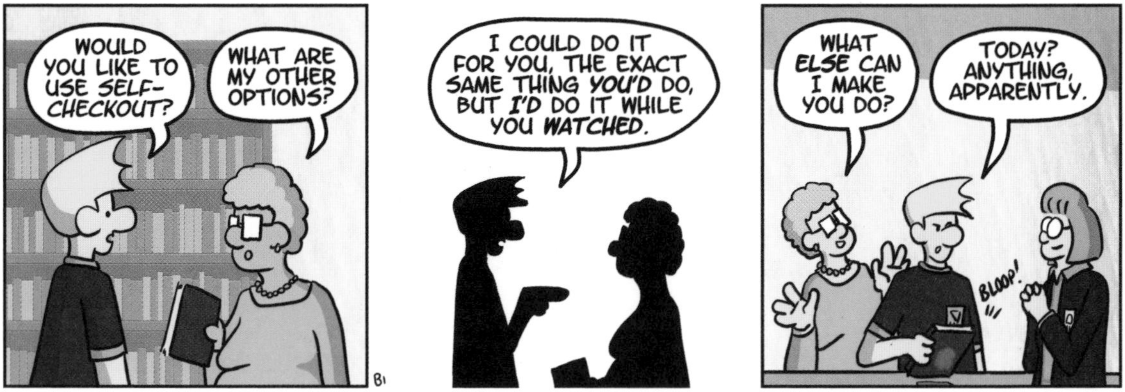
WOULD YOU LIKE TO USE SELF-CHECKOUT?
WHAT ARE MY OTHER OPTIONS?
I COULD DO IT FOR YOU, THE EXACT SAME THING *YOU'D* DO, BUT *I'D* DO IT WHILE YOU *WATCHED*.
WHAT *ELSE* CAN I MAKE YOU DO?
TODAY? ANYTHING, APPARENTLY.
BLOOP!

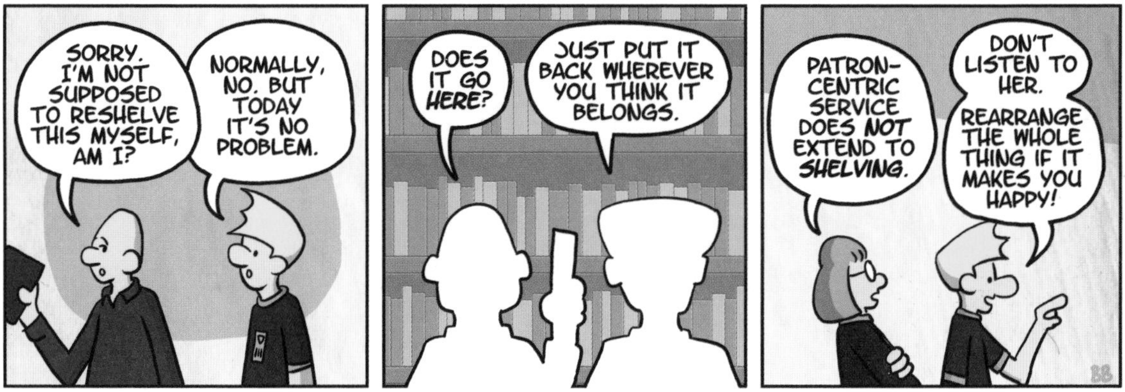
SORRY. I'M NOT SUPPOSED TO RESHELVE THIS MYSELF, AM I?
NORMALLY, NO. BUT TODAY IT'S NO PROBLEM.
DOES IT GO *HERE*?
JUST PUT IT BACK WHEREVER YOU THINK IT BELONGS.
PATRON-CENTRIC SERVICE DOES *NOT* EXTEND TO *SHELVING*.
DON'T LISTEN TO HER.
REARRANGE THE WHOLE THING IF IT MAKES YOU HAPPY!

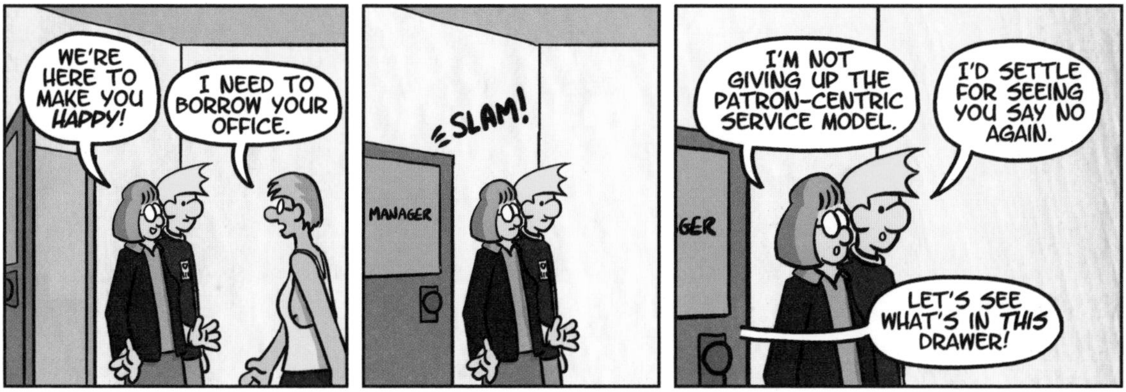
WE'RE HERE TO MAKE YOU *HAPPY*!
I NEED TO BORROW YOUR OFFICE.
SLAM!
MANAGER
I'M NOT GIVING UP THE PATRON-CENTRIC SERVICE MODEL.
I'D SETTLE FOR SEEING YOU SAY NO AGAIN.
GER
LET'S SEE WHAT'S IN *THIS* DRAWER!

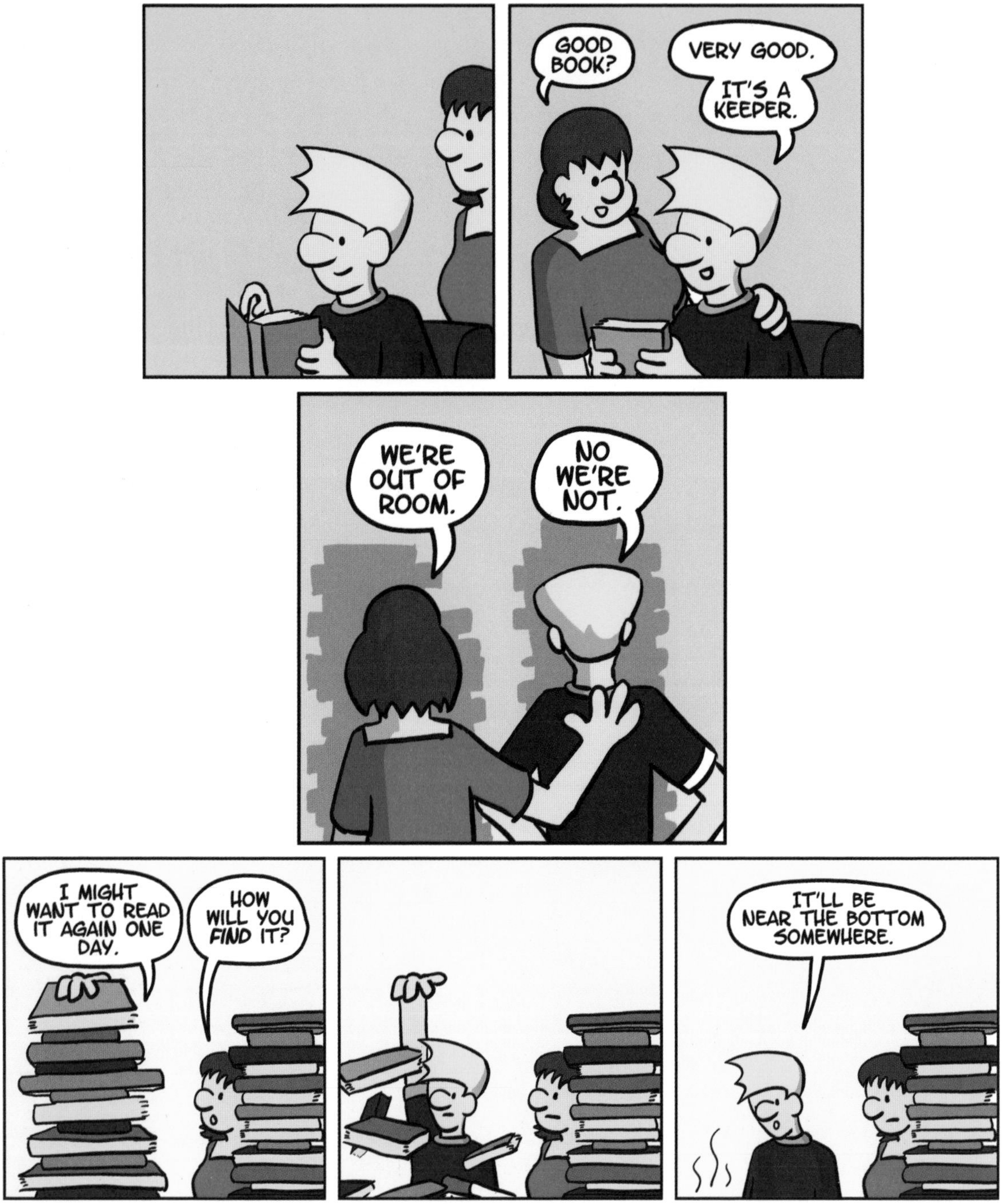
GOOD BOOK?
VERY GOOD.
IT'S A KEEPER.
WE'RE OUT OF ROOM.
NO WE'RE NOT.
I MIGHT WANT TO READ IT AGAIN ONE DAY.
HOW WILL YOU FIND IT?
IT'LL BE NEAR THE BOTTOM SOMEWHERE.

Reads Well With Others

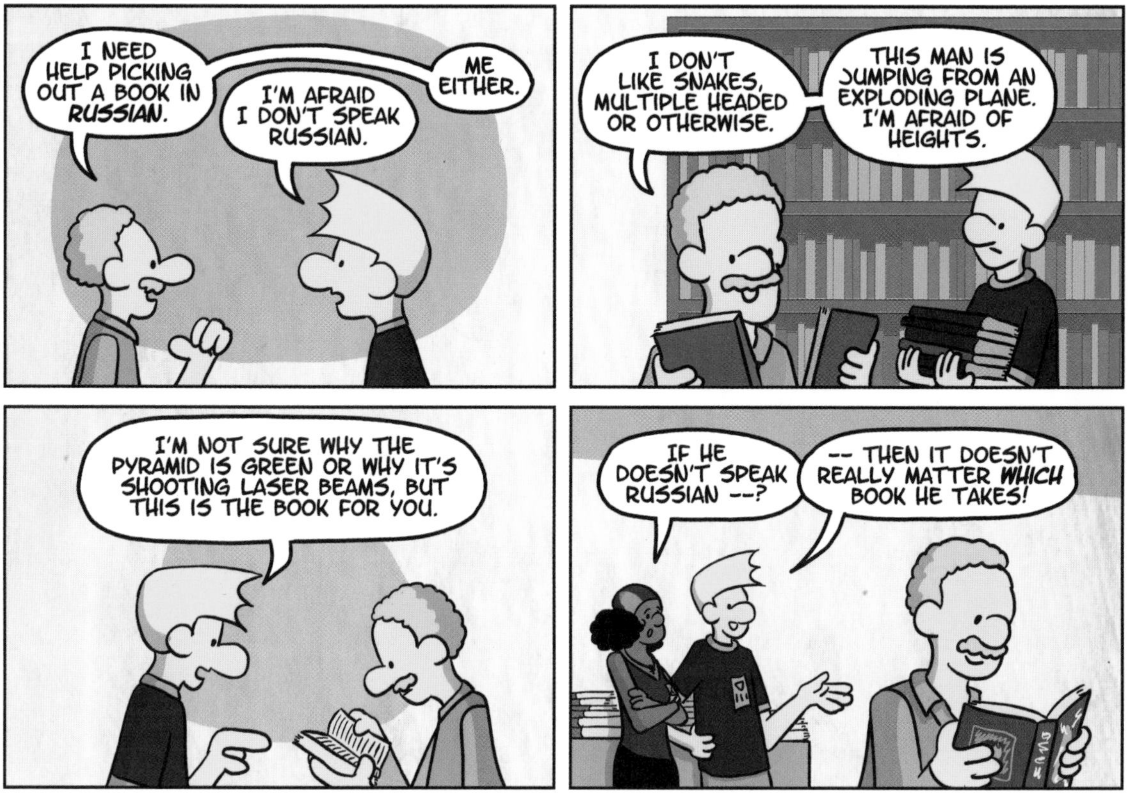

I NEED HELP PICKING OUT A BOOK IN **RUSSIAN**.
I'M AFRAID I DON'T SPEAK RUSSIAN.
ME EITHER.
I DON'T LIKE SNAKES, MULTIPLE HEADED OR OTHERWISE.
THIS MAN IS JUMPING FROM AN EXPLODING PLANE. I'M AFRAID OF HEIGHTS.
I'M NOT SURE WHY THE PYRAMID IS GREEN OR WHY IT'S SHOOTING LASER BEAMS, BUT THIS IS THE BOOK FOR YOU.
IF HE DOESN'T SPEAK RUSSIAN --?
-- THEN IT DOESN'T REALLY MATTER ***WHICH*** BOOK HE TAKES!

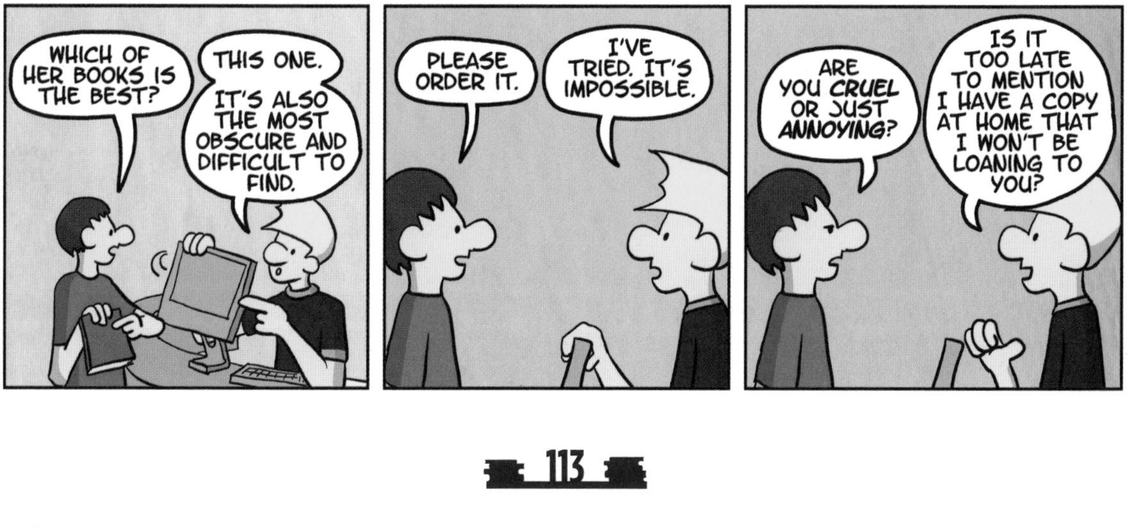

WHICH OF HER BOOKS IS THE BEST?
THIS ONE.
IT'S ALSO THE MOST OBSCURE AND DIFFICULT TO FIND.
PLEASE ORDER IT.
I'VE TRIED. IT'S IMPOSSIBLE.
ARE YOU ***CRUEL*** OR JUST ***ANNOYING***?
IS IT TOO LATE TO MENTION I HAVE A COPY AT HOME THAT I WON'T BE LOANING TO YOU?

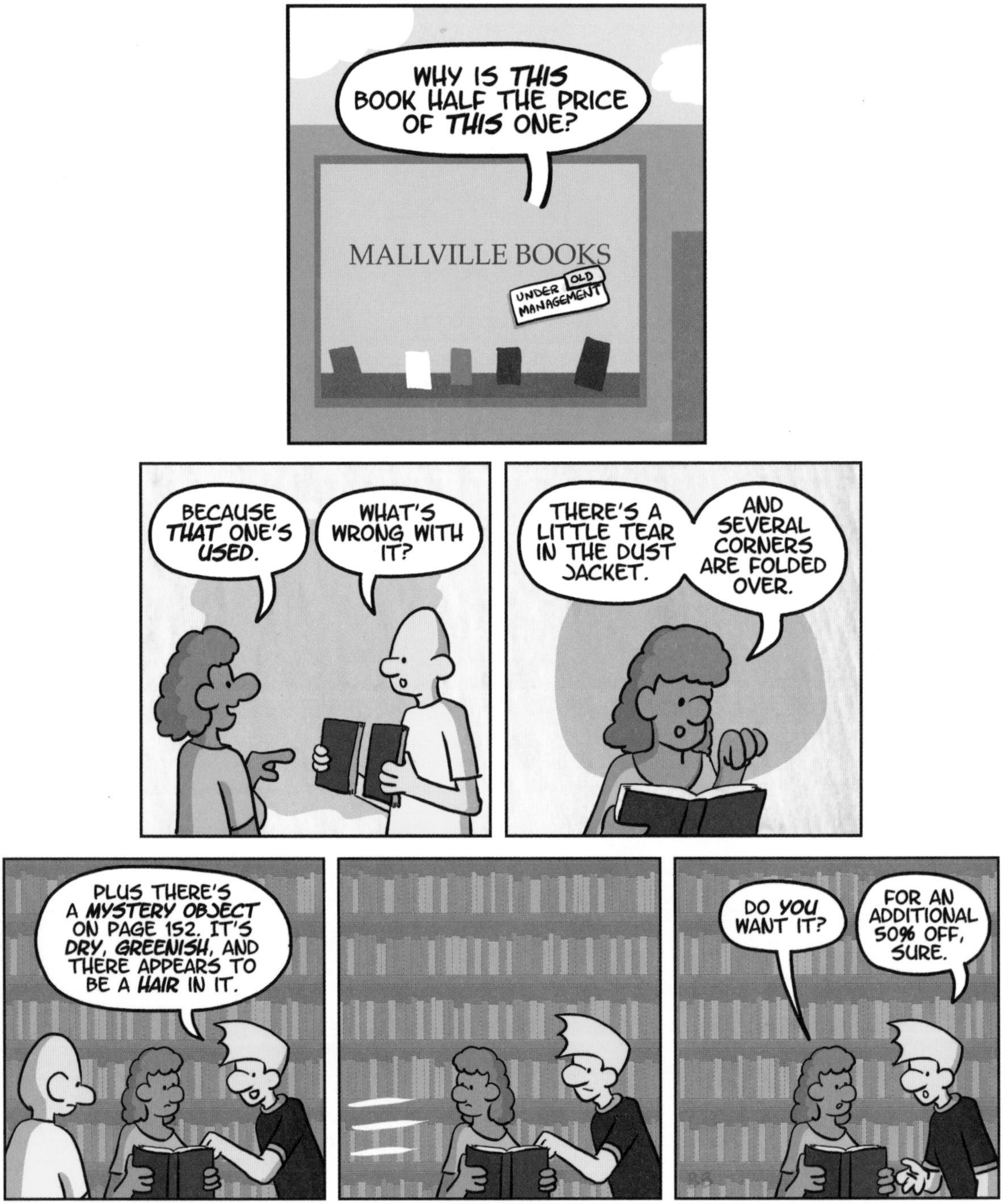
WHY IS THIS BOOK HALF THE PRICE OF THIS ONE?
MALLVILLE BOOKS
UNDER OLD MANAGEMENT
BECAUSE THAT ONE'S USED.
WHAT'S WRONG WITH IT?
THERE'S A LITTLE TEAR IN THE DUST JACKET.
AND SEVERAL CORNERS ARE FOLDED OVER.
PLUS THERE'S A MYSTERY OBJECT ON PAGE 152. IT'S DRY, GREENISH, AND THERE APPEARS TO BE A HAIR IN IT.
DO YOU WANT IT?
FOR AN ADDITIONAL 50% OFF, SURE.

Reads Well With Others

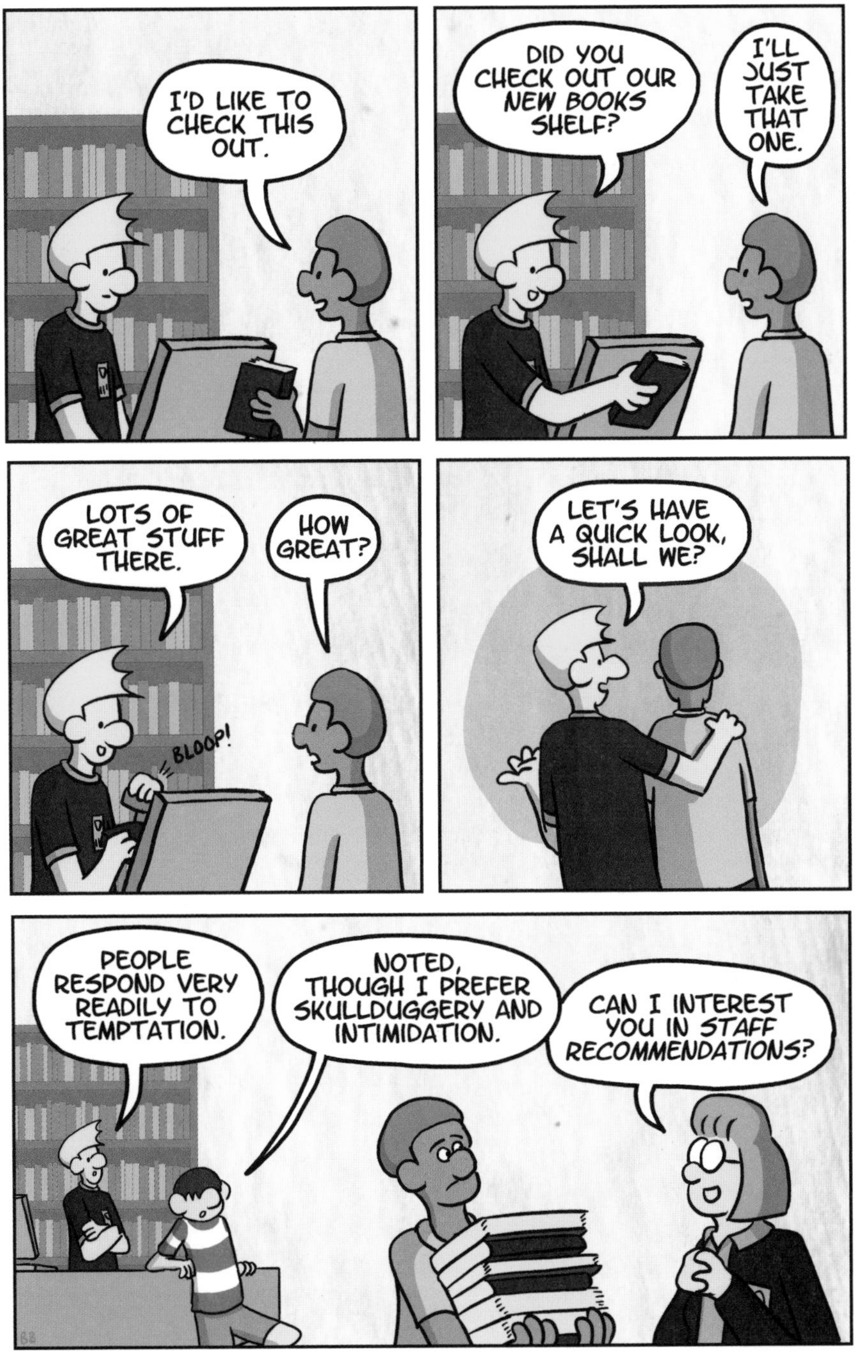
I'D LIKE TO CHECK THIS OUT.
DID YOU CHECK OUT OUR NEW BOOKS SHELF?
I'LL JUST TAKE THAT ONE.
LOTS OF GREAT STUFF THERE.
HOW GREAT?
BLOOP!
LET'S HAVE A QUICK LOOK, SHALL WE?
PEOPLE RESPOND VERY READILY TO TEMPTATION.
NOTED, THOUGH I PREFER SKULLDUGGERY AND INTIMIDATION.
CAN I INTEREST YOU IN STAFF RECOMMENDATIONS?

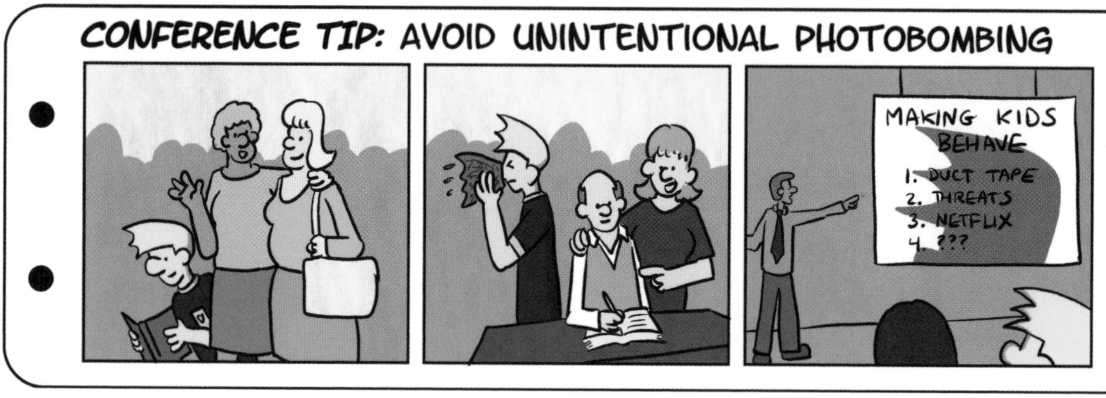
CONFERENCE TIP: AVOID UNINTENTIONAL PHOTOBOMBING
MAKING KIDS BEHAVE
1. DUCT TAPE
2. THREATS
3. NETFLIX
4. ???

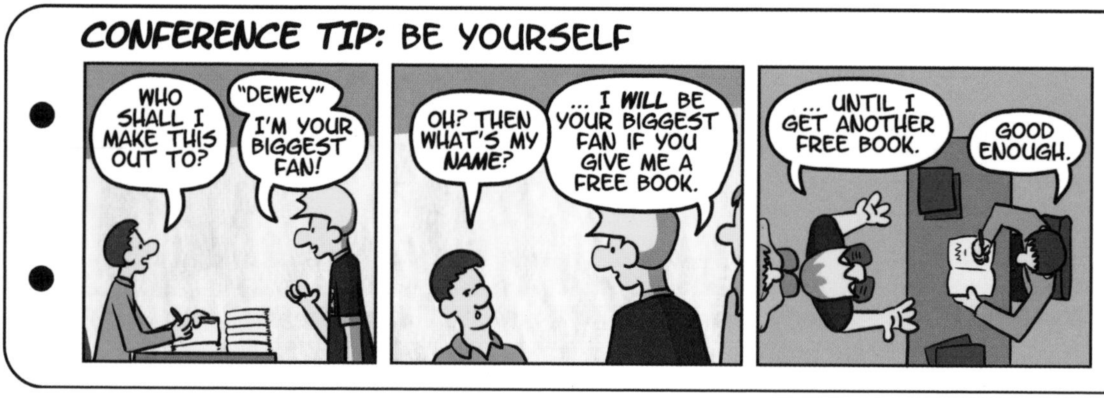
CONFERENCE TIP: BE YOURSELF
WHO SHALL I MAKE THIS OUT TO?
"DEWEY"
I'M YOUR BIGGEST FAN!
OH? THEN WHAT'S MY *NAME*?
... I *WILL* BE YOUR BIGGEST FAN IF YOU GIVE ME A FREE BOOK.
... UNTIL I GET ANOTHER FREE BOOK.
GOOD ENOUGH.

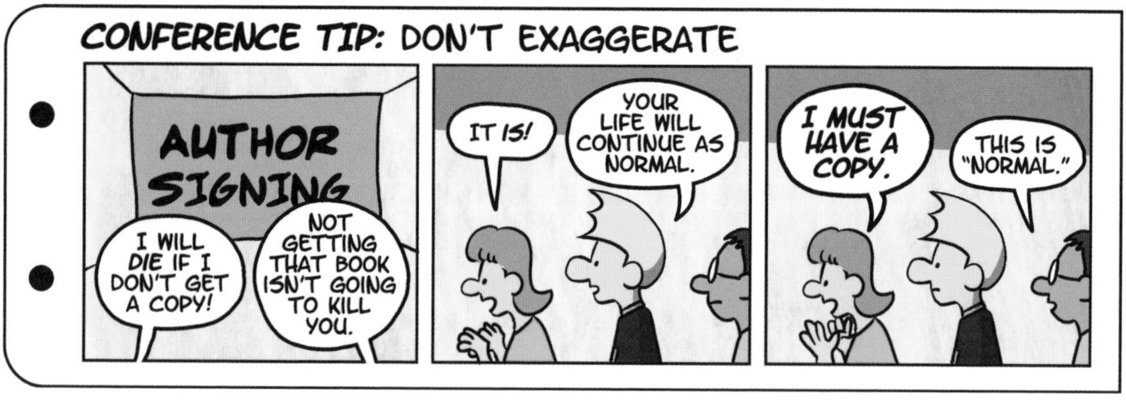
CONFERENCE TIP: DON'T EXAGGERATE
AUTHOR SIGNING
I WILL *DIE* IF I DON'T GET A COPY!
NOT GETTING THAT BOOK ISN'T GOING TO KILL YOU.
IT *IS*!
YOUR LIFE WILL CONTINUE AS NORMAL.
I MUST HAVE A COPY.
THIS IS "NORMAL."

CONFERENCE TIP: ENJOY YOUR DOWN TIME

I'M WORRIED ABOUT WHAT'S GOING ON IN MY LIBRARY.
I'D BETTER CALL.
NO ONE IS ANSWERING!
MAYBE IT BURNED DOWN.
... OR MAYBE IT'S JUST NOT OPEN YET BECAUSE OF THE TIME DIFFERENCE.

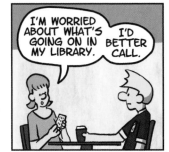

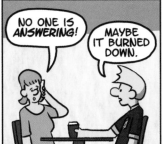

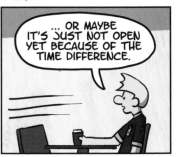

CONFERENCE TIP: GO FOR GOLD

JENNY STAR
MANAGER
MIDWEST PUBLIC LIBRARY
ALA Member
Conference Virgin
Blogger
@unshelfeed
Read Responsibly
Library Superhero
Unshelved
Be Informed.
Speaker
Reviewer
Interpreter
Geek
Manager
Roundtable member
Advocate
Libraries For All
Will work for books
Furry
Visitor
Ask me about my condition
Cataloger
I NY
Nerd
WINNER

CONFERENCE TIP: COLLECT 'EM ALL

I'LL GIVE YOU FIVE PENS FOR YOUR COFFEE MUG.
I'LL BID THREE GALLEYS AND AN AMBIGUOUS STUFFED ANIMAL.
COME ON, PEOPLE. IT HAS A BOOK ON IT.
I WANT MORE.
DOESN'T ANYONE WANT ANOTHER TOTE BAG?

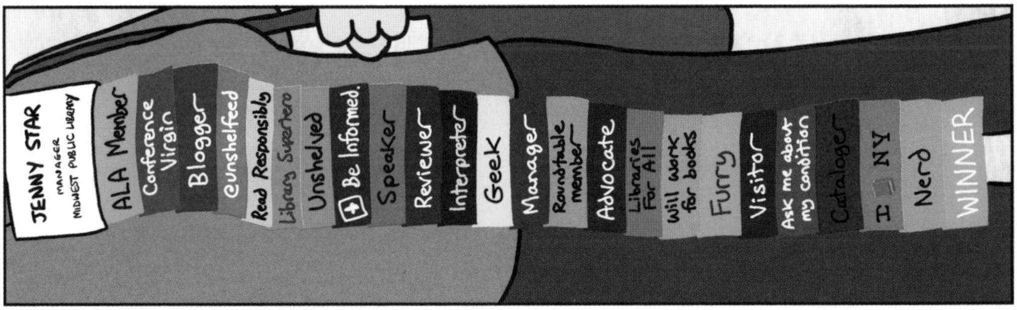

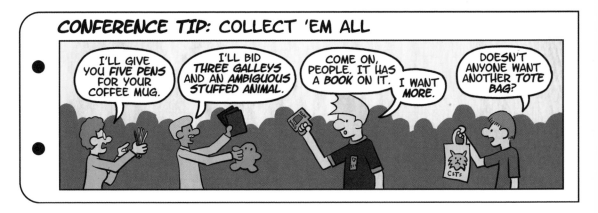

CONFERENCE TIP: SHOOT FOR THE MOON

I NEED EVERYTHING YOU PUBLISH PLUS THAT TABLE AND YOUR RENTAL CAR.
ARE YOU CRAZY?
IMPOSSIBLE.
FINE, GIVE ME THOSE TEN BOOKS.
HE WOULDN'T GIVE ME ANYTHING.
I LET HIM TALK ME DOWN.

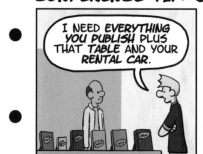

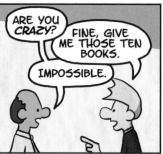

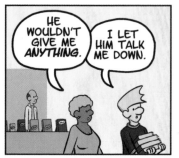

CONFERENCE TIP: KNOW YOUR LIMITATIONS

IF I GIVE YOU THIS BOOK, WHAT WILL YOU DO TO PROMOTE IT?
TWEET IT. PIN IT. POST IT ON MY WALL. BLOG IT TO THE MOON. MY REVIEW WILL SHAKE THE WORLD!
TELL A FRIEND. MAYBE TWO.
THAT WAS YOUR THRESHOLD?
HONESTY WAS MY THRESHOLD.

CONFERENCE TIP: KEEP YOUR DISTANCE

I LOVE YOUR BOOKS!
I KNOW WE'RE GOING TO BE BEST FRIENDS.
I MADE YOU THESE COOKIES.
GLUTEN FREE!
HOW ABOUT I CHEW THEM FOR YOU?
AND THEN FEED YOU LIKE YOU'RE A BABY BIRD!
MEET THE AUTHOR!
SECURITY?
BB

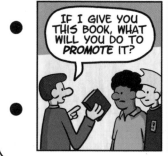

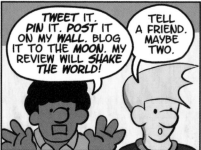

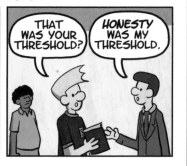

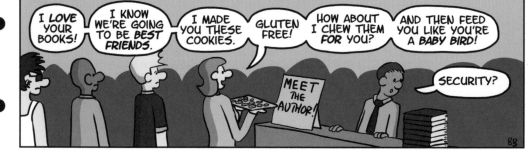

CONFERENCE TIP: CHOOSE LIFE

ZOMBIE BOOKS ARE *IN*!
I DON'T THINK THAT'S TRUE ANY MORE.
REALLY?
READERS ARE FICKLE.
MY BOSS IS GOING TO KILL ME.
MAYBE YOU'LL COME BACK AS THE ***SALESPERSON OF THE LIVING DEAD!***
BB

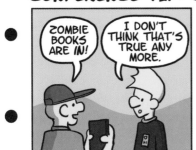

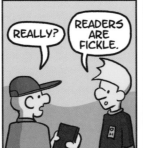

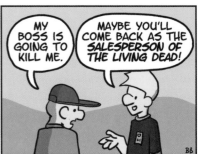

CONFERENCE TIP: THERE'S NO SUCH THING AS A FREE BREAKFAST

WHEN IS ***BREAKFAST*** SERVED?
AFTER THE SALES PITCH.
WAKE ME WHEN IT'S OVER.
IF YOU SLEEP THEY WON'T FEED YOU.
WHAT IF I CLAP WILDLY?
SKY'S THE LIMIT.
CAVIAR FOR MADAM?
BB

CONFERENCE TIP: HAVE A HEART

WOULD YOU LIKE A FREE BOOK? THE AUTHOR IS SIGNING.
NO THANKS.
MEET THE AUTHOR
DID I MENTION THE AUTHOR IS--
RIGHT THERE? YES, I SAW HIM.
MEET THE AUTHOR
TRY THIS ONE AND I'LL GIVE YOU TWO BONUS BOOKS.
I'M IN.
I'M OUT.
MEET THE AUTHOR

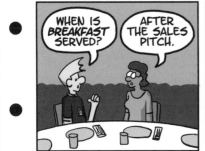

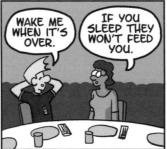

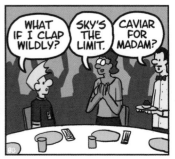

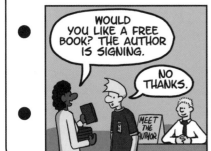

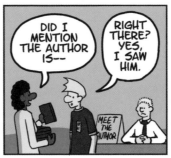

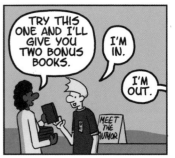

More UNSHELVED by Gene Ambaum & Bill Barnes

Unshelved

What Would Dewey Do?

Library Mascot Cage Match

Book Club

Read Responsibly

Frequently Asked Questions

Reader's Advisory

Large Print

Too Much Information

Bibliovores

Books by Gene Ambaum

Poopy Claws (with Sophie Goldstein)

Fifty Shades of Brains (as BF Dealeo)

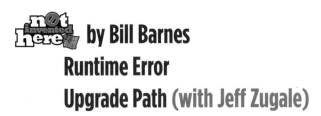 by Bill Barnes

Runtime Error

Upgrade Path (with Jeff Zugale)